I0831260

THE *Elegies* OF *Maximianus*

THE *Elegies* OF *Maximianus*

Edited and translated by

A. M. Juster

Introduction by

Michael Roberts

PENN

UNIVERSITY OF PENNSYLVANIA PRESS

PHILADELPHIA

Published by
University of Pennsylvania Press
Philadelphia, Pennsylvania 19104-4112

Printed in the United States of America on acid-free paper
10 9 8 7 6 5 4 3 2 1

Library of Congress Cataloging-in-Publication Data

Names: Maximianus, active 6th century, author. | Juster, A. M., editor, translator. | Roberts, Michael, writer of introduction. | Container of (expression): Maximianus, active 6th century. Elegiae. | Container of (expression): Maximianus, active 6th century. Elegiae. English
Title: The elegies of Maximianus / edited and translated by A. M. Juster ; introduction by Michael Roberts.
Description: 1st edition. | Philadelphia : University of Pennsylvania Press, [2018] | Bilingual; text in Latin and English; includes substantial annotations in English. | Includes bibliographical references.
Identifiers: LCCN 2017033938 | ISBN 978-0-8122-4979-8 (hardcover : alk. paper)
Classification: LCC PA6511.M6 A2 2018 | DDC 871/.02—dc23
LC record available at https://lccn.loc.gov/2017033938

Contents

Preface

My goal with this book is to provide a faithful—but not "literal"—translation that also works as poetry. I try to replicate the feel of the Latin elegiac distich with couplets in alternating iambic hexameter and iambic pentameter while allowing myself the customary substitutions of formal poetry in English. When possible, I imitate Maximianus's pronounced internal rhyme, alliteration, and assonance, all of which are much more common in Late Antiquity than in the classical era. I also try to mimic his love of the spondee. (See Cupaiuolo 1997 at 381.)

The commentary is the only one in English other than the Webster edition of 1900. I try to explain facets of the text that might be unclear to a reader while also conceding confusion on many points in the hope of spurring future scholarship. Those concessions are important because I believe too much of the scholarship has stifled debate by interpreting the text rigidly rather than acknowledging its intentional and unintentional ambiguities.

No scholar has comprehensively traced the reception of the elegies in later literature, and I do not try to do so myself, but I note some instances of Maximianus's influence, again in the hope of spurring future scholarship. I include the *Imitatio Maximiani* and *Le regret de Maximian* for that same reason but leave translation of those texts to interested scholars. I want to bring Maximianus to as wide an audience as possible, so I also include some notes that are unnecessary for classics scholars but possibly helpful to academics and students still refining their Latin.

Most textual analysis of the elegies ended over a century ago with the very different editions of Baehrens and Webster. Although Webster's commentary is frustratingly erratic, his editorial choices are far more cautious and thoughtful than those of Baehrens. Baehrens's editing reflects to a greater extent the late nineteenth-century bias toward aggressive emendations motivated by a misguided desire to "classicize" the Latin of Late

Antiquity. Too much of the Maximianus scholarship of the past century relies on the flawed Baehrens text.

Future research and translations would benefit from a text of Maximianus derived from a new analysis of the many surviving manuscripts, but I am not the right person for that task. Accordingly, I rely on the Webster text as my starting point. When I emend the text, I flag the change with an asterisk and state my reasons for doing so in the notes. For those interested in the manuscript tradition, see Schetter (1970) at 3–9; Agozzino (1970) at 23–27; Spinazzè (2011) at 43–49, 52–61; D'Angelo (2005) at 467–471. For those who want to consider the many variations in the manuscripts in more detail than I provide in my commentary, I recommend the work of Öberg (1999) at 88–91 and 153–183; see also Prada (1918). For comments on the manuscript tradition, I also recommend Perroni's review of Schetter (1979 at 144–150).

I rejected well-intentioned advice and did not punctuate the text but left it as I believe it stood in the sixth century. Punctuation of texts of Maximianus's elegies has tended to push readers toward the editor's often debatable interpretations, and I think it is better to acknowledge uncertainties created by the difficulty of the Latin, the suspect parts of the text, and the poet's deliberate ambiguities. In other words, I want to stimulate debate, not stifle it. With the same rationale, I try to highlight disagreements between scholars about the meaning of lines instead of pronouncing a definitive answer where there is uncertainty.

Methods of citation vary greatly. Mine reflects my legal training and should be easy for anyone to follow. Where citations to texts vary, as is the case with Boethius *Consolatio philosophiae*, I have relied on the choice made by the Monumenta.ch database. For ease of use I have avoided abbreviations except "OLD" for the 2006 combined edition of the *Oxford Latin Dictionary*.

Many wonderful people have generously and graciously assisted me with this project. The two anonymous reviewers were painstaking and thoughtful. Aaron Poochigian was the reader of my first draft, and he patiently answered many questions over many years. Roger Green, Julia Hejduk, Joel Relihan, Aaron Pelttari, Anna Maria Wasyl, Cillian O'Hogan, and Ian Fielding carefully read all or large parts of subsequent drafts. Genevieve Liveley, James Uden, and Patrick McBrine regularly responded to pleas for help as I was wrestling with the text. Robert Kaster provided invaluable assistance tracking down and analyzing "epigrams" of Maximianus referenced in the literature as well as answering occasional questions about rhetoric. I tapped the expertise in elegy of my former collaborator, Robert Maltby, on several occasions. Mark Tizzoni helped me with questions relating to Eugene of Toledo. Sharon James answered some questions relating to interpretation of certain terms in light of the elegiac tradition. James Adams helped me with several questions related to sexual vocabulary. James O'Donnell and Shane Bjorlie rescued me from the unfamiliar prose of Cassiodorus, and Eric Hutchinson was helpful with the *Appendix Maximiani*. Danuta Shanzer provided helpful input on several points, and Jay Wickersham helped me obtain microfilmed dissertations. Finally, Michael Roberts did a superb job helping me with the final edits, but all mistakes are mine.

I am grateful for the hospitality of the Library of Congress, the Georgetown University Library, Harvard University's Widener Library, and the Dumbarton Oaks Library. I am grateful to Eva Oledzka of the Bodleian Library, who helped me on questions relating to the key manuscript for the *Appendix Maximiani*. I am also grateful for the patient and skilled assistance of Deborah Brown of Dumbarton Oaks, who taught me new tools of research and patiently answered many questions, and to the Widener Library's Stephen Kuehler for his diligence and creativity in tracking down sources. I also thank Herbert Golder for running excerpts from this translation in Arion, and Eric Halpern of the University of Pennsylvania Press for publishing my work for a second time.

Finally, I want to thank Laura Mali-Astrue for her unfailing linguistic and emotional support during all the hours that I traded the frustrations of twenty-first-century Washington for the satisfactions of sixth-century Italy.

THE *Elegies* OF *Maximianus*

Introduction

MICHAEL ROBERTS

Despite increasing critical attention in the last half century or so, the *Elegies* of Maximianus are not widely known among readers of Latin literature. This is true even though in their meter and erotic subject matter they recall the heyday of Latin love elegy in the Augustan period. Indeed they are often described as a late epigone of that genre, a final example of ancient love elegy, a genre otherwise not practiced in Late Antiquity.[1] The relative neglect that these in many ways remarkable poems have experienced in the modern era contrasts with their extensive use as a school text in the Middle Ages, when they were valued, somewhat surprisingly, for the moral instruction they provided. Schetter, in his fundamental study of the manuscript tradition of the poems, listed fifty-two medieval manuscripts, though no complete manuscripts before the eleventh century, as well as twenty-three florilegia containing Maximianus excerpts.[2] While they are unlikely to regain the popularity they enjoyed in the medieval period, the poems certainly deserve a wider readership. Juster's new translation will help bring them that expanded audience.

The Poet

The only evidence for the date and identity of our poet derives from the *Elegies*. Even his name, Maximianus, depends on a reference in elegy 4, where an observer says of the speaker of the poem "Maximianus loves the singer" (*cantantem Maximianus amat*, 4.26). The name Maximianus is attested a number of times in the sixth century. Most promisingly a person of that name is addressed in an official letter of Cassiodorus (*Variae* 1.21, translated by Juster in Appendix A; the same *vir illustris* is also mentioned in *Variae* 4.22.3), but the date of these letters may be too early for our poet.

In the absence of any corroborative evidence for the poet outside his works, even the existence of Maximianus as a real historical figure has been questioned. In 1900 Webster roundly declared the content of the poems, and with it the reality of the protagonist, fiction.[3] It is certainly true that the argument for a poet named Maximianus depends on the balance of probabilities, not definitive proof. But it may be that the insertion of the name of the poet in elegy 4 serves as a kind of *sphragis*, or signature, in the manner of other poets who wished to include their names in their works. Generally scholars admit the identification, while aware that the evidence for it is not conclusive. The suggestion by a recent editor that Maximianus is to be identified not with the poet but with a different historical figure, the subject of the anonymous poet's mockery, is unpersuasive.[4]

Determination of the date of the poem likewise relies primarily on internal evidence. The third elegy features, in addition to Maximianus himself and the object of his amorous attentions, Aquilina, the figure of Boethius, who can be no other than the famous author of the *Consolation of Philosophy*. In the poem the poet describes himself as still young, inexperienced in love (3.7–8)—he is still attended by a *paedagogus*—while Boethius features as an older and wiser mentor on affairs of the heart. The dramatic date, then, would be perhaps in the second or third decade of the sixth century, prior to Boethius' imprisonment in 523/4. All the elegies, however, presuppose an elderly speaker, in some cases looking back at youthful erotic experiences. If this can be taken as autobiographically accurate it would suggest a date for the composition of the poems roughly in the second quarter of the sixth century, with the lapse of a substantial span of years since the experience described in elegy 3.

The other piece of evidence regularly invoked to supply a criterion for dating concerns the embassy to the Greek East that provides the occasion for the poet's encounter with a "a girl from Greece" (*Graia puella*) in elegy 5 (1–4). His mission is to conclude a treaty between "twin realms" (*gemini . . . regni*, 5.3), that is, between Ostrogothic Italy and the Eastern Roman Empire. Scholars have identified the embassy variously with one sent by the Ostrogothic king Theodahad in 534–535 or by Totila in 546 or 549.[5] If, as is often argued, the North African poet Corippus imitates Maximianus in his epic on the exploits of the general John Troglita, the *Iohannis* (dated to 548), then the last date is ruled out.[6] The 534–535 date would receive some corroboration if poems 3 and 4 of the *Appendix Maximiani*, which describe in glowing terms a fortress to Theodahad, could be securely attributed to the poet of the *Elegies*. All these arguments, however, rely on the assumption that the *Elegies* are reliable evidence for the life of the poet. This can by no means be taken for granted. At most the presence of Boethius and the expectation that an audience would find the dispatch of an embassy from Italy to the East credible suggest the mid-sixth century as a likely date.[7]

A few references in the poems have been taken to supply biographical data. In elegy 5 the poet twice describes himself as from Etruria (5.5 and 5.40). In both cases, though, his Etruscan origin contrasts with the Greek guile of his seductress; the word may convey no more than that he is a simple Italian. Elegy 1 adds the detail that he walked the streets of Rome in his youth, the cynosure of womanly gaze (1.63–64). Like many of his reminiscences of his youthful glories in that poem, it invites taking with a large dose of salt. It would be unwise, for instance, to give too much credence to his self-described brilliance as an orator and poet and to the accolades he received as an advocate (1.9–14). On the other hand, his poetry makes clear he had received the thorough literary education characteristic of the schools of Late Antiquity. His works show knowledge of the writers most familiar to late Latin poets, Virgil, Horace, Ovid, Juvenal, and the poets of the first century CE generally.

The Poems

The 686 lines of Maximianus' *Elegies* have traditionally been divided into six separate poems, corresponding to discrete subject matter: poems 2–5 describe the poet's relations with four different women; the first and largest poem of the collection sets the theme of old age and its decrepitude, a theme taken up in the short concluding poem, poem 6. Whatever age he was at the time of the experiences he describes in the individual poems, he views them all from the perspective of an old man. Importantly the division into separate poems has manuscript authority, even though the evidence of the manuscripts is not unambiguous.[8] In particular, transitional passages at the beginning and end of poems occasion uncertainty in specifying where exactly the division between poems should be made. Recently two scholars have revived the nineteenth-century suggestion that Maximianus' work should be seen as a single continuous poem, without any division into separate elegies.[9] Although the poems are closely interrelated and amount to a mutually complementary treatment of love and age, the sixfold division has usually been retained, conforming as it does to the sequence of distinct episodes or compositions that make up the collection.

Elegy 1 is the longest in the corpus: 292 lines, almost 43 percent of the whole. It establishes the voice of the speaker: a querulous old man, full of the indignities of aging, which he contrasts with the vigor and prestige he enjoyed in his youth. The first eight lines establish two key themes: regret that he continues to live rather than enjoying a timely death and, in a line evoking a number of classical texts, recognition that the man he once was has gone forever: "I am not who I was, my greatest part has perished" (1.5).[10]

After this introduction the poem launches into a hyperbolic description of the young Maximianus' many talents. In part the highly colored account can be seen as a characterization of an old man viewing through rose-tinted glasses his glorious youth; in part a rhetorical ploy to make his present misery all the more pitiable; but there's also an element of poetic tour de force as the poet paints a picture of the perfect Roman "gentleman." Maximianus distinguishes himself as orator, poet, and advocate; he excels in hunting, wrestling, footraces, and singing lyrics from tragedy. He possesses good looks complemented by moral qualities: ability to withstand wind, rain, and water. Needing little sleep, he can drink even the wine god Bacchus under the table. Neither adversity nor poverty faze him.

At this point, for the first time the theme of love enters the picture. Such are Maximianus' qualities that all the girls flirt with him, while their parents want him as their son-in-law. But Maximianus holds aloof; none is worthy of him. The section ends (85–100) with the description of an ideally beautiful girl who alone could rouse his desire.

From this point on the poem turns to the evils of age and its degrading effects. The abilities he so prided himself on in his youth have gone (127–130): singing voice, oratory, even writing poetry (though, since he makes this last claim in a poem, there are reasons to be skeptical).[11] As an old man he has lost all five senses; in physical decay he is a prey to multiple diseases. All his former pleasures are now denied him or may positively do him harm. No longer able to enjoy his wealth, he just keeps watch over it for his heir. Foolish and garrulous, he is an object of mockery to those around him. His posture, bent toward the ground, supporting himself with a stick, prompts him to pray to earth, his mother, to take him once more in her embrace and bring his suffering to an end. In the second couplet of the poem Maximianus had described his current life as "a punishment" (*poena*, 1.4); his description of the sufferings of old age amply justifies this characterization. The term runs as a leitmotif through that description. The speaker's present existence is a kind of living death.

The first poem ends with a recognition of the pain that recollection of past glories brings to the wretched. Poem 2 similarly derives from a contrast between past happiness and present misery, but this time in the experience of love. (The effect of aging on love only receives a passing mention in poem 1.)[12] It concerns his relations with Lycoris—the name is also that of the lover of Cornelius Gallus, writer of love elegy in the first century BCE. The two had enjoyed a harmonious relationship for many years, but now she scorns her aged former lover and is repelled by his appearance. Our speaker wishes he had died before receiving this slight. His loss of physical appeal and, as we learn later (2.57–58), sexual capacity contrasts with Lycoris' retention of her beauty, despite grey hairs. In the last part of the poem (45–72) he attempts to persuade Lycoris to display affection for him on the grounds of the pleasure he has given her in the past and to think of him as a revered father, if no other relationship is possible.

Poem 3 initiates a sequence of three narrative elegies, recounting episodes from the poet's amatory career. In poem 3 Maximianus is very young, with no experience of love (3.7–8), in poem 5 he is an old man (5.40 and 5.42). The two couplets with which poem 3 begins, with their reference to tales of youth and age, seem to act as an introduction to the whole three-poem sequence.

The third elegy finds Maximianus smitten with love for an equally young and inexperienced girl, Aquilina, who returns his love. The couple meet resistance to their desires—an overbearing *paedagogus* on his side, a harsh mother on hers—but such is the force of their love that they learn to communicate through secret signs and finally to arrange assignations. When Aquilina's mother finds out about the relationship, she gives her daughter a beating, only for the girl to display her wounds to her lover as evidence of the force of her passion, thereby still further intensifying the young man's longing. At this point Boethius, hailed as "great searcher of important things" (*magnarum scrutator maxime rerum*, 3.47) intervenes. He diagnoses the situation and, laughing at Maximianus' scruples about forcing himself on Aquilina, urges him to do just that. Nevertheless Boethius first takes matters in hand himself, bribing the girl's parents to turn a blind eye to the affair. The parents' acquiescence, however, has a surprise effect. Now that the barriers to their love are removed, passion cools, the pair separate, and Boethius congratulates Maximianus on his newfound devotion to celibacy. Only the last couplet sounds a discordant note: the separation leaves the couple sad and unfulfilled.

The poet's age at the time of his second erotic misadventure, that described in poem 4, is left unspecified if, as seems most likely, the last three couplets of the fourth elegy as it is normally printed actually introduce poem 5.[13] Clearly, though, he is now older and more experienced than in the previous poem. This time he has fallen in love with the musician, dancer, and singer Candida, fair in both looks and name. His behavior shows clear signs that he is in love, including singing snatches of songs from her repertoire. It is this that prompts the observation "Maximianus loves the singer" (4.26). But disaster strikes when he talks in his sleep, naming Candida and summoning her to a tryst. Lying beside him is the girl's father. He hears Maximianus' words and begins to put two and two together. Although we do not hear what further action the father takes, Maximianus regrets the blow to his prestige the incident apparently caused, contrasting this past episode with his present situation as an old man, when he is free from any reproach because to his shame he lacks the capacity for sexual exploits, although he still has the desire for them.

The fifth poem takes place when Maximianus has become an old man; it illustrates his continuing sexual desire. Sent on a mission to the East to arrange a treaty between Ostrogothic Italy and the Eastern Empire he falls under the spell of an unnamed Greek girl—she too a dancer, musician, and singer—who feigns love for him and serenades him by his window, evoking in Maximianus pity for her apparent suffering and genuine love for her. He describes her alluring movements and physical beauty, succumbing entirely to her charms. A first night of lovemaking, somewhat against the odds given his age, proves successful, but on the second night his powers fail him. The girl attempts to rouse him manually, without success. When she accuses him of having another lover, Maximianus first pleads the burden of official business as excuse for his failure before admitting his loss of sexual potency.

The poem now takes an unexpected turn. Much of its second half is addressed to the penis (*mentula*), initially in a lament for the demise of Maximianus' member, now inert and crestfallen, as good as dead. The poet's response to the girl's lament, that it shows she suffers from a worse disease (i.e., she is sexually frustrated), prompts a furious rejoinder, a forty-four-line hymn to the penis, this time as principle of cosmic order and harmony and of procreation and attraction between the sexes, a power to which all are subject. The speech ends with a celebration of the role of the penis in lovemaking: it conquers only to be conquered but then will conquer again, a description of the sequence of tumescence, detumescence, and future retumescence. Only one couplet follows the Greek girl's speech. She leaves Maximianus, her grief exhausted. Her speech has been for him a kind of funeral rite.

The last poem in the collection is only twelve lines long, a kind of epilogue or coda. It begins "please stop these miserable complaints" (6.1), for, it argues, to linger over such shameful episodes only invites reproach. After six lines devoted to the commonplace of consolation literature that all humans must die, an enigmatic final couplet seems to offer some prospect of continued existence for Maximianus, probably through the survival of his poetry, though the language chosen suggests an analogy between such survival and the revival of sexual potency, just as impotence is figured as death.

The theme of death in the last eight lines of poem 6 picks up on the metaphorical death that Maximianus suffers in poem 5. But it also looks back to the first eight lines of poem 1, in which Maximianus speaks of his desire for the release of death. In this way, despite their disparity in length, poems 1 and 6 form a kind of frame for the collection. They are also the only poems in which the poet does not speak of a specific lover. The most widely accepted scheme for the structure of the collection, as proposed most influentially by Schetter, in fact sees a chiastic structure: 1 corresponds to 6 in their common themes of aging and death; 2 to 5, both treating the poet's erotic experiences when old; 3 and 4 then recount youthful misadventures.[14] This presupposes that poem 4 describes a youthful exploit, even though there is no unambiguous evidence of the age of Maximianus at the time of his affair with Candida. He's unlikely to be the same age as the inexperienced tyro in love of poem 3. Since poems 3 and 5 represent extremes of youth and age, it seems more plausible to locate poem 4 somewhere between the two.

An alternative structure for the collection is possible.[15] Although poem 2 is like the next three poems in specifying a particular lover, in other respects it is significantly different. Poems 3 to 5 are all largely narrative, recounting episodes in Maximianus' erotic career. Poem 2 does not detail a specific event but rather characterizes the poet's reaction to a situation, his rejection by Lycoris, concluding with an appeal to her to view him more sympathetically. In this respect it is more akin to the procedures of classical love elegy, which does not typically contain a large element of narrative.[16] The affiliations of the second poem are rather with its predecessor, elegy 1. Both poems deal with the problems of old age: the first gives a general characterization of the woes of aging; the second an illustration of how these problems manifest themselves specifically in erotic relationships. The two complement each other. Poems 3 to 5 then follow a sequence of increasing age, from the naïve youth at one extreme to the aging but still susceptible figure at the other, with the Maximianus of poem 4 somewhere in between. But ultimately there is no need to decide for one or the other of these schemes. There is no reason why they cannot coexist. Poems 3 and 4 and 2 and 5 do have elements in common; one system of organization can overlay the other.

Genre and Style

Because they treat of love and are in the elegiac meter Maximianus' poems are most often classified as a late example of the Latin love elegy that flourished in the Augustan period. The name of the poet's lover in the second poem, Lycoris, reinforces that connection. The originator of Latin love elegy, Cornelius Gallus, addressed his poems to a woman of that name. Although Maximianus will not have read Gallus' poetry—it exists now only in fragments—he will have known of him and his beloved from references in Virgil, Ovid, and Martial. Of the three surviving love elegists, Ovid, with his *Amores*, has the most profound influence, both in themes and language; Tibullus and Propertius generally were not much read in Late Antiquity after the fourth century, and the evidence for their influence on Maximianus is questionable.

The sixth-century poet shares with the love elegy of Ovid a number of motifs. The young lovers of poem 3 learn to communicate with each other through nonverbal signals, a frequent subject in the *Amores* (1.4.13–28, 2.5.15–20, 3.11.23–24).[17] In the same poem Boethius' use of bribery to persuade Aquilina's parents to acquiesce in the affair recalls Ovid's invoking of the myth of Jupiter and Danae to illustrate the persuasive power of money in overcoming parental opposition (3.8.31–34). The final reversal, by which the young lovers' passion abates once their way is made clear, also finds Ovidian antecedents. The Augustan poet speaks both of the appeal of the forbidden and the lack of appeal of the permissible: "what is allowed has no attraction" (2.19.3).[18] Poem 5, too, in its general theme of impotence, invites comparison to Ovid, who devoted one of his *Amores* to the subject. There are similarities in detail too. For instance, the Greek girl of poem 5 in her physical appearance shares traits with Corinna

(1.5.17–24), and Ovid, like Maximianus, is susceptible to the attractions of a dancer (2.4.29–30).[19]

Despite the coincidence of meter and subject matter Maximianus' *Elegies* are very different from anything in the love elegy of the classical period, most obviously in the personality of the poet and the treatment of old age. The Augustan poets adopt the persona of obsessive lovers in thrall to their mistresses, in part in rebellion against the cultural norms of the society they lived in. Theirs is a poetry of young men; love, like soldiery, is an activity for the young; for the old it is simply disgusting (Ovid, *Amores* 1.9.4). Maximianus, on the other hand, is a respectable member of society, entrusted with an important diplomatic mission. His poetry looks at love and past erotic encounters from the perspective of an old man and documents the uncomfortable persistence of love and sexual desire in the elderly.

In other respects, too, the *Elegies* differ from or are in contradiction with the classical elegiac ethos.[20] Poem 1 speculates on the possibility of marriage and the qualifications a future wife should have; poem 2 looks back on a long-standing relationship with a woman, Lycoris, that in old age has grown sour. Such concerns for a lifelong alliance are alien to the Latin love elegy. The first poem shows further points of divergence from Ovid and the classical tradition. The poet's very exacting standards for a future bride contrast with Ovid's declaration in *Amores* 2.4 that there is no one style of beauty that attracts him; Rome is full of desirable women of all kinds. As subsequent poems show, Maximianus' discrimination in seeking a marriage partner does not prevent him from having lovers or seeking relationships. But his persona remains very different from Ovid's. It is perhaps significant of the changed ethos that while in Ovid's *Ars amatoria* it is girls who in the theater "come to view and come to be viewed themselves" (*Ars amatoria* 1.99), in the first elegy it is Maximianus who is "examined everywhere by all the girls" (1.64).

Of all the poems in the collection, elegy 5 most immediately invites comparison with Ovid. It shares the subject of impotence with *Amores* 3.7. In both poems the woman attempts to rouse her lover's dormant member manually (*Amores* 3.7.73–74; *Elegies* 5.57–58) and indignantly accuses her partner of having another lover (*Amores* 3.7.80; *Elegies* 5.61–62). But beyond this the two poems are very different in nature. Ovid is a young man. There is no reason to think his impotence is anything but temporary, even though, in his despondency, he wonders what old age has in store for him, if his youth occasionally fails him in this way (*Amores* 3.7.17–18).

Maximianus is old; his impotence is part of his condition, not a passing aberration. If in classical elegy love is a young person's pursuit, then the poetry of Maximianus, despite its echoes in subject and theme of the Augustan author, is a kind of antielegy.[21]

Despite the prominence of classical love elegy as foil to Maximianus' poetry, other genres exert influence on the poems in a way familiar to readers of late Latin poetry, which is often marked by a certain generic indeterminacy. For instance, the *Elegies* show some affinities with satire, most prominently in the long section on the woes of old age in poem 1, which recalls in general terms the section on the same subject in Juvenal's tenth satire (10.187–288). In elegy 3, Boethius' congratulations to Maximianus for overcoming his erotic desires (3.87–90) evoke a similar context in a satire of Horace, where the elder Cato offers congratulations to a young man who has also gained control of his sexual impulses, though by a rather different strategy, by patronizing a brothel (1.2.31–35). In addition to these parallels with satire the poet's erotic imbroglios are also from time to time reminiscent of comedy and mime. Poem 5 is particularly generically diverse, including two speeches by the *Graia puella*, the first in the form of a mock epitaph, the second a quasi-philosophic account of universal order, variously described as Lucretian and/or Neoplatonic. One further *comparandum* deserves mention. The poet Orientius in his *Commonitorium*, a poem of Christian moral instruction in elegiac couplets dating to the first decades of the fifth century, includes a passage itemizing the physical decay of old age (1.417–436). The context is a denunciation of love and of female beauty: good looks are only transitory, of no value in the larger Christian scheme of things.

As the example of Orientius suggests, the elegiac meter was not exclusively dedicated to the subject of love. While in Latin literature, because of the prominence of Augustan love elegy, this association is often made, in fact elegiacs had always been something of a multipurpose meter. Already Ovid employs it for a wide range of subjects: not just for the erotic, but for a poetic calendar of the Roman year and for his poems from exile. In Late Antiquity the meter is employed, for instance, for poems on the miraculous rebirth of the phoenix and on the martyrdom of St. Hippolytus, and for a final book of an otherwise prose work on agriculture, dedicated to the subject of pruning.[22] In particular, elegy, for etymological reasons, was associated with expressions of grief. Maximianus' choice of the meter for his complaints about old age, therefore, had special appropriateness, while the large narrative content of poems 3 to 5, though untypical of love elegy, had ample precedent in the elegiac tradition.

Already in the classical period it was normal for the elegiac couplet to encompass a complete unit of sense. The pentameter, which occupies the second half of the couplet, begins in the same way as the preceding hexameter, but then doubles back on itself; the second half of the line mirrors the first, thereby creating a sense of closure. Maximianus' elegiacs conform to this pattern. The relation between couplets tends to be paratactic and cumulative. More extended sentence structure, as for instance in the first two couplets of poem 5, which set the scene for the narrative that follows, is rare. Within the couplet, too, certain regularities are apparent. There is often, though by no means invariably, a break in the clause structure between hexameter and pentameter: the relation between the two halves of the couplet may be that of subordinate and main clause, or it may be complementary, enumerative, or synonymic (i.e., the two lines phrase the same idea differently). All are familiar patterns in Latin dactylic poetry. Figures of repetition—anaphora (repetition of the same word at the beginning of successive parallel syntactic units), polyptoton (repetition of the same word in different inflectional forms), and antithesis—may serve to articulate structure within and between couplets. Maximianus' general conformity in clause structure to elegiac tradition accords with the tendency of his prosody, which is largely correct by classical standards, despite a few false quantities.

Interpretation

The generic indeterminacy of the *Elegies* is matched by uncertainty about the collection's interpretation. The overarching themes of love and old age that predominate in the first and last pairs of poems (1 and 2, and 5 and 6), culminate in a kind of funeral dirge for Maximianus' fading powers, a condition he represents as a sort of living death. Some have seen here a serious or moralizing purpose, with a lesson to be drawn on the false pleasures of love and the evils of age. Others have found any suggestion of moral seriousness hard to sustain and have been more inclined to detect parodic or ironic intent. A further question concerns the poem's relation to Christianity. What does it mean to write such a set of poems in what is now a fully Christian society? Does Maximianus intend a critique of Christian opinion or is there a covert Christian message? Both positions have been maintained.[23] It is relevant that early in the sixth century Ennodius, at that time deacon of Milan, could have Cupid in an epithalamium denounce the deleterious effect of "chill virginity" (*frigida . . . virginitas*, *Carmina* 1.4.57–58) that "takes possession of the bodies of men," and celebrate the force of human procreation. Christian opinion was not, then, necessarily hostile to physical love.

The same kind of interpretative questions that apply to the collection as a whole also arise with regard to individual poems, especially poems 3 and 5. In the former the main issue is the role of Boethius. After urging Maximianus to abandon all scruples in pressing his attentions on Aquilina, the philosopher apparently plays the role of pander by bribing the girl's parents to acquiesce in the relationship. The situation is further complicated by Boethius' compliment to the young man after he has abandoned the affair and welcomed "holy chastity" (*sancta . . . virginitas*, 3.83–84), praising him for his conquest of erotic desire. Some have seen this as the older man's intent all along, to effect a homeopathic cure, curing like with like.[24] Others have found this hard to believe and have detected a satirical intent.[25] The poet's description of Boethius when he is first introduced as "great searcher of important things" (3.47) can accordingly be read either at face value or ironically. Boethius' role in this poem as a healer of Maximianus has further suggested to some an analogy with the role of personified Philosophy in his *Consolation of Philosophy*, who cures the spiritual sickness of the prisoner. (Maximianus certainly knew that work.) Finally there is intriguing evidence in an epigram of Ennodius (*C.* 2.132, translated by Juster in Appendix C), that Boethius had a reputation as a lover, making him an appropriate adviser on erotic matters.[26]

In poem 5 the same critical division between a serious and a parodic reading centers on the two speeches of the *Graia puella*, the first mourning the death of the *mentula*, the second celebrating it as a principle of cosmic order.[27] It is hard, though, to read at least the first speech, a funeral lament for Maximianus' moribund penis, as anything but parody. The longer speech, in praise of the *mentula* as cosmic principle, certainly has parallels in content with Lucretius' proem to the *De rerum natura*, celebrating the generative power of Venus as originator of universal peace and harmony. But to my mind the lines near the end of the speech that laud the penis in metaphorical terms for its ability to rouse itself continually for new conquests undercut the philosophical seriousness of what precedes.

Whatever line a reader takes on these problems of interpretation, it is undeniable that individual poems allow a variety of approaches, and definitive solutions are hard to come by. The same is true of the collection as a whole. The poems prompt an integrative reading but also frustrate it. That is part of their appeal. There are recurrent themes—love and chastity, sexuality, old age and death—but the tone of the poems and the attitude they adopt to their subject prove elusive.

The Appendix Maximiani

Two manuscripts of Maximianus contain a further six short poems attributed to the poet of the *Elegies*. They have come to be known as the *Appendix Maximiani*.[28] The authenticity of the attribution to Maximianus is a matter of debate. There are a few similarities of language, especially in the first poem of the *Appendix*, but metrical irregularities in some of the poems count against the attribution. One scholar believed that they were youthful productions of Maximianus.[29] In the absence of conclusive evidence scholars have generally been inclined to deny the poems' authenticity.

The poems of the *Appendix* fall into three pairs, associated by subject matter. Poems 1 and 2 are erotic in nature; both describe a beautiful woman and show strong Ovidian influence. Poems 3 and 4, the most interesting and assured of the group, describe a fortress of Theodahad, Ostrogothic king (534–536). (Poem 3, alone in the *Appendix*, is in dactylic hexameters rather than elegiac couplets.) The fortress is a symbol of the protection and prosperity Theodahad offers his people. Praise of the building serves to praise its builder. The last two poems both begin with the same antithesis, between country and city, and surely refer to the same opulent city dwelling; in both cases the amenities of the country have found a place in the city, in the first by introducing there a well-watered grove, in the second a stream that feeds fishponds.

Notes

1. The poems are described by Jacques Fontaine, in his review of Schetter (1970), as "the swan song of ancient elegy" (*REL* 48 [1970], 694) and by Pinotti (1989), 183, as "the last representative of erotic elegy."

2. Schetter (1970), 1–8.

3. Webster (1900), 9–11.

4. Öberg (1999), 11–45.

5. For 534–535 see Romano (1979), 318–319; for 546 Boano (1949), 202–203; for 546 or 549 Schneider (2003), 50–52. Boano also raises the possibility of some earlier, less well attested, embassy.

6. Boano (1949), 200–203, believes Corippus imitated Maximianus, Schneider (2003), 66–67, the reverse. I have some reservations whether the similarities are sufficiently distinctive to prove imitation in either direction.

7. Ratkowitsch's (1986) proposed ninth-century date for the *Elegies* has not won acceptance.

8. As established by Schetter (1970), 158–162.

9. Spaltenstein (1983), 65–72, and Schneider (2003), 21–36. Fo (1986), 9–21, makes a persuasive case for retaining the traditional division.

10. *Non sum qui fueram; periit pars maxima nostri.*

11. The wording "I don't write fawning poems" (*non blanda poemata fingo*, 129) could possibly mean that he still composes, but that his poetry is no longer enticing.

12. Maximianus describes the gifts of Venus as no longer giving him pleasure (1.163). Lines 125–126 also probably contain a double entendre.

13. Line 4.55 refers to older age, *serior aetas*. These couplets fit well with poem 5. The ending of poem 4 has been much discussed; see, for example, Fo (1986–1987), 102–105, and Schneider (2003), 222. Division at 4.55 has some manuscript authority.

14. Schetter (1970), 161–162.

15. Fo (1986), 15–18.

16. Fo (1986–1987), 94–96.

17. The Ovidian word for these signals is *notae*: so Maximianus 3.14.

18. *Quod licet ingratum est.* See also 2.19.36 and 3.4.17 and 25–26.

19. Both have breasts that invite cupping with the hand (*Am.* 1.5.20; *El.* 5.27–28) and below those trim breasts a flat belly or full thighs (*Am.* 1.5.21; *El.* 5.30).

20. On the non-elegiac in the *Elegies*, where elegiac is taken to refer to love elegy, see Consolino (1997), 375–376 and 391–394; Pinotti (1989), 189–191; Gärtner (2004), 146–147 (on elegy 5); and Goldlust (2011), 165–169.

21. Goldlust (2011), 167.

22. Respectively Lactantius *De ave phoenice*; Prudentius *Peristephanon* 11; Palladius *De re rustica*, book 14.

23. Ratkowitsch (1986), 63–127, in arguing for a ninth-century date, describes the collection as cautionary moral reading for monks; Schneider (2003), 110–129, sees it as an assertion of the pleasures of the body in response to Christian asceticism.

24. Ratkowitsch (1986), 95–96. For a discussion of the issues surrounding the poem see Fo (1986–1987), 96–102.

25. Webster (1900), 94–95, Szövérffy (1968), 361.

26. See Shanzer (1983), 183–195. She characterizes the poet's attitude to Boethius as "gently ironic" (189).

27. Fo (1986–1987), 108–111, argues for the serious philosophical content of the woman's final speech; Webster (1900), 106, and Szövérffy (1968), 362–364, see it as satirical or parodic.

28. The title derives from Schetter (1960), 117, who first edited poem 6 from a newly discovered manuscript and showed what had previously been edited as a single poem by Garrod actually consisted of two poems, the present 4 and 5. The most important subsequent treatment is Fo (1984–1985), 151–230.

29. Romano (1979), 309–329.

Elegies

~ Elegy 1

aemula quid cessas finem properare senectus
cur et in hoc fesso corpore tarda venis

solve precor miseram tali de carcere vitam
mors est iam requies vivere poena mihi

non sum qui fueram periit pars maxima nostri
* hoc quoque quod superest languor et horror habent

lux gravis in luctu rebus gratissima laetis
quodque omni peius funere velle mori

dum iuvenile decus dum mens sensusque maneret
orator toto clarus in orbe fui

saepe poetarum mendacia dulcia finxi
et veros titulos res mihi ficta dabat

saepe perorata percepi lite coronam
et merui linguae praemia grata meae

quae cum defectis iam sint immortua membris
heu senibus vitae portio quanta manet

nec minor his aderat sublimis gratia formae
* quae si mihi desint cetera multa placent

~ Elegy 1

Jealous old age, why hold back hastening the end
        and why come slowly for this weary body?

Release my wretched life, I beg, from such a prison!
        Death is now rest, my life a punishment.

I am not who I was; my greatest part has perished.
        Fatigue—and dread too—cling to what survives.

Life is grave during grief, most dear in happy times;
        each wish to die is worse than any death.

While youthful handsomeness, while mind and senses stayed,
        I was a famous speaker everywhere.

I often fashioned sweet deceptions of the poets,
        and fictions kept providing me true honors.

I often won a wreath with closing legal pleas
        and earned some welcome prizes with my language.

Since what is worn out now in body parts has died,
        alas, how much life remains for old men?

It helped with these (no less than heavenly) good looks,
        which, if they left me, would delight most others.

quin etiam virtus fulvo pretiosor auro
per quam praeclarum plus micat ingenium

si libuit celeres arcu temptare sagittas
occubuit telis praeda petita meis

si placuit canibus densos circumdare saltus
prostravi multas non sine laude feras

dulce fuit madidam si fors versare palaestram
implicui validis lubrica membra toris

nunc agili cursu cunctos anteire solebam
* nunc tragicos cantus exuperare melos

augebat meritum dulcis mixtura bonorum
ut semper varium plus micat artis opus

nam quaecumque solent per se perpensa placere
alterno potius iuncta decore placent

has inter virtutis opes tolerantia rerum
spernebat cunctas insuperata minas

vertice nudato ventos pluviasque ferebam
non mihi solstitium non grave frigus erat

innabam gelidas tiberini gurgitis undas
nec timui dubio credere membra freto

quamvis exiguo poteram requiescere somno
et quamvis modico membra fovere cibo

at si me subito vinosus repperit hospes
aut fecit laetus sumere multa dies

cessit et ipse pater bacchus stupuitque bibentem
et qui cuncta solet vincere victus abit

Still, character is valued more than yellow gold,
for it outshines innate ability.

If it were sport to try swift arrows with a bow,
the quarry fell when hunted by my weapons.

If it was pleasing to surround dense woods with dogs,
I took down many beasts (not without praise).

To hit a sweaty gym, if just by chance, was sweet.
I grappled greasy limbs with sturdy muscles.

Sometimes I'd outdo everyone with nimble feet.
Sometimes my tragic songs surpassed their ditties.

A mixture of sweet qualities improved my worth,
just as the varied artwork glitters more,

for that which tends to please considered by itself
is better blended with contrasting beauty.

Along with these fine traits, my steadfast fortitude
in matters fended off all of these "threats":

I tolerated wind and rain with head exposed;
for me no summer's heat, no chill was harsh.

I swam the icy currents of the Tiber's waves
and did not fear to trust my limbs in rapids.

I could refresh myself with sleep, albeit brief,
and nourish limbs with scraps, however small,

but if a wine-soaked host abruptly sought me out
or good times led to drinking many days,

even old Bacchus marveled at my binge and yielded,
and he who vanquishes all snuck off, vanquished.

haut facile est animum tantis inflectere rebus
ut res oppositas mens ferat una duas

hoc quoque virtutum quondam certamine magnum
socratem palmam promeruisse ferunt

hinc etiam rigidum memorant valuisse catonem
non res in vitium sed male facta cadunt

* intrepidus quaecumque forent ad utrasque ferebam
cedebant animo tristia cuncta meo

pauperiem modico contentus semper amavi
et rerum dominus nil cupiendo fui

tu me sola tibi subdis miseranda senectus
cui cedit quicquid vincere cuncta potest

in te corruimus tua sunt quaecumque fatiscunt
ultima teque tuo conficis ipsa malo

ergo his ornatum meritis provincia tota
optabat natis me sociare suis

sed mihi dulce magis resoluto vivere collo
nullaque coniugii vincula grata pati

ibam per mediam venali corpore romam
spectandus cunctis undique virginibus

quaeque peti poterat fuerat vel forte petita
erubuit vultum visa puella meum

et modo subridens latebras fugitiva petebat
non tamen effugiens tota latere volens

sed magis ex aliqua cupiebat parte videri
laetior hoc potius quod male tecta fuit

It isn't easy focusing upon great things
so thought sustains two opposites as one.

In the same vein, they say that in this test of genius,
the famous Socrates once earned a palm.

Next they declare stern Cato had the power too;
no acts, save those done wrongly, count toward guilt.

Undaunted, on each side I'd argue what might be;
depressed, they all conceded to my logic.

Content with less, I always loved great poverty
and was the lord of goods by wanting nothing.

Only you overcome me, miserable old age,
which can defeat whatever conquers all.

We have collapsed toward you, whatever cracks is yours,
and you're consumed at last by your own evil.

Equipped with these endowments, therefore, the whole province
hoped to introduce me to their daughters,

although I lived more sweetly with my neck unyoked
and never bore the welcome chains of marriage.

I would proceed through central Rome, its flesh for sale,
examined everywhere by all the girls,

and a young girl who could be sought, or had been sought
perhaps, when glimpsed would blush at my expression,

and, barely smiling, looked for hideouts—wishing, though,
that her coquettishness not fully hide her.

She wished instead for part of her to be revealed;
she cheered up when she was more badly hidden.

sic cunctis formosus ego gratusque videbar
omnibus et sponsus sic generalis eram

sed tantum sponsus nam me natura pudicum
fecerat et casto pectore durus eram

nam dum praecipuae cupio me iungere formae
permansi viduo frigidus usque toro

omnis foeda mihi atque omnis mihi rustica visa est
nullaque coniugio digna puella meo

horrebam tenues horrebam corpore pingues
non mihi grata brevis non mihi longa fuit

cum media tantum dilexi ludere forma
maior enim mediis gratia rebus inest

corporis has nostri mollis lascivia partes
incolit has sedes mater amoris habet

quaerebam gracilem sed quae non macra fuisset
carnis ad officium carnea membra placent

sit quod in amplexu delectet stringere corpus
ne laedant pressum quaelibet ossa latus

candida contempsi nisi quae suffusa rubore
vernarent propriis ora serena rosis

hunc venus ante alios sibi vindicat ipsa colorem
diligit et florem cypris ubique suum

aurea caesaries demissaque lactea cervix
* vultibus ingenuis visa decere magis

nigra supercilia frons libera lumina nigra
urebant animum saepe notata meum

So I seemed beautiful and lovable to all,
and so to each I was a standard suitor—

but *just* a suitor, since my nature made me chaste
and I was steadfast in my virgin soul,

for while I longed to wed a truly gorgeous girl,
I lingered in a frigid, wifeless bed.

They each seemed gross to me and each uncouth to me,
and not one girl deserved to be my wife.

I shuddered at the slender, shuddered at the fat;
short wasn't right for me—nor tall for me.

I loved to frolic only with a middling figure—
for the greater charm is in the midsized things.

Within these body parts sweet lasciviousness
resides; Love's mother rules these spots.

I searched for someone thin, but not one who was scrawny;
some limbs with meat enhance the carnal function.

In an embrace let flesh that pleases be caressed
so on both sides bones pressed down do not hurt.

I hated white except upon a cheerful face suffused
with pink that blossomed with distinctive roses.

Venus herself demands her color over others,
and Cypris loves her flower everywhere.

A lowered milky neck and flowing golden hair
appeared to fit far more with modest looks.

Black brows, a confident expression, and black eyes
inflamed my soul (as I have often written).

flammea dilexi modicumque tumentia labra
quae gustata mihi basia plena darent

in tereti collo visum est pretiosius aurum
gemma et iudicio plus radiare meo

singula turpe seni quondam quaesita referre
et quod tunc decuit iam modo crimen habet

diversos diversa iuvant non omnibus annis
omnia conveniunt res prius apta nocet

exultat levitate puer gravitate senectus
inter utrumque manens stat iuvenile decus

hunc tacitum tristemque decet fit clarior ille
laetitia et linguae garrulitate suae

cuncta trahit secum vertitque volubile tempus
nec patitur certa currere quaeque via

nunc quod longa mihi gravis est et inutile aetas
vivere cum nequeam sit mihi posse mori

o quam dura premit miseros condicio vitae
nec mors humano subiacet arbitrio

dulce mori miseris sed mors optata recedit
* et cum tristis erit praecipitata venit

me vero heu tantis defunctum in partibus olim
vivum tartareas constat inire vias

iam minor auditus gustus minor ipsa caligant
lumina vix tactu noscere certa queo

nullus dulcis odor nulla est iam grata voluptas
sensibus expertem quis superesse putet

I loved a bit of pout and sultry scarlet lips,
which, being tasted, gave me ample kisses.

Some gold appeared more precious on a silky neck
and, in my view, a jewel bedazzled more.

Each ancient issue that old men rehash is shameful—
and what occurred back then keeps its verdict.

Diverse things please diverse types. Nothing satisfies
all ages; what was fitting once is wrong.

A boy exults in folly, an old man in sternness,
and a youth's deeds remain between them both.

Silence and sadness suit one man; another is
more famous for his chatter and his joy.

Time rolling on disturbs and drags with it all things
and lets nobody run a certain route.

Since now for me my long old age is harsh and futile,
since I can live no longer, let me die.

O how life's brutal contract burdens wretched men!
Death does not acquiesce to human will.

Death's sweet for wretches, but when welcomed death retreats,
and when it's sad it comes all in a rush.

Alas, with me long truly dead in many parts,
it's clear I enter hellish roads alive.

Taste fades now, hearing fades; even my eyes are fogging.
I barely can discern what's real by touch.

No scent is sweet, no pleasure gratifying now.
Who could believe one goes on lacking senses?

en lethaea meam subeunt oblivia mentem
nec confusa sui iam meminisse potest

ad nullum consurgit opus cum corpore languet
* atque intenta suis astupet ipsa malis

carmina nulla cano cantandi summa voluptas
effugit et vocis gratia vera perit

non fora sollicito non blanda poemata fingo
litibus haut rabidis commoda iura sequor

ipsaque me species quondam dilecta reliquit
et videor formae mortuus esse meae

pro niveo rutiloque prius nunc inficit ora
pallor et exanguis funereusque color

aret sicca cutis rigidi stant undique nervi
et lacerant uncae scabida membra manus

quondam ridentes oculi nunc fonte perenni
deplangunt poenas nocte dieque suas

et quos grata prius ciliorum serta tegebant
desuper incumbens hispida silva premit

ac velut inclusi caeco conduntur in antro
torvum nescio quid heu furiale vident

iam pavor est vidisse senem nec credere possis
hunc hominem humana qui ratione caret

si libros repeto duplex se littera findit
largior occurrit pagina nota mihi

claram per nebulas videor mihi cernere lucem
nubila sunt oculis ipsa serena meis

Watch Lethean amnesia steal upon my mind;
bewildered now, it can't recall itself.

It does not rise for work when flesh is languishing
and is benumbed, intent on its own woes.

I sing no songs; my greatest joy, reciting, flees,
and the true charm of words is vanishing.

I don't disturb the courts; I don't write fawning poems.
I don't pursue awards with savage lawsuits,

and even my own once-loved looks abandon me,
and I am looking dead in my appearance.

In place of red and snowy white, a sallowness
and deathly bloodless color stain my face.

Skin shrivels dry, tight muscles stiffen everywhere,
and clawlike hands keep scratching itchy limbs.

Now, with a never-ending stream, once-laughing eyes
bemoan their punishment through night and day,

and where a welcome wreath of brows was sheltering,
a drooping thatch harasses from above

and they are shrouded as if closed in some dark cave.
Alas, they witness something grim and frenzied!

An old man is a fright to witness, and you doubt
a man who lacks his faculties is human.

If I revisit books, their letters split in pairs;
for me familiar writing seems much larger.

It seems that I detect a brilliant light through haze;
the clouds themselves are clear inside my eyes.

* eripitur sine nocte dies caligine caeca
septum tartareo quis neget esse loco

talia quis demens homini persuaserit auctor
ut cupiat voto turpior esse suo

iam subeunt morbi subeunt discrimina mille
iam dulces epulae deliciaeque nocent

cogimur a gratis animum suspendere rebus
atque ut vivamus vivere destitimus

et me quem dudum iam nulla adversa nocebant
ipsa quibus regimur nunc alimenta gravant

esse libet saturum saturum mox esse pigebit
praestat ut abstineam abstinuisse nocet

quae modo profuerat contraria redditur esca
fastidita iacet quae modo dulcis erat

non veneris non grata mihi sunt munera bacchi
nec quicquid vitae fallere damna solet

sola iacens natura manet quae sponte per horas
solvitur et vitio carpitur ipsa suo

non totiens experta mihi medicamina prosunt
* non aegris quicquid ferre solebant opes

sed cum materia pereunt quaecumque parantur
fit magis et damnis tristior urna suis

non secus instantem cupiens fulcire ruinam
diversis contra nititur obicibus

donec longa dies omni compage soluta
ipsum cum rebus subruat auxilium

Day passes without night. Within deep darkness who
denies his jailing in a hellish place?

What expert is so mad he would convince a man
that in his prayer he wants to be more loathsome?

First, illnesses encroach, uncounted risks encroach,
then banquets, sweets, and pleasures take their toll.

We're forced to give up fondness for the pleasant things,
and we stop living so that we might live,

and I, who for so long no adversaries harmed,
I'm ruled by foods that now themselves oppress.

It's better being full; soon being full annoys.
It's best I fast; it's painful to have fasted.

With food that served well once, the opposite returns;
repelled, one throws away what once was sweet.

No food, no gifts of wine, are welcome to me now,
nor anything that tends to mask life's losses.

Just nature lying ruined lingers, which in time
degrades and is consumed by its own weakness.

The proven treatments often do not help me much,
nor do what tends to do the job for pains,

but what's prepared as medication goes to waste,
and the urn gets much sadder with the losses.

Not unlike one who wants to brace a threatened ruin,
one leans against assorted reinforcements

until time's passage undermines the help itself
with the whole structure broken into pieces.

quid quod nulla levant animum spectacula rerum
nec mala tot vitae dissimulare licet

turpe seni vultus nitidi vestesque decorae
quis sine iamque ipsum vivere turpe seni

crimen amare iocos crimen convivia cantus
o miseri quorum gaudia crimen habent

quid mihi divitiae quarum si dempseris usum
quamvis largus opum semper egenus ero

immo etiam poena est partis incumbere rebus
quas cum possideas est violare nefas

non aliter sitiens vicinas tantalus undas
captat et appositis abstinet ora cibis

efficior custos rerum magis ipse mearum
conservans aliis quae periere mihi

sicut in auricomis dependens plurimus hortis
pervigil observat non sua poma draco

hinc me sollicitum torquent super omnia curae
hinc requies animo non datur ulla meo

quaerere quae nequeo semper retinere laboro
et retinens semper nil tenuisse puto

stat dubius tremulusque senex semperque malorum
credulus et stultus quae facit ipse timet

laudat praeteritos praesentes despicit annos
hoc tantum rectum quod sapit ipse putat

se solum doctum se iudicat esse peritum
et quod sit sapiens desipit inde magis

What of the fact no public shows uplift the spirit?
One cannot hide so many of life's pains.

It shames the old—their swanky clothes and polished looks;
without these things now, living shames the old.

It's a vice loving jokes—the feasts, the songs a vice.
O wretches, whose delights display their vice!

For me, what are great riches? If you banned their use,
despite great wealth, I always would be poor.

Indeed, it's still a burden owning purchased assets;
while you possess them harming them is wrong.

As when parched Tantalus tries reaching nearby streams
and his mouth always misses offered foods,

I have myself become more watchman of my assets—
saving for others what is lost for me.

As in the garden draped with many golden leaves,
the snake on watch does not protect its apples,

so restless worries torture me above all else,
so rest is never given to my spirit.

I cannot gain from what I always saved from work
and always think my holdings held no value.

A wary, shaking old man always stays convinced
of woes—and what he fears the dope provokes.

He praises bygone years, despises present times;
he thinks that only what he knows is true.

He deems that only *he* is skillful, *he* is smart,
then acts more foolish since he would be wise.

multa licet nolis referens eademque revolvens
horret et alloquium conspuit ipse suum

deficit auditor non deficit ipse loquendo
o sola fortes garrulitate senes

omnia nequicquam clamosis vocibus implet
nil satis est horret quae placuere modo

arridet de se ridentibus ac sibi plaudens
incipit opprobrio laetior esse suo

hae sunt primitiae mortis his partibus aetas
defluit et pigris gressibus ima petit

non habitus non ipse color non gressus euntis
non species eadem quae fuit ante manet

labitur ex umeris demisso corpore vestis
quaeque brevis fuerat iam modo longa mihi est

contrahimur miroque modo decrescimus ipsa
diminui nostri corporis ossa putes

nec caelum spectare licet sed prona senectus
terram qua genita est et reditura videt

fitque tripes prorsus quadrupes ut parvulus infans
et per sordentem flebile repit humum

ortus cuncta suos repetunt matremque requirunt
et redit ad nihilum quod fuit ante nihil

hinc est quod baculo incumbens ruitura senectus
assiduo pigram verbere pulsat humum

et numerosa movens certo vestigia plausu
talia rugato creditur ore loqui

Rehashing and repeating (though you do not want
  that much this way), he shakes and spits his speech.

A listener just fades; *he* doesn't fade while talking.
  O old men, only forceful with their chatter!

In vain he fills up everything with shouted words.
  Nothing's enough; he dreads what was once pleasing.

He mocks his being mocked and, clapping for himself,
  he starts to be more happy in his shame.

These are first fruits of death; age creeps throughout these limbs
  and searches for the depths with sluggish steps.

Not posture, not one's own complexion, not one's gait—
  no feature stays the same it was before.

My clothes are sliding off my drooping body's shoulders,
  and now what was once short for me is long.

We just compress and shrink extraordinarily;
  you'd think our body's bones themselves diminished.

He can't see sky, but an old man keeps peering down
  at earth, from which he came and shall return,

and is three-footed, even four, just like a tiny child,
  and, sadly, crawls upon the filthy ground.

All creatures trace their roots and go back to their mother,
  and what was nothing once returns to nothing.

It's why a failing old man, leaning on his staff,
  keeps pounding stubborn earth with constant blows

and making many footsteps with a steady beat,
  his wrinkled mouth is thought to speak this way:

suscipe me genetrix nati miserere laborum
membra peto gremio fessa fovere tuo

horrent me pueri nequeo velut ante videri
horrendos partus cur sinis esse tuos

nil mihi cum superis explevi munera vitae
redde precor patrio mortua membra solo

quid miseros variis prodest extendere poenis
non est materni pectoris ista pati

his dictis trunco titubantes sustinet artus
neglecti repetens stramina dura tori

quo postquam iacuit misero quid funere differt
heu tantum adtracti corporis ossa vides

cumque magis semper iaceam vivamque iacendo
* quis suo vitali me putet esse loco

iam poena est totum quod vivimus urimur aestu
officiunt nebulae frigus et aura nocet

ros laedit modicoque etiam corrumpimur imbre
veris et autumni laedit amoena dies

hinc miseros scabies hinc tussis anhela fatigat
continuos gemitus aegra senectus habet

hos superesse reor quibus et spirabilis aer
et lux qua regimur redditur ipsa gravis

* ipse etiam cunctis requies gratissima somnus
avolat et sera vix mihi nocte redit

vel si lassatos umquam dignabitur artus
turbidus in quantis horret imaginibus

"Pick me up, Mother! Pity struggles of your child!
I long to warm weak limbs upon your lap.

Boys dread me; I cannot be looked at as before.
Why do you let your children be so dreadful?

With no one left for me, I have consumed life's gifts.
Return dead limbs, I beg, to native soil.

Why add assorted punishments for wretched men?
No mother's heart should have to suffer that."

That said, returning to his lonely rough straw bed,
he props up quaking limbs with his tree trunk.

While prone how does he differ from a wretched corpse?
Alas, you see just bones in withered flesh.

And when instead I rest, and live by always resting,
who for his part would think I was alive?

All that we're living through is pain: we're scorched by heat;
clouds punish; cold and wind are wreaking havoc;

dew causes harm (we're even ruined by light rain);
and pleasant days of spring and fall annoy—

hence this vile itching, hence a raspy cough fatigues.
Our sick old age involves incessant whines.

It lingers, I believe, for those for whom fresh air
and even light, which guides us, grow burdensome.

Even the rest most dear to us —sleep—slips away
from me and rarely comes back late at night,

or, if it ever deems my weary body worthy,
confused, it horrifies in many visions!

mollia fulcra tori duris sunt cautibus aequa
parva licet magnum pallia pondus habent

cogor per mediam turbatus surgere noctem
multaque ne patiar deteriora pati

vincimur infirmi defectu corporis et qua
noluero infelix hac ego parte trahor

omnia naturae solvuntur viscera nostrae
et praeclarum quam male nutat opus

his veniens onerata malis incurva senectus
cedere ponderibus se docet ipsa suis

ergo quis has cupiat per longum ducere poenas
paulatimque anima deficiente mori

morte mori melius quam vitam ducere mortis
et sensus membris hic sepelire suis

non queror heu longi quod totum solvitis anni
improba naturae dicere iussa nefas

deficiunt validi longaevo tempore tauri
et quondam pulcer fit modo turpis equus

fracta diu rabidi conpescitur ira leonis
* lentaque per senium caspia tigris erit

ipsa etiam veniens consumit saxa vetustas
et nullum est quod non tempore cedat opus

set mihi venturos melius praevertere casus
atque infelices anticipare dies

poena minor certam subito perferre ruinam
quod timeas gravius sustinuisse diu

Soft cushions of a couch are like rough, jagged rocks;
	though light, thin blankets have a heavy weight.

Vexed in the middle of the night, I'm forced to rise,
	and greatly suffer not to suffer worse.

I'm conquered by frail flesh's weakness and, depressed,
	I'm dragged into this role that I resist.

My body's organs are all being broken down,
	and this exquisite structure badly totters!

Encroaching old age, bent by these oppressive woes,
	directs itself to yield to its own burdens,

thus who would wish to bear these punishments for long
	and slowly die with a declining mind?

Better to die a death than lead a life of death
	and bury senses here in one's own limbs.

Alas, long years, I don't protest; you break it all.
	it's wrong to call the laws of nature evil.

The mighty bulls diminish in the course of time,
	and someday a fine horse becomes repulsive.

Long broken down, the angry lion's rage is checked;
	a Caspian tiger will be slow in dotage.

With coming epochs even rocks themselves erode,
	and there's no work which does not yield with time,

but it is better to forestall my coming woes
	and to anticipate unhappy days.

It is less pain to bear sure ruin all at once;
	It's harder putting up with what you dread.

at quos fert alios quis posset dicere casus
hoc quoque difficile est commemorasse seni

iurgia contemptus violentaque damna secuntur
nec quisquam ex tantis praebet amicus opem

* ipsi me pueri atque ipsae sine lite puellae
turpe putant dominum iam vocitare suum

irrident gressum irrident iam denique vultum
et tremulum quondam quod timuere caput

cumque nihil videam tamen hoc spectare licebit
ut gravior misero poena sit ista mihi

felix qui meruit tranquillam ducere vitam
et laeto stabiles claudere fine dies

dura satis miseris memoratio prisca bonorum
et gravius summo culmine mersa ruit

But who can talk about the other woes he bears?
Recalling this is hard, too, for old men.

Invective, scorn, and heavy losses follow next;
no friend (of many) offered any help.

Without dispute the boys and girls themselves believe
it's shocking now to name me as their "master."

They mock my walk; they finally now mock my face
and palsied head, which once inspired fear,

and while I may see nothing, this I can still see,
so for a wretch like me such pain is graver.

Happy is he who earned the tranquil life he led
and closed routine days with a happy end.

Recalling bygone joys is quite rugged for the sad,
and from the highest peak their plunge drops harder.

~ Elegy 2

* en dilecta mihi nimium formosa lichoris
cum qua mens eadem res fuit una mihi

post multos quibus indivisi viximus annos
respuit amplexus heu pavefacta meos

iamque alios iuvenes aliosque requirit amores
me vocat imbellem decrepitum senem

nec meminisse volet transactae dulcia vitae
nec me quod potius reddidit ipsa senem

immo etiam causas ingrata ac perfida fingit
ut spretum vitio iudicet esse meo

haec me praeteriens cum dudum forte videret
expuit obductis vestibus ora tegens

hunc inquit dilexi hic me complexit amavit
huic ego saepe nefas oscula blanda dedi

nauseat et priscum vomitu ceu fundit amorem
imponit capiti plurima dira meo

en quid longa dies nunc affert ut sibi quemquam
quondam dilectum prodere turpe putet

~ Elegy 2

Behold the gorgeous Lycoris, much loved by me,
    with whom my world was one, my soul as well.

After the many years that we had lived together,
    alas, dismayed, she kissed off my embrace

and now is chasing new young men and new desires;
    she's calling me "a gutless, weak old man"

and wishes to forget our sweet transpired life—
    not that she left me, an old man, instead.

Indeed, ungrateful and untrue, she makes up claims
    so she can judge rejection is my fault.

By chance not long ago she saw me passing by;
    while clothing covered up her mouth, she spat.

She said, "I liked *him*? Did he love me during sex?
    Damn it! I often gave him tender kisses!"

She's nauseous and she spews "past love" as if it's vomit;
    she lays a slew of curses on my head.

See what long life now brings: that she could think to screw
    a person whom she previously loved.

nonne fuit melius tali me tempore fungi
quo nulli merito despiciendus eram

quam postquam periit quicquid fuit ante decoris
extinctum meritis vivere criminibus

iam nihil est totum quod viximus omnia secum
tempus praeteriens horaque summa trahit

atque tamen nivei circumdant tempora cani
et iam caeruleis infecit hora notis

praestat adhuc nimiumque sibi pretiosa videtur
atque annos mecum despicit illa suos

et fateor primae retinet monimenta figurae
atque inter cineres condita flamma manet

ut video pulcris etiam vos parcitis anni
nec veteris formae gratia tota perit

reliquiis veterum iuvenes pascuntur amorum
* et si quid nunc est quod fuit ante placet

ante oculos statuunt primaevi temporis actus
atque in praeteritum luxuriantur opus

* set quia nos totus membrorum deserit usus
* nullus in amplexu quod memoretur habet

* et solus miseris superest post omnia luctus
quot bona tunc habui tot modo damna fleo

omnia nemo pati non omnes omnia possunt
efficere hoc vincit femina victa viro

ergo velut pecudum praesentia sola manebunt
nil de transactis quod memoretur erit

Wouldn't it have been better to have died right then,
when I was—rightfully—despised by no one,

than, after any charm had perished that once was,
to live on dead with merited indictments?

All that we lived is nothing; at the final hour
time passing drags off everything with it,

and yet, as snowy hair envelops he with age,
and time now stains her face with deep blue marks,

she stands out even now, and to herself she looks
so precious, and resents her years with me,

and, I concede, a trace of youthful shape endures
and fire stays preserved within her ash.

Indeed, time, I observe you spare the beautiful;
all charm of bygone beauty does not perish.

Young men are fed by remnants of their former loves
and if what was before still is, it's pleasing.

They focus on the exploits of their youthful years
and revel in their past accomplishments,

but, since all function of our "parts" has gone away,
nobody has a memory of sex

and after everything, just grief survives for wretches.
I had great joys then; now I mourn huge losses.

No one endures it all; no one can do it all.
Won by a man, a woman wins this way.

Thus, as with sheep, where just the present will remain,
none of our actions will be what's recalled,

cum fugiunt et bruta novos animalia campos
ac repetunt celeres pascua nota greges

* sub qua decubuit requiescere diligit umbra
taurus et amissum quaerit ovile pecus

dulcius in solitis cantat philomela rubetis
fitque suum rabidis dulce cubile feris

tu tantum bene nota tibi atque experta relinquis
hospitia et potius non manifesta petis

nonne placet melius certis confidere rebus
eventus varios res nova semper habet

sum grandaevus ego nec tu minus alba capillis
par aetas animos conciliare solet

si modo non possum quondam potuisse memento
sit satis ut placeam me placuisse prius

permanet invalidis reverentia prisca colonis
quod fuit in vetulo milite, miles amat

rusticus expertum deflet cessisse iuvencum
cum quo consenuit victor honorat equum

non me adeo primis spoliavit floribus aetas
* en versus facio et mea facta cano

sit gravitas sitque ipsa tibi veneranda senectus
sit quod te nosti vivere velle diu

quis suam in alterius condemnet crimine vitam
et quod pertendit claudere certet iter

dicere si fratrem seu dedignaris amicum
dic patrem affectum nomen utrumque tenet

and while brute beasts avoid the unfamiliar fields
    and flocks return in haste to well-known pastures,

a bull delights where he has lain to rest in shade
    and the lost ewe keeps looking for her fold.

The nightingale sings sweeter in familiar brush,
    and for the savage beasts their lairs are sweet.

Only you leave what's proven and well-known to you,
    and seek instead unclear accommodations.

Isn't it more enjoyable to trust sure things?
    Something new always has uncertain outcomes.

I'm ancient, and you have no less white hair than I;
    the same age tends to bring together minds.

If I can't do it now, recall that I once could.
    Past pleasing should suffice for me to please.

The old respect remains for feeble tenant farmers;
    a soldier loves what was in some old soldier.

The peasant mourns his trusty ox that's been retired;
    the victor hails the steed with which he aged.

So far age has not stripped my early blossoming.
    Look! I write verses and recite my works.

You should respect old age itself and dignity;
    Let life be lengthy, which you knew you want.

Who would condemn another's life for its wrongdoing
    and try to block the path on which he travels?

If you refuse to say "my brother" or "my friend,"
    say "Father"—either name connotes affection.

vincat honor luxum pietas succedat amori
    plus ratio quam vis caeca valere solet

his lacrimis longos quantum fas flevimus annos
    est grave quod doleat commemorare diu

May honor conquer decadence, may duty follow love;
  reason, more than blind power, tends to win out.

I wept long years, as much as proper, with these tears;
  it's hard recalling pain for this long time.

~ Elegy 3

nunc operae pretium est quaedam memorae iuventae
  atque senectutis pauca referre meae

quis lector mentem rerum vertigine fractam
  erigat et maestum noscere curet opus

captus amore tuo demens aquilina ferebar
  pallidus et tristis captus amore tuo

nondum quid sit amor vel quid venus ignea noram
  torquebar potius rusticitate mea

nec minus illa meo percussa cupidine flagrans
  errabat tota non capienda domo

carmina pensa procul nimium dilecta iacebant
  solus amor cordi curaque semper erat

nec reperire viam qua caecum pasceret ignem
  docta nec alternis reddere verba notis

tantum in conspectu studium praestabat inane
  anxia vel solo lumine corda fovens

me pedagogus agit illam tristissima mater
  servabat tanti poena secunda mali

~ Elegy 3

It is now worthwhile to recall some of my youth
 and say a bit regarding my old age,

from which a reader may uplift a mind undone
 by change and try to grasp a sad affair.

Seduced by love for you, I went mad, Aquilina,
 morose and pale, seduced by love for you.

I did not know what love or fiery lust was yet;
 instead I suffered from my awkwardness.

She, smoldering, not any less love-struck than me,
 would wander unrestrained all through the house.

Beloved carding combs, raw wool were tossed aside,
 and love alone became her heart's obsession.

She found no method that would feed the hidden fire,
 no guidance for response with two-way signals.

She showed so much affection in her foolish gaze
 with just one glance relieving anxious feelings.

Her tutor chased me. Her grim mother guarded her,
 a second punishment for such misfortune.

pensabant oculos nutusque per omnia nostros
quaeque solet mentis ducere signa color

dum licuit votum tacite compressimus ambo
et varia dulces teximus arte dolos

at postquam teneram rupit verecundia frontem
nec valuit penitus flamma recepta tegi

mox captare locos et tempora coepimus ambo
atque superciliis luminibusque loqui

fallere sollicitos suspensos ponere gressus
* et muta nullo currere nocte sono

nec longum genetrix furtivum sensit amorem
et medicare parans vulnera vulneribus

increpitat caeditque foventur caedibus ignes
ut solet adiecto crescere flamma rogo

concipiunt geminum flagrantia corda furorem
et sic permixto saevit amore dolor

tunc me visceribus per totum quaerit anhelis
emptum suppliciis quem putat esse suis

nec memorare pudet turpesque revolvere vestes
immo etiam gaudens imputat illa mihi

pro te susceptos iuvat inquit ferre dolores
tu pretium tanti dulce cruoris eris

sit modo certa fides atque inconcussa voluntas
quae nihil imminuit passio nulla fuit

his egomet stimulis angebar semper et ardens
languebam nec spes ulla salutis erat

Throughout it all they scrutinized our eyes and nods—
and coloring that tends to signal thoughts.

When possible, in silence we both stifled longing
and hid our sweet deceits in different ways,

though after modesty emerged on her young face,
deep hidden passion failed to be concealed.

Soon both of us began to seek out times and places,
to converse with eyebrows and our eyes,

to dupe the guards, to put a foot down gingerly,
and in the night to run without a sound.

But not for long! Her mother sensed our secret love
and, getting set to treat the wounds with wounds,

she nagged and slapped; the blaze was kindled by her slaps
like tinder tossed on pyres to stoke the flames.

Our fiery hearts ignite a doubled frenzied passion,
and so an anguish mixed with love is raging,

then, with a panting heart, she looks around for me,
who she believes her purchase through her pleas.

She's shameless rolling back stained clothes to recollect;
joyful, she even credits them to me.

She says, "I'm glad to suffer pains endured for you.
You'll be the sweet return on so much blood.

Just let your faith be certain and your will unbroken;
passion that ruined nothing never was."

I constantly endured these goads, and while in love
I languished, and I had no hope of rescue.

prodere non ausus carpebar vulnere muto
set stupor et macies vocis habebat opus

hic mihi magnarum scrutator maxime rerum
solus boeti fers miseratus opem

nam cum me curis intentum saepe videres
nec posses causas noscere tristitiae

tandem prospiciens tali me peste teneri
mitibus alloquiis pandere clausa iubes

dicito et unde novo correptus carperis aestu
dicito et edicti sume doloris opem

non intellecti nulla est curatio morbi
et magis inclusis ignibus antra fremunt

dum pudor est tam foeda loqui vitiumque fateri
agnovit taciti conscia signa mali

mox ait occultae satis est res prodita causae
pone metum veniam vis tibi tanta dabit

prostratus pedibus verecunda silentia rupi
cum lacrimis referens ordine cuncta suo

* fac ait an placitae potiaris munere formae
respondi pietas talia velle fugit

solvitur in risum exclamans pro mira voluntas
castus amor veneris dicito quando fuit

parcere dilectae iuvenis desiste puellae
impius hic fueris si pius esse velis

unguibius et morsu teneri pascuntur amores
vulnera non refugit res magis apta plagae

Unthreatened, I was bothered by a silent wound,
        though shock and wasting took the place of words.

Boethius, great searcher of important things,
        only you, showing pity, bring assistance,

for while you often saw me focused on my worries,
        you could not know the reasons for my woes.

Sensing at last that I am gripped by violent sickness,
        you softly order opening what's closed:

"Speak! From whom did you catch this new ignited fever?
        Speak! And accept the cure for your claimed pain!

There is no treatment for undiagnosed disease,
        and caverns bellow more with smothered flames."

When it was shameful to confess and talk of sin,
        he recognized clear signs of silent pain.

He quickly said, "The matter's cause is clear enough.
        Don't fret; great strength will give you much forgiveness."

I broke my shamefaced silence, prostrate at his feet,
        while through tears sharing everything in sequence.

"Do it," he said, "Or could a 'gift' of beauty please you?"
        "Honor avoids such wishing," I replied.

He broke up laughing, shouting, "What a wondrous will!
        Speak up! When was a love from Venus chaste?

Young man, refrain from sparing your delightful girl!
        If you'd be 'proper' here, you'll be improper!"

Tender affairs are fed by scratches and a bite;
        a violent business does not shun more blows.

interea donis permulcet corda parentum
et pretio faciles in mea vota trahit

auri caecus amor nativum vincit amorem
coeperunt natae crimen amare suae

dant vitiis furtisque locum dant iungere dextras
et totum ludo concelebrare diem

permissum fit vile nefas fit languidus ardor
vicerunt morbum languida corda suum

illa nihil quaesita videns procedere causam
odit et illaeso corpore tristis abit

proieci vanas sanato pectore curas
et subito didici quam miser ante fui

salve sancta inquam semperque intacta maneto
virginitas per me plena pudoris eris

quae postquam perlata viro sunt omnia tanto
meque videt fluctus exuperasse meos

macte inquit iuvenis proprii dominator amoris
et de contemptu sume trophaea tuo

arma tibi veneris cedantque cupidinis arcus
cedat et armipotens ipsa minerva tibi

sic mihi peccandi studium permissa potestas
abstulit atque ipsum talia velle fugit

ingrati tristes pariter discedimus ambo
* discidii ratio vita pudica fuit

Meanwhile, he pacifies her parents' hearts with "gifts"
and lures soft touches to my goal with cash.

Blind love of money overcomes parental love;
they both begin to love their daughter's guilt.

They give us room for secret sins; they acquiesce
to holding hands and filling days with play.

A sanctioned sin becomes cheap; lust becomes depleted.
Exhausted hearts defeated their disease.

She, seeing no pursuit advancing, hates the cause
and leaves dejected with an unspoiled body.

I banished phantom worries from a chastened heart
and quickly found out what a wretch I was.

I said, "Hail holy chastity, and always stay
untouched. Through me you'll be most modest."

Once everything had been conveyed to this great man
and he observed I rose above my moods,

he said, "Well done, young man, the lord of your own love!"
and "Gather up some trophies of your scorn.

To you may Cupid's bow and arms of Venus yield,
and even bold Minerva yield to you.

And so a sanctioned license stole my zeal for sinning,
and even longing for such things departed.

We split up, equally resentful and unhappy;
the reason for the split was modest life.

~ Elegy 4

restat adhuc alios turpesque revolvere casus
atque aliquot molli pascere corda ioco

conveniunt etenim delirae ignava senectae
aptaque sunt operi carmina vana meo

sic vicibus variis alterni fallimur anni
et mutata magis tempora grata mihi

virgo fuit species dederat cui candida nomen
* candida diversis nam bene compta modis

huic ego per totum vidi pendentia corpus
cymbala multiplices edere pulsa sonos

nunc niveis digitis nunc pulsans pectine cordas
arguto quicquam murmure dulce loqui

sic me diversis tractum de partibus una
carpebat variis pulcra puella modis

hanc ego saltantem subito correptus amavi
et coepi tacitus vulnera grata pati

singula visa semel semper memorare libebat
haerebant animo nocte dieque meo

~ Elegy 4

It still remains to tell of other shameful falls
    and gratify some hearts with gentle humor.

Since idle deeds, in fact, befit deranged old men,
    my foolish poems are fitting as my work,

and so I am beguiled each year by sundry changes,
    and I'm more grateful for the changing seasons.

There was a girl whose incandescence nicknamed her
    "Candida"—chic because of smart, fresh styles.

I saw the cymbals hanging all around her body
    making shifting sounds when they were struck.

First with strings struck by snowy fingers, then a pick,
    she warbled something in a sweet, clear whisper.

So, with me being lured by one with shifting parts,
    the gorgeous girl was "plucking" different ways.

I loved her, being quickly smitten by her dancing,
    and started bearing welcome wounds in silence.

Each glance each time was always pleasing to recall;
    they stuck inside my mind through night and day.

saepe velut visae laetabar imagine formae
et procul absenti voce manuque fui

saepe velut praesens fuerit mecum ipse loquebar
* cantabam dulces quos solet illa modos

o quotiens demens quotiens sine mente putabar
nec puto fallebar non bene sanus eram

atque aliquis cui caeca foret bene notus voluptas
cantat cantantem maximianus amat

certe difficile est abscondere pectoris aestus
panditur et clauso saepius ore furor

nam subito inficiens vultum pallorque ruborque
internum clausae vocis habebat opus

nec minus ipsa meas prodebant somnia curas
somnia secreto non bene fida meo

nam cum sopitos premerent oblivia sensus
confessa est facinus nescia lingua suum

candida clamabam propera cur candida tardas
nox abit et furtis lux inimica redit

proximus ut genitor mecum comitatus amatae
virginis herbosa forte iacebat humo

illius ad nomen turbatos excutit artus
exilit et natam credit adesse suam

omnia collustrans toto me pectore somnum
* prospicit efflantem nec meminisse mei

vana putas an vera sopor ludibria iactat
* an te verus ait pectoris ardor agit

I'd often gladden at her figure's lifelike image,
though I was far removed from voice and touch.

I'd even often speak as if she were with me;
I kept on singing her sweet melodies.

Oh, often I was thought demented, often mindless,
nor was I tricked, I think; I was quite mad,

and some for whom my secret love was well-known said:
"She sings; Maximianus loves the singer."

It's surely difficult to hide a fevered heart;
lust, usually closed-lipped, is opened wide.

Yes, blush and paleness, quickly coloring my face,
performed the task of cloistered, private speech.

My dreams themselves no less betrayed anxieties—
the dreams unwisely trusted with my secret—

for when amnesia had submerged my drowsy senses,
my unknowing tongue confessed its crime:

I cried, "Candida, hurry! Why delay, Candida?
Night flees and light, unkind to trysts, returns!"

Just as, by chance, my girlfriend's father sprawled upon
the grassy soil while nestled close to me,

he jumps up at that name and shakes his restless limbs,
and he believes his daughter is nearby.

Observing everything, he sees me slumbering
with my whole chest and being inattentive.

"Do you believe sleep throws off true or false illusions?"
he says, "Or does the heart's true passion move you?

credo equidem assuetas animo remeare figuras
et fallax studium ludit imago suum

stat tamen attonitus perplexaque murmura captat
et tacitis precibus dicere plura rogat

sic ego qui cunctis sanctae gravitatis habebar
proditus et vitio sum miser ipse meo

et nunc infelix tota est sine crimine vita
et peccare senem non potuisse pudet

deserimur vitiis fugit indignata voluptas
* et quod non possum non voluisse meum est

hoc etiam meminisse licet quod serior aetas
intulit et gemitus quos mihi laeta dedit

* quis ad has possit naturae adtingere partes
clarus et ut sapiens noxia saepe velit

interdum rapimur vitiis trahimurque volentes
et quod non capiunt pectora bruta volunt

I truly think known shapes return within the mind
        and a false image plays with one's desire."

He stands, still dazed, and hears my muddled murmuring,
        and with hushed questions asks for more disclosure.

So I, who everyone considered a grave saint,
        am wretched and revealed by my own vice,

and all my dreary life now is without reproach
        and humbles an old man unfit to sin.

We're left behind by vice; the scornful pleasure flees
        and what I cannot do I haven't wanted.

One may remember this as well: that older age
        produced and gave me numerous laments.

But who could influence these parts of nature when
        one famed and wise keep wanting what is wrong?

We're sometimes dragged by faults and ravaged willingly,
        and brutish hearts can't get the things they want.

~ Elegy 5

missus ad eoas legati munere partes
tranquillum cunctis nectere pacis opus

dum studio gemini componere foedera regni
inveni cordis bella nefanda mei

hic me suspiciens etruscae gentis alumnum
involvit patriis graia puella dolis

nam cum se nostro captam simularet amore
me potius vero fecit amore capi

pervigil ad nostras astabat nocte fenestras
nescio quid graeco murmure dulce canens

nunc aderant lacrimae gemitus suspiria pallor
et quicquid nullum fingere posse putes

sic velut afflictam nimium miseratus amantem
efficior potius tunc miserandus ego

haec erat egregiae formae vultusque modesti
grata micans oculis nec minus arte placens

docta loqui digitis et carmina fingere docta
et responsuram sollicitare lyram

~ Elegy 5

Dispatched for diplomatic service in the East
 to close a quiet deal for worldwide peace

while I attempted forging ties between twin realms,
 I came upon wars toxic to my heart.

Here, sizing me up as a cloddish Tuscan son,
 a girl from Greece ensnared me with her tricks,

for though she faked that she had fallen hard for me,
 she made me truly fall in love instead.

Outside my windows she remained on watch all night—
 in soft tones sweetly singing something Greek.

Her tears, groans, sighs and pallor were now coming—
 and things that you would think no one could fake,

so pitying too much—as with a humbled lover—
 I then became more pitiful instead.

This one had special beauty and a modest face
 with bright eyes no less pleasing for their art,

with fingers trained to strum, and trained to write her songs
 and stimulate a lyre that would respond.

illam sirenis stupefactus cantibus aequans
efficior demens alter ulixes ego

et qui non poteram tantas evadere moles
nescius in scopulos et vada caeca feror

quis referat gressus certa sub lege moventes
suspensosque novis plausibus ire pedes

grande erat inflexos gradibus numerare capillos
grande erat in niveo pulla colore coma

urebant oculos stantes duraeque papillae
et quas astringens clauderet una manus

* ah quantum mentem stomachi iunctura movebat
atque sub exhausto pectore pingue femur

terrebar teneros astringere fortiter artus
visa per amplexus ossa sonare meos

grandia clamabat tua nunc me brachia laedunt
non tolerant pondus subdita membra tuum

dirigui quantusque fuit calor ille recessit
et nata est venae causa pudenda meae

* non lac sic tenerum permixta coagula reddunt
nec liquidi mollis spuma liquoris erit

succubui fateor graiae tunc nescius artis
succubui tusca simplicitate senex

qua defensa suo superata est hectore troia
unum non poterat fraus superare senem

muneris iniuncti curam studiumque reliqui
deditus imperiis saeve cupido tuis

Stunned by her songs, I would compare her to the Sirens,
and while mad I became the new Ulysses,

and I, who was unable to evade such reefs,
was borne off-guard to unseen shoals and rocks.

Who can describe steps moving to a steady beat
that went with fresh applause and arching feet?

It was intense to count her layered waves of hair;
it was intense—dark hair on snowy skin…

Her breasts were standing firm and burning up my eyes,
and with one hand each could be cupped while squeezed.

Ah, how her stomach (joined below by fleshy thighs . . .)
and her exhausted chest aroused my spirit!

I was scared squeezing her frail limbs aggressively;
bones seemed to crack because of my embraces.

She shouted, "Now your massive arms are hurting me!
My limbs can't stand to be beneath your bulk!"

I froze, and what had been great lust for her receded,
and my old pecker was a cause of shame.

The well-stirred rennet does not make so firm a curd,
nor will there be light foam on flowing fluid.

I yielded, I confess, unschooled about Greek tricks;
I yielded, an old man with Tuscan dullness.

Couldn't deceit, through which Hector-guarded Troy
was beaten, triumph over one old man?

I lost concern and fondness for the ordered duties,
cruel Cupid, while enthralled by your commands.

nec memorare pudet tali me vulnere victum
subditus his flammis iuppiter ipse fuit

set mihi prima quidem nox affuit ac sua solvit
munera grandaevo vix subeunda viro

proxima destituit vires vacuusque recessit
ardor et in venerem segnis ut ante fui

illa velut proprium repetens infesta tributum
instat et increpitat debita redde mihi

sed nihil hic clamor nil sermo mitis agebat
quod natura negat reddere nemo potest

erubui stupui quia tunc verecundia mentem
abstulit et blandum terror ademit opus

contrectare manu coepit flagrantia membra
meque etiam digitis sollicitare suis

nil mihi torpenti vel tactus profuit ignis
perstitit in medio frigus ut ante foco

quae te crudelis rapuit mihi femina dixit
cuius ab amplexu fessus ad arma redis

iurabam curis animum mordacibus uri
nec posse ad luxum tristia corda trahi

illa dolum credens non inquit fallis amantem
plurima certus amor lumina semper habet

* quin potius placito noli inquit parcere ludo
proice tristitias et renovare ioco

obtundunt siquidem curarum pondera sensus
intermissa minus sarcina pondus habet

It's no disgrace recalling loss from such a wound—
Jove was himself subjected to these lusts.

Though my first night had come and paid its pending debt
(one barely handled by an ancient man),

the next one sapped my strength, and hollow passion shrank,
and I was sluggish, as before, at sex.

The hostile girl, as if demanding her own tax,
pursues and snarls, "Return what's owed to me!"

But here no bluster, no sweet talk was motivating;
what nature cancels, no one can restore.

I blushed, I froze. Since shame then made me lose my mind
and panic cut off the alluring task,

she started fondling my burning prick by hand
and she aroused me with her fingers too.

Even the strokes of passion did not help my numbness;
frost stayed within the hearth, as in the past.

"What bitch has stolen you from me?" she said, "From whose
grasp do you come back tired to my arms?"

I swore my spirit was inflamed by gnawing cares;
sad hearts cannot be drawn to easy living.

Sensing a trick, she says, "You do not fool your lover!
Constant love always has its many eyes."

She says, "What's more, do not reject our pleasing play!
Give up your frowns and be restored by fun!

Indeed, if loads of burdens make your senses dull,
'some easing of the weight' relieves the load."

tunc egomet toto nudatus corpore lecto
effusis lacrimis talia verba dedi

* cogimur heu senes crimen vitiumque fateri
ne meus extinctus forte putetur amor

me miserum cuius non est culpanda voluptas
vindicor infelix debilitatis ope

en longo confecta situ tibi tradimus arma
arma ministeriis quippe dicata tuis

fac quodcumque potes nos cessimus hoc tamen ipso
grandior est hostis quod minus ardet amor

protinus argutas admovit turpiter artes
meque cupit flammis vivificare suis

ast ubi dilecti persensit funera membri
nec velut expositum surgere vidit opus

erigitur viduoque toro laniata recumbens
vocibus his luctus et sua damna fovet

mentula festorum cultrix operosa dierum
quondam deliciae divitiaeque meae

quo te deiectam lacrimarum gurgite plangam
quae de tot meritis carmina digna feram

tu mihi flagranti succurrere saepe solebas
atque aestus animi ludificare mei

tu mihi per totam custos gratissima noctem
consors laetitiae tristitiaeque meae

conscia secreti semper fidissima nostri
astans internis pervigil obsequiis

Then, with my body fully naked on the bed,
I spoke with streaming tears some words like these:

"Alas, old men are forced to cop to blame and guilt,
in case it's thought, perhaps, my love is quenched.

I am a wretch whose appetite is not to blame!
Jinxed, I'm excused by virtue of my weakness.

Look! I give you these arms weak from long disuse—
the arms assigned, of course, for your deployments.

Do what you can; I've yielded. For this reason, though,
the foe is stronger since love simmers less."

She shamefully applied her cunning arts at once
and wanted to revive me with her lusts,

but when she recognized the cherished member's death,
and saw the tool not rise, as if laid out,

and torn—prone on her widowed bed—she grew aroused
and nursed her grief and damage with these words:

"Prick, busy celebrator of the holidays,
an old delight and treasure that was mine,

with what fierce flood of tears should I lament your fall?
What songs worth such great service should I bring?

You often were inclined to help me while aroused
and tease me for my spirit's sultriness.

You were my dearest guardian all through the night,
and partner in my happiness and sadness,

always most trustworthy when privy to our secrets,
standing tall on watch in private rites.

quo tibi fervor abit per quem feritura placebas
quo tibi cristatum vulnificumque caput

nempe iaces nullo ut quondam perfusa rubore
pallida demisso vertice nempe iaces

nil tibi blandities nil dulcia carmina prosunt
non quicquid mentem sollicitare solet

* hic velut exposito merito te funere plango
occidit assueto quod caret officio

hanc ego cum lacrimis deducta voce canentem
irridens dictis talibus increpui

* dum defles nostri languorem femina membri
ostendis morbo te graviore premi

illa furens nescis ut cerno perfide nescis
non fleo privatum set generale chaos

haec genus humanum pecudum volucrumque ferarum
et quicquid toto spirat in orbe creat

hac sine diversi nulla est concordia sexus
hac sine coniugii gratia summa perit

haec geminas tanto constringit foedere mentes
unius ut faciat corporis esse duo

pulcra licet pretium si desit femina perdit
et si defuerit vir quoque turpis erit

haec si gemma micans rutilum non conferat aurum
* aeternum fallax mortiferumque genus

tecum pura fides secretaque certa loquuntur
o vere nostrum fructiferumque bonum

Where did the heat, by which you pleased in foreplay, go?
Where is your crested, wound-inflicting head?

Of course, no longer do you lie engorged with red.
Of course, you lie pale with your drooping crown.

No flattery, no charming songs encourage you,
nothing that tends to stimulate the mind.

I mourn for you here as befits a laid-out corpse;
what lacks its customary use has died."

As she was singing this in tears, her voice subdued,
I mockingly derided her with these words:

"Woman, while you lament the slackness of my prick,
you show you suffer from a worse disease."

She raged, "You're clueless, traitor! Clueless, as I see it!
I mourn a public, not a private, hell.

It makes the human race, the herds, the birds, the beasts
and everything that breathes throughout the world.

Without it there's no union of the different sexes;
the highest grace of marriage dies without it.

It brings together coupled minds with its strong bond
so that the pair combine to be one flesh,

Though pretty, if it goes, a woman loses value,
and, if it's gone, a man will be grotesque too.

If this bright gem does not embellish ruddy gold,
a birth is fake and moribund forever.

With you, pure vows and trusted secrets are declared,
O truly fruitful benefit of mine!"

* vale inquam felix semper felicibus apta
* et mihi cognatis utere deliciis

cedunt cuncta tibi quodque est sublimius ultro
cedunt imperiis maxima sceptra tuis

nec subtracta gemunt set se tibi subdita gaudent
vulnera sunt irae prosperiora tuae

ipsa etiam totum moderans sapientia mundum
porrigit invictas ad tua iussa manus

sternitur icta tuo votivo vulnere virgo
et perfusa novo laeta cruore iacet

fert tacitum ridetque suum laniata dolorem
et percussori plaudit amica suo

non tibi semper iners non mollis convenit actus
mixtaque sunt ludis fortia facta tuis

nam nunc ingenio magnis nunc viribus usa
nunc his quae veneris sunt inimica malis

nam tibi pervigiles intendunt saepe labores
* imbres insidiae iurgia damna nives

tu mihi saepe feri commendas corda tyranni
sanguineus per te mars quoque mitis erit

et post extinctos debellatosque gigantes
excutis irato tela triscula iovi

tu cogis rabidas affectum discere tigres
per te blandus amans redditur ipse leo

mira tibi virtus mira est patientia victos
diligis et vinci tu quoque saepe voles

"Go happily," I say, "Be primed for happy things
and handling for me those kinds of pleasures!"

"All freely yield to you and, what is more sublime,
your country's greatest ruler yields as well.

They don't mourn capture, but rejoice obeying you;
wounds from your anger are more fortunate.

Even Wisdom herself, directing all the world,
extends unvanquished hands at your command.

A virgin, cut down by a prayed-for wound, is struck
and lies with joy immersed in her fresh blood.

Bloodied, she bears and mocks her grief without a sound,
and claps for her abuser as a friend.

No weak or lazy act is ever suitable for you,
and fearless deeds are mixed up with your games—

yes, first with wit, then with the use of heavy force,
then with these schemes that are opposed to Venus.

Yes, sleepless struggles—plots, storms, snow, domestic strife,
financial losses—often target you.

You often recommend fierce tyrants' hearts to me.
Blood-drenched Mars also would be mild for you,

and after Giants are defeated and destroyed,
you shake off three-pronged bolts from angry Jove.

You force the frenzied tigers to discover passion;
Through you a lion's made a fawning lover.

Your power stuns, your patience stuns, you love the conquered;
you love to win and being won again.

cum superata iaces vires animosque resumis
atque iterum vinci vincere rursus amas

ira brevis longa est pietas recidiva voluptas
et cum posse perit mens tamen una manet

conticuit tandem longo satiata dolore
me velut expletis deserit exequiis

You gather strength and spirits as you lie down beaten,
 and like to win once more, then being won.

Your rage is brief, your joy recurring, your faith constant,
 and when strength fails, your will still stays unbroken."

At last she shuts up, satisfied by boundless grief.
 She leaves me as if my last rites were over.

Elegy 6

claude precor miseras aetas verbosa querelas
        numquid et hic vitium vis reserare tuum

sic satis indignum leviter tetigisse pudorem
        contractata diu crimina crimen habent

omnibus est eadem leti via non tamen unus
        est vitae cunctis exitiique modus

hac pueri atque senes pariter iuvenesque feruntur
        hac par divitibus pauper egenus erit

ergo quod attritum quodque est vitabile nulli
        festino gressu vincere praestat iter

infelix ceu iam defleto funere surgo
        hac me defunctum vivere parte puto

Elegy 6

Chatty old age, please stop these miserable complaints!
And do you want to show your failure here?

So, having lightly touched on scandal is enough;
repeatedly massaging wrongs is wrong.

Death's journey is the same for all; the type of life
and exit, though, is not the same for all.

Old men, young men, and boys are snatched the same for it.
The needy poor will match the rich for it,

thus it is better to endure a road that's worn
and unavoidable with rapid steps.

Morose, I rise now as if mourned at my last rites;
I think I'm living partly dead this way.

Appendices

Appendix A

Cassiodorus, *Variae* 1.21

Maximiano V.I. et Andreae V.S. Theodericus Rex

[1] Provocandi sumus affectuosis civium studiis ad augmenta civitatis, quia nemo potest diligere quod habitatores intellegit non amare. unicuique patria sua carior est, dum supra omnia salvum fore quaeritur, ubi ab ipsis cunabulis commoratur. Quapropter votis paribus invitemur ad dona, quatenus quod sponte tribuimus, duplicata gratia conferamus. Et ideo nulli grave sit Romanis fabricis deputatae pecuniae reddere rationem, cum pura conscientia desideret se probari, quando fructum laboris sui capit, dum ad nos prospera de se pervenire cognoscit.

[2] Quocirca praesenti decernimus iussione Romanae civitatis fabricas vos debere discutere, si labor operis concordat expensis: vel, si apud aliquem constet residere pecuniam, quae non sit fabricis expensa, deputatae rei reddat erogandam. Quibus rationibus evidenter expressis ad nos instructionem fidelissimam destinate, ut indicio nostro respondere videamini qui estis ad indaginem veritatis electi. Nullum enim de largitate nostra fraudari velle credimus, quando in tali negotio et de propriis facultatibus eum impendere posse iudicamus.

[3] Aves ipsae per aera vagantes proprios nidos amant: erratiles ferae ad cubilia dumosa festinant voluptuosi pisces campos liquidos transeuntes cavernas suas studiosa indagatione perquirunt cunctaque animalia ubi se norunt refugere longissima cupiunt aetate constare. Quid iam de Roma debemus dicere quam fas est ipsis liberis plus amare?

Appendix A

Cassiodorus, *Variae* 1.21

King Theoderic to Maximianus, Illustrious Man, and Andreas, Admirable Man

[1] We should be inspired to improvement of the community by the citizens' zealous actions because nobody can value what he knows the residents do not love. For each person his own native city is more precious than any other, since where he has resided from his own cradle is considered above all to be safe. Consequently, we should be encouraged to make a donation so that what we offer voluntarily we contribute with twice the gratitude, and thus it should be burdensome to no one to render an account of the funds allocated for the Romans' public projects because one with a clean conscience desires approval, provided that he obtains the fruit of his labor when he knows that a favorable report comes to us about it.

[2] Accordingly, by this decree we now declare that you should examine public projects of the Roman citizenry with regard to whether the work of their projects is commensurate with their expenses; or, if it is decided that money which has not been expended on public works remains with anyone, let it return to the project for which it was allocated. With these accounts clearly rendered, send us your most accurate statement so that you who are selected as the hunter of the truth will be seen as having responded to our directive. We believe, indeed, no one wants defrauding based on our generosity, since we declare that one can invest in such work—and with one's own resources.

[3] Birds themselves drifting through the air love their own nests, wandering beasts hurry to their bushy lairs, delightful fish traversing the watery plains search for their dens with an eager hunt, and all the animals desire for the longest time to remain when they know they find refuge. What should we say now about Rome other than it is right for its own free people to love it more?

Appendix B

The Appendix Maximiani

I praemia tot formae numeret . . .

praemia tot formae numeret quis voce facunda
quaeve potest laudes dicere musa tuas
quamvis votivas intendam promere voces
deficiunt verba pectus anhelat amans
esse Paris vellem Helenae quid fama teneris
in pretio potuit te dare nuda Venus
dum similes auro crines religantur in auro
vincuntur meritis flava metalla tuis
cilia blanda micant grato distincta nitore
utque ebenus pulchro ebore mixta nitent
regnat in ore decus quod tinxit rubor alumnus
ut cedant labiis victa roseta tuis
lactea colla tibi fulgent quasi lilia multa
vernantur meritis membra decora tuis
quisne parum tumidas delecto ventre papillas
non tractet manibus poma fecunda suis
quam castigato planus sub pectore venter
quantum et quale latus quam iuvenile femur
inguina pulcra latet magnae sub imagine formae
his nequeo testis inscius esse quidem

II lux oculis lux blanda . . .

lux oculis lux blanda, meis lux mentibus apta
sic se fert clarum lucifer ante diem

Appendix B

The Appendix Maximiani

---

1 *To Most of You*

Who in fine voice could count your many points of beauty?
    What Muse is able to express your praises?
No matter how I try to speak in promised speech,
    words fall short as my lover's chest is heaving.
I would be Helen's Paris. What famed worth you have!
    Nude Venus could have given birth to you.
Although your locks resembling gold are bound in gold,
    gilt metal is defeated by your merits.
Coy lashes flutter with a pleasing, striking style
    and ebony shines mixed with gorgeous ivory.
Grace rules upon a face a nurtured blush has tinged
    as vanquished roses lose out to your lips.
Your milky neck is blooming like abundant lilies;
    your gorgeous limbs are budded with your charms.
Who would not stroke with his own hands your perky breasts,
    plucked ripened fruit with just a bit of bulge?
How flat a stomach underneath the shapely chest!
    Such a fine, splendid side! How young a thigh!
Below great beauty glimpsed there lurks a gorgeous groin;
    for that I'm surely not a clueless witness!

2 *Soft Light*

Light from your eyes, soft light, light fixed within my thoughts,
    is like what Venus brings before bright day.

me veneris retines constrictum blanda catenis
dum me subdideris tunc ego liber ero
non aliter Leander gelidis remeabat in undis
inter quas dubium vincere fecit amor
haud secus Achilles arsit Briseide flava
idem victus erat cognitor ipse sui
sic Phoebum quondam cruciavit pectore Daphne
incenditque animum plusque negando magis
nos aliter sors ista cremat plus denique fervet
quem tu respicies corpore grata trahis
nunc anulus cuperem fieri dilectus in auro
ut manibus teneris tu mea membra regas
obsequio facili semper tibi vinctus haberer
circulo dum religo corpus idemque tuum
si nostram in ceris cupias mutare figuram
applicitum labiis oscula blanda dabis

III quisquis ad excelsi tendis

quisquis ad excelsi tendis fastigia montis
et varium miraris opus dum singula lustras
aspice devictas ullo sine funere gentes
non opus est conferre manus caecoque furore
casibus incertis dubiam committere vitam
cedant arma loco pugnant pro milite rupes
turriti scopuli atque adiectae molibus arces
undarum minae praeruptaeque undique ripae
et tremulum quo pergis iter pendente ruina
promittunt certam per tot discrimina vitam.
stat muris innixa domus compendia parvum
distendunt spatium recubans de culmine cuncta
prospicit et placido fruitur custodia lecto
nec munisse locum satis est iuvat eminus arcem
conspicere et blando vocat intra moenia vultu
quae tibi pro tali solvantur munere vota
Theodade potens cuius sapientia mundo
prospiciens castris ne quid minus esset in istis
artem naturae permiscuit utile pulchro

Gentle, you hold me fettered by sweet chains of love;
	when you subdue me, then I shall be free.
Leander swam no differently back through cold waves
	between which passion had to conquer risk.
Achilles burned no less for golden-haired Briseis;
	so too the champion was himself defeated.
Daphne once likewise tortured Phoebus in his heart
	and stoked his soul increasingly with snubs.
Such fate consumes us differently as he you see
	just burns more; you seduce with your fine body.
Now I would wish to be a cherished golden ring
	so you would guide my parts with tender hands.
With loyal service I'd be always tied to you,
	while with a band I'd bind your flesh—mine too.
If you intend to move my image onto wax,
	you'll give me gentle kisses pressed on lips.

3 *Panegyric to Theodahad*

You who encamp on lofty mountain peaks
and marvel seeing varied building features:
observe tribes conquered with no trace of death!
There is no use for force, nor life at stake
endangered by dark rage at risky odds.
Here let arms yield; cliffs fight instead of troops.
Stone towers and peaks raised upon the crags,
the waves' threats and on every side steep banks,
and the rough path you take with looming ruin—
for a safe life they promise many hazards.
A house stays propped on walls; short paths extend
across cramped space. Skyward the lolling guard
gazes and lazes in his peaceful bed.
Here building is not enough; the distant fort
delights and gently summons one inside.
What vows are paid to you for such a gift,
mighty Theodahad, who, wisely watching
the world so nothing's lacking in these forts,
united nature's art with noble craft?

magna quidem virtus bello prosternere gentes
sed melius nec bella pati cum laude quietis
et titulo pietatis erit tot credere demptos
quot populos tua castra regunt instante ruina

IV De saxo vario decore ornato

quod micat ornatum pulchro munimine saxum
hoc quondam nullis utile rebus erat
hic tantum pelagi volucres residere solebant
cum freta turbatis aestuarentur aquis
nunc servant nova castra viros licet horrida bella
stent circum hoc septus vertice tutus eris
saxa lacus rupes pontes pugnacula turres
tot species vitae quot loca mortis habent
viderat hunc scopulum lustrans sua litora solers
theodadus atque aridi squalida terga soli
aspera nulla potens producere germina tellus
at melius dixit condita ferre potes
caeduntur scopuli decorantur culmina muri
fitque decus subito nuper id horror erat
nunc varios fructus diversaque pignora servat
dives ab ingrato cespite facta magis
resque vilis nimium pretii est modo reddita tanti
quantum tuta salus grataque vita valet
at tibi dent superi tranquillae tempora vitae
per quem nos scopuli duraque saxa iuvant
ipsaque si posset grates natura referret
quae quas non genuit laeta ministrat opes

V quis tam diverso concludens . . .

quis tam diverso concludens atria cultu
miscuit urbanis ruris amoena locis
inter tecta domus sylvas miramur et undas
atque uno fruimur tempore cuncta simul
hic gelidi fontes hic dulces arboris umbrae

What power in a war to slaughter tribes!
But peace with praise, with no war waged, is better,
and it is thought your legacy will be
the throngs who your forts rule removed from crisis.

4 *On a Rock Arrayed with Varied Splendor*

Though well-hewn stone is gleaming as a proud defense,
 this site was not useful in the past.
Here only seabirds were accustomed to reside
 when stormy waters in the strait were churned.
New forts now guard men; though cruel wars may still persist,
 you will be safe encircled by this peak.
Stones, lakes, cliffs, bridges, forts and towers have
 as many kinds of life as scenes for death.
Touring his shores, the wise Theodahad observed
 this rock, and to dry soil's uneven surface
declared, "Harsh earth, unable to produce new growth,
 you can more fittingly support construction."
Boulders were hewn, and summits of the walls adorned,
 and glory sprang where there was horror once.
It guards assorted treasures now and varied crops
 that have produced more wealth from meager soil,
and something cheap is changed soon into worth as great
 as wellness and a happy life is valued,
but may the gods bestow calm times of life on you
 through whom the stones and rugged cliffs delight us
and Nature, if she could, would even offer thanks
 for works she did not make that served with joy.

5 *Villa*

Who, covering his palace with diverse adornment,
 mixed city sites with pleasant country places?
We're awed by woods and water all around the house,
 and we are reveling in them together.
Here are the icy springs, here gentle shade from trees;

hic videas toto quidquid in orbe placet
impendet vitreis sublimis platanus undis
aspectoque suo gurgite sylva tremit
dumque niger patula contexitur arbore lucus
frigida torpentes adiuvat umbra lacus
aestibus in mediis viridi sub fronde canora
vernat avis resonant atria tecta nemus
et quae sola nimis poterant divisa placere
amplius haec duplo mixta decore nitent

VI De viridario

haec quondam rapido fugiens per devia cursu
perdebat meritum rustica lympha suum
quae nunc tecta colens excelsaque culmina lustrans
mitior urbanis luxuriatur aquis
ducitur ad varios per stagna micantia quaestus
et quas non genuit solvere discit opes
ecce peregrini ludunt in gurgite pisces
miranturque novos perspicuosque lacus
et se felici conclusos carcere gaudent
quos placido melius nunc fovet unda sinu

here you could see what pleases all the world:
above the limpid ripples looms a splendid plane tree,
and looking at the brook the forest quivers
and, as a spreading tree enshrouds the darkened grove,
cool shadow on the lake enhances stillness.
In midday heat beneath green leaves, a singing bird
exults; the house, roof and forest echo,
and things that would delight when set off by themselves,
more fully shine when mixed with twice the grace.

6 *From the Arboretum*

Once racing with great swiftness through a winding course,
the country river was diminishing
where, serving homes and washing lofty buildings now,
it plays more placidly in city waters.
It's drawn for different uses through the gleaming pools
and learns to loosen things it did not make.
Watch the fish frolic in an unfamiliar stream
and marvel at their newfound clear lagoons,
and those now better nourished in a placid harbor
rejoice enclosed inside a happy jail.

Appendix C

Ennodius, *De Boetio spata cincto*

Languescit rigidi tecum substantia ferri,
    Solvitur atque chalybs more fluentis aquae.
Emollit gladios inbellis dextra Boeti.
    Ensis erat dudum, credite, nunc colus est.
In thyrsum migrat quod gestas, improbe, pilum.
    In Venerem constans linque Mavortis opem.

Appendix C

Ennodius, *On Boethius's Broadsword Being Sheathed*

With you, the essence of the rigid iron droops
    and, like the flowing water, it is drained.
Boethius's weak right hand enfeebles blades;
    what was your sword, bastard, is now a distaff.
The spear you falsely bear becomes a drunkard's wand;
    leave work of war while standing firm in love.

Appendix D

Imitatio Maximiani (Anonymous)

musa senectutis istic cantatur amarae

fortia quid subito dissolvis membra senectus
quae sibi bellipotens potuit nec subdere quisquam
tu me pestifero subdis fugienda mucrone
quae placidam properans spolias virtute iuventam
quicquid ad astra volat quicquid generatur in arvis
colla superba tibi lacerate pectore flectit
fulgida famosae fugerunt tempora vitae
non sum, qui dudum fueram, cum viveret in me
virtus, qua pugnans cunctos superare solebam
corniferos potui cervos prostrare sagitiis
cum canibus densas nimium perstringere silvas
si sub fronde lepus, si ramis damma sub altis
mansisset, nostro delusa est territa gestu
firma per undisonos credebam brachia fluctus
cum niueum quercus pondus curvaret ad arva
si iuvenis mecum voluit contendere cursu
post me confusus fracta virtute remansit
nudato gelidos tolerabam vertice nimbus
nocte meos parvus claudebat somnus ocellos
optabam placida caeli splendentis ab arce
auroram laetus teneris lusurus in arvis
ire frementis equi sonitu studioque volebam
per plateas magna mecum comitante caterva
comtus eram gemmis et mundo fulgidus auro
splendebat roseo vestis perfusa colore
morbida languentis subito si membra videbam

claudebam manibus demisso uertice vultum
nunc tussis gemitus languor mea viscera frangunt
et dolor ardenti succendit lampade pectus
brachia fessa ruunt consumptis viribus aptis
nocte dieque gravi franguntur crura dolore
invalidus per rura trahor reptando bacillo
nec possum recubans maeroris surgere lecto
nam vocem ut servus nostram persenserit aure
subducit nostris fugiens solacia membris
nec tolerare potest longos ancilla labores
noxia quos misit spinosa fronte senectus
solve tenebroso miseram de carcere vitam
turbida viventi quae nulli parcere nosti

Appendix E

Le regret de Maximian (Anonymous)

Herkneþ to mi ron,
As hic ou tellen con
Of helde al hou hit ges:
Of a modi mon,
Þat muchel of murþe won
In prude and al in pes.
His nome wes maximian;
Swech nes neuere nan
Iwis wiþ-houten les.
Clerc he wes foul goed,
As moni mon hounder-stod;
Ihereþ al hou hit wes.

Is wille he heuede I-nou,
And pal wor prude he drou
And oþere murþes mo;
He wes feirest mon
Wiþ-houten apselon,
Þat seþþen wes and þo.
Þo laste his lif so longe,
Þat he bigon to ounstronge,
As fele men tideþ swo.
Þo gon him rewen sore
Al his wilde lore,
Þo helde him wroute wo.

Þo his helde him com,
His bok an honde he nom

And gon of reuþe rede;
Hof his herte hord
He makede moni a word,
Hof hal his liues dede.
Menen he gon his mone,
Hou feble weren his bone;
His heu bigon to shede,
So clene he wees agon,
Þat strengþe neuede he non;
His herte bigon to blede.

Ofte ich grunte and grone,
Wen iche wondri hone,
And þenke on childes dede.
For þissen ille wone
Nis her boten a lone;
Her beþ blissen gnede.
To wepen and to wone,
To makien muchele mone,
Al me hit deþ for nede.
An ende ounder þe stone.
Wiþ flesse and eken wiþ bone
Wormes shulen we fede.

Uuen blostmen brekeþ on brere,
Ich makede murie bere
Ich wes hof bliþe mod.
Helde, þe worste I-fere,
Of blisse þu makest me skere,
Þu meniest al mi blod.
To longe hic habbe I-ben here:
Bi mo þen pritti ȝere
Ich wes to ouer-mod.
Nou ich wolde ich were
As þau I neuere nere;
Þis life nis noþing goed.

Kare and kunde of helde
Makeþ me for to helde,

Þat I ne may stonden opriȝt.
For-þi min herte keldeþ,
And mi bodi ounbeldeþ
Þat wilen wes so liȝt.
Makeþ min heer so þenne,
Of-comen is worldes wenne,
Þis day me þinkeþ niȝt.
Deþ is þat I munne,
Me saiþ þat hit is sunne,
So me is nou I-diȝt.

Ar rich were þus hold,
Ich wes of speche bold,
And mon of glade chere;
Proud in euchan pres,
And wlonk in euchan res,
And lef to ben I-fere.
Ich wes hot and am kold,
Wat helpeþ al itold?
Of liue ich wolde ich were.
Me were leuere deed,
Þen eni gold so reed,
And seþþen leid on bere.

ȝong ich wes, I-cnowe,
Mine lokes were I-þrowe,
And nou her nabbi non;
Me wes hem lef to showen,
Þe wind hem to-wowen,
Mi ler wes wiit so swon.
As I stod in a snowe,
Heye houpon a lowe,
I tolde hit riche won.
Hounten herd I blowen,
Hertes bigounnen to þrowen,
Ne stunte me non ston.

Mi main þat wes so strong,
Mi middel small and long,

I-brout hit is to grounde.
Nis þer non so wlonk
Of speche ne of þonk,
Þat bodi had boten a mounde.
Þer I be men among,
Ne gladieþ me no song,
Ne gomen of haueke ne of hounde.
Ich am I-wend to helde,
Þat makeþ me for to ounbelde,
And al nis boten a stounde.

Þo ich wes ȝoung and wis,
And werede grei and gris,
Ich heuede frendes þo.
Foul soþ I-seid hit Iis,
Þe mon þat is of pris,
He haueþ frendes þe mo.
Mi mureþ nowit nis,
Agon hit is I-wiis,
Mine frendes beþ also.
Crist, al so he king iis
So soþliche and so wiis,
Me bringe of þisse wo.

Iche nuste non I-wis
Þat werede grei and gris,
So murie so me wes þo,
Ne more heuede of his;
And nou nowiit hit nis,
And al hit is ago;
So gentil ne so wiis,
Ne mon of more pris;
Me may wel ben wo.
Þis world wrechede iis,
Þat ich wot wel I-wiis,
And moni men tideþ swo.

Fair ich wes and fre,
And swete forto se;

Þat laste luitel stounde.
Gladdore gome wiþ gle
Ne miȝte neuere be
In middelert I-founde.
Helde ounhende is he,
He chaugeþ al mi ble,
Mi miȝte is al aswounde.
Ac henne woldi flee,
For ich am on of þee,
Þat ofte sikeþ ounsounde.

Ich mourne and sike sore,
For I ne may be namore
Mon as ich wes þo;
So crafti clerc of lore,
So godlich ounder gore,
And al hit is ago.
Ich walke as water in wore.
Louerd Crist, þin ore!
Wi is me so wo?

Riche I wes and riȝt
Borlich I-wis and liȝt,
As ich am ounderstonde.
Of herte ich wes wel liȝt,
Soþliche wiis and briȝt,
And franc mon of honde.
Þer nis clerk ne kniȝt,
Ne mon of more miȝt,
Þat leuere wes in londe.
I-tint is al mi fiȝt,
Þis day me þencheþ niȝt,
And þus ich am I-bounde.

Fair I wes in hewe,
And of treuþe trewe;
Þat laste luitel stounde.
Þee þat her me knewe,
Ich hem sore rewe;

And þat ich habbe I-founde.
Wen rose blostme blewe,
Me wes murþe newe,
And nou ich am aswounde.
Wo is me þe siþe,
Ne worþe I neuer eft bliþe,
I-brout ich am to grounde.

Þe wimmen þat I se,
Þat gladieþ hem wiþ me,
Hy brekeþ min herte a-two;
For ich wes on of þee,
Þat gladdoust wes woned to bee,
In londe þat were þo.
Nou am ich liih þan tre,
Þat loren haueþ his ble,
Ne greneþ hit nammo.
Henne wold I fle,
Ich ne wot weder ich te;
Helde me doþ so wo.

I-tint is al mi plawe,
Þat I wes woned to haue,
Þe wile I wes so liȝt.
Hold ich am and ounmon,
Ich lerne for to gon,
And þenche on children briȝt.
Helde wiþ-houten hawe
Makeþ þat I ne may wawe
Mi bodi wiþ-houten miȝt.
Deþ ich wolde fawe,
For I ne may tellen no sawe,
So helde me haueþ I-diȝt.

Ich wolde ich were on rest,
Wel owe leiid in a chest;
Mi blisse is al forlore.
Mi murþe wes monne mest,
Þat ilke wile þat hit I-lest,

And nou me is wo þerfore.
Ne gladieþ me no geest,
Ne ioie of more feest.
Wat solde ich I-bore?
Þis world me þinkeþ west,
Deþ ich wilni mest,
Win is he me I-core?

Mi ler þat wes so briȝt
Al so þe strerre a-niȝt,
Falew hit is and won;
Mi bodi þat wes so tuiȝt,
So stiþ and stod opriȝt—
Ich wes a modi mon.
Astunt is nou mi fiiȝt,
Mi main and eke mi miiȝt,
Of reuþes is mi ron.
Nis non so modi kniȝt,
Þat him ne beþ so I-diiȝt,
Wen helde him sieþ on.

Wilde ich wes her þo,
Wildere þen þe ro,
Are I bi-gon to hore.
Helde is min I-fo,
And þat ich wilnede þo,
And nou nulli nammore,
Nulli nout don so.
I lerne for to go,
And stonde and sike sore.
Mi wele is went to wo,
Al so is oþres mo
Þat habbeþ I-liued so ȝore.

As I rod þoru-out rome,
Richest alre home,
In murþes al so ich wolde,
Leuedies wiit so swon,
Maidenes so briȝt so bon,

Comen for me biholde.
"Lo! Wer riit þe mon,
Þat heiȝte maximion,
Wiþ his bernes boldes."
Nes þer non of þee,
Þat dourste me I-see
In hire cloþes holde.

Reuþfoul is mi reed;
Hoe makeþ me selden gled,
Mi wif þat sholde be.
Of me hoe is al seed,
Hoe saiþ ich waste breed.
Mine frend me nulleþ I-se.
Ich telle me for a queed,
Þe wile ich miȝt, en heueed
I-beten nedde ich hoe.
Crist þou do me reed!
Me were leuere deed,
Þen þus aliue to bee.

Iich may seien alas,
Þat ich I-boren was;
I liued ich have to longe.
Were ich mon so ich was,
Min heien so grei so glas,
Min her so feir bihonge,
And ich hire heuede bi þe trasce
In a derne place,
To meken and to monge:
Ne sholde hoe neuere at-witen
Min helde ne me bifliten,
Wel heye I shulde hire honge.

Commentary

Title: Most references to this text call them *Elegiae*, a default title in the absence of evidence of the original title. Disputable manuscript evidence suggests that Maximianus called these poems *Nugae*. See Ellis (1884a) at 8–9; Gagliardi (1988) at 28; but see Butrica (2005) at 563.

Around 1200 the French grammarian Alexander de Villa Dei criticized what he called *nugis* of Maximianus in lines 3–4 and 25 of his popular grammar book, *Doctrinale puerorum*. See Copeland and Sluiter at 576–577; see also Ellis (1884a) at 8; d'Andeli (1914) at 28–29.

> Iamque legent pueri pro *nugis Maximiani*
> Quae veteres sociis nolebant pandere caris (3–4)
>
> Proderit ista tamen plus *nugis Maximiani* (25)

This title, embraced by Schneider (2003) (albeit with parentheses signaling tentativeness), suggests that Maximianus placed himself in the tradition of non-epic and sexually explicit poets, such as Martial and Catullus, who popularized *nugae* as part of the Roman literary vocabulary. Horace's *Art of Poetry* and the *Satires* of both Juvenal and Persius included *nugae* as a description of that kind of poetry, although scholars have disagreed sharply about the best way to translate the term.

Without attempting to settle all the issues surrounding translation of *nugae*, I caution readers against interpreting it as a frothy word, which it became in the nineteenth century when it became associated with the word "bagatelle." To import that interpretation into classical usage is a mistake. For Martial and Catullus, the slangy *nugae* was a broad and supple term that indicated that their poems did not aspire to the heights of epic poetry. See Copley, "Catullus, c. I" at 29–31 in Gaisser (2007); Galán Vioque (2002) at 104. The label of *nugae* for a collection of poems did not necessarily mean that it included frivolities; it also could have described poems that dealt with issues of everyday life—seriously or humorously. "Details" would be one apt translation.

Later manuscripts also carry the titles *De senectute* and *Proverbia Maximiani*, see Ellis (1884a) at 8–9, but there is no reason to believe that these titles reflect anything more than a scribe's sincere longing for a title. In the absence of evidence of the author's intention, I retain the conventional "*Elegies*," although these poems are as much satires in the tradition of Horace as they are love elegies in the tradition of Ovid, Propertius, and Tibullus.

Structure: I retain the division of the text into six elegies despite doubt about Maximianus' intent; the manuscripts usually have no divisions. See Wasyl (2011) at 113–120; Schneider (2001) at 445–464; Goldlust (2011) at 157–158; Spaltenstein (1977) at 81–101; Fo (1986) at 9–21; Cupaiuolo (1997) at 388–389; Franzoi (2011) at 160–162. Some recent editors present the text without divisions; Prada (1919) presents elegy 1 as the first book and the rest of the text as a second book.

Date of the author and the text: The term *senectus* ("old age") had a different sense in an era when people typically lived a hard and short life. See generally Parkin (2003) at 15–35. In *Consolatio philosophiae* 1.1.8 Boethius refers to himself as a *senis* ("old man") even though he was probably in his mid-forties when he wrote the line. Maximianus refers to his own *serior aetas* ("older age") at 4.55; the common assumption that Maximianus was in his sixties or seventies when he wrote these elegies is probably wrong. My best guess, based primarily on internal evidence of the manuscripts, is that he was in his mid-to-late fifties when he completed these elegies around 539 AD, a period shortly after Cassiodorus *Variae* and Boethius *Consolatio philosophiae* became available—and just before Belisarius reclaimed Ravenna and the remnants of the Roman Empire for Justinian in May 540.

My dating of this text assumes the following: (a) Elegy 3 is accurate in indicating Maximianus was younger, by perhaps three to five years, than Boethius, who was born in 480 AD, cf. Arcaz Pozo (2011) at 16, but see Bertini (1981) at 273–283 (arguing for a birth date around 495); (b) Maximianus probably did not complete these elegies until after he read Cassiodorus *Variae*, which did not circulate until around 538 but which might have been available to a select few earlier, cf. Bjornlie (2009) at 149; (c) Maximianus probably did not complete these elegies after 540 AD because he refers to the Ravenna/Constantinople division of power in elegy 5 without noting Justinian's final conquest in 540; (d) Maximianus is the likely author of the *Panegyric to Theodahad* and other poems associated with Theodahad in the *Appendix Maximiani*, thus the diplomatic service mentioned in the *Elegies* most likely occurred during Theodohad's brief reign from 534 to 536 AD; (e) Maximianus was probably the addressee of Cassiodorus' letter to Maximianus in the *Variae* regarding the restoration of historic buildings in Rome, which means that Maximianus must have achieved a certain professional stature between the time that Cassiodorus started government service in 507 and the death of Theoderic in 526 (see note to 2.45–50 discussing Spaltenstein's point that Maximianus echoes Cassiodorus' letter to Maximianus, an observation that bolsters the argument that Maximianus was a real individual, not a pseudonym or a fiction), but see Boano (1949) at 208; and (f) the elegies had to be completed no later than 548 or 549 (and realistically at least several years earlier) in order to influence Corippus *Iohannis*. See Mastandrea (2003–2004) at 327; Boano (1949) at 200–204; Anastasi (1951) at 47–66.

My best guess is that Maximianus completed these elegies around 539 AD just as the last Ostrogoth holdouts in Italy were being defeated by Justinian. The Plague of Justinian brought *Yersinia pestis* to Ravenna and Rome around 543 AD and wiped out about one-third of their populations; it is the most likely date of Maximianus' death, though it is highly speculative. That speculation is strengthened by the fact that nothing in the elegies (or the *Appendix Maximiani*) mentions an event after 540 AD. Moreover, the text does not seem to include vocabulary or phrasing that emerged after 540 AD.

Two recent analyses are unduly confident that Maximianus remained in Constantinople after finishing his diplomatic assignment of elegy 5. See Vitiello (2014) at 92–93; Mastandrea in "Linee per una biografia ipoetica di Massimiano" in Franzoi and Spinazzè at 28. In their defense, though, Justinian did send one of his key functionaries, Athanasius, to meet with Theodahad in 535 to negotiate an end to hostilities. It is likely that Athanasius met Maximianus during these negotiations if Maximianus was indeed close to Theodahad, as the *Appendix Maximiani* and elegy 5 suggest. Corippus, the first poet to incorporate phrases of Maximianus into his own poetry, was a subordinate of Athanasius in North Africa who subsequently moved to Constantinople. A plausible explanation for the improbable survival of Maximianus' poetry (given that it is not a Christian work and no mention of it survives from his lifetime) is that Corippus encountered Maximianus or an intimate of Maximianus through Athanasius (or otherwise) in Constantinople, and through that encounter obtained a copy of the elegies. If that hypothesis explains transmission, it increases the probability that Maximianus lived comparatively peacefully in Constantinople during Justinian's conquest of Italy.

Elegy 1

1.1 Webster (1900) argues at 59–60 that *aemula* ("Jealous") has "a tinge of the late Latin meaning, *invida*" and thus *cessas* is oxymoronic with *aemula* as well as *properare*." The term *aemula*, in fact, suggests a softer, less angry characterization than *invida*. Cf. Prudentius *Cathemerinon* 10.101–102 (*iam nulla deinde senectus / frontis decus invida carpet*). Spaltenstein (1983) at 80 has only one citation, Virgil *Aeneid* 5.415–416, that arguably supports his claim that *aemula* used with *senectus* was formulaic.

The phrase *finem properare* ("hastening the end") appears to be original with Maximianus, although *mortem properare* appears in the poetry of Virgil, Tibullus, and other Roman poets. Tyson (1996) at 50, Öberg (1999) at 184, Franzoi (2011) at 163, and Goldlust at 126 note the parallel of *properata . . . senectus* in Boethius *Consolatio philosophiae* 1.1.1.5.

1.2 Webster correctly notes at 60 that *tarda* ("slowly"—the adjective is used here as adverb) is a standard epithet for *senectus* ("old age"). Cf. Horace *Sermones* 2.2.88, Ovid *Tristia* 4.7.23, Tibullus 2.2.19; Navarro Antolín (1996) at 438 ("*tardus* alludes to the slow, laborious walk of the elderly"). Tyson at 50 notes *tarda in senectute* appears as far back as Ennius. For variants of *tarda*, see Franzoi and Spinazzè at 127.

The phrase *fesso corpore* ("weary body") is common and perhaps an echo of

Virgil *Aeneid* 4.522–523 (*fessa . . . corpora*). Öberg at 184 notes the similar *effeto corpore* in Boethius *Consolatio philosophiae* 1.1.1.10. Augustine in *In Ioannis evangelium* 7.19.26 uses this phrase in a line (*in corpore fessi et incurve senis mortuae sunt vires*) that also includes the uncommon term *incurva* used by Maximianus later in this elegy. Cf. note to 1.261.

1.3 The phrase *tali de carcere* ("from such a prison") could foreshadow Maximianus' conversation with Boethius in elegy 3, both for evoking the setting of *Consolatio philosophiae* and for its Neoplatonic image of the soul imprisoned by the body. Cf. Goldlust at 126 (who overreaches by claiming that this image is Neoplatonic "sans doute"); cf. Agozzino (1970) at 121. The prison of the body is also a favorite image of other Christian authors. See, e.g., Ambrose *Expositio evangelii secundam Lucam* 2.59 (*corporeae carcere*). However, non-Platonists, particularly Stoics, also use this metaphor. See, e.g., Cicero *De re publica* 6.14 (*corporum vinculis . . . e carcere*); see generally Courcelle (1965) at 406–443.

Maximianus' desire to release his *life*, rather than his *soul*, from the prison of his body reflects his materialistic perspective, a perspective influenced by Horace and probably Lucretius. Given Boethius' familiarity with Lucretius, it is possible Maximianus had access to *De rerum natura*. See generally O'Daly (1991) at 35–44. For a comparison of attitudes toward aging and death between the opening of this elegy and the opening of Boethius *Consolatio philosophiae*, see Consolino (1997) at 368–369; Fielding (forthcoming) at 20–25.

The phrase *miseram . . . vitam* ("my wretched life") is a familiar phrase in classical and Christian literature. See, e.g., Cicero *Tusculanae disputationes* 5.50; Augustine *Sermones* 30.305.4.

1.4 Death as a rest or a relief from life's burdens is a cliché of both Roman and Christian poetry. See Webster at 58–59, 61. Spaltenstein at 81, who is too quick to denigrate Maximianus, sees a nonexistent tension between *carcere* ("prison") in line 3 and *poena* ("punishment") in line 4 instead of a perfectly logical extension of a trope in a way that is striking because it lacks the usual religious sentiment of the era. Öberg at 184 overreaches by arguing this line echoes Virgil *Aeneid* 8.540 (*quas poenas mihi, Turne, dabis*).

1.5 Ovid, Tibullus, and Propertius often use the first person plural for the first person singular, particularly in such phrases as *nostra puella* ("my girl").

Webster at 61 and Tyson at 53 overread *pars maxima nostri* ("my greatest part") by arguing that the phrase is wordplay on Ovid's *pars pessima nostri*, a reference to his own penis. But see Arcaz Pozo at 68; cf. Ovid *Amores* 3.7.69; note to 6.12. This suggestion is unlikely because the poem's somber tone doesn't break into an intermittently more lighthearted mode for at least another twenty lines. It may be true, though, that the use of *maxima* in this line is a self-reference and an example of Maximianus' linguistic playfulness even without a sexual reference. The suggestion of Uden and Fielding (2010) that the phrase reverses Ovid *Amores* 1.15.42 (*vivam parsque mei multa superstes erit*) has merit. See Uden and Fielding (2010) at 443; but see Adams (1982) at 45. This phrase may also echo Horace *Carmina* 3.30.7 (*multa pars mihi*). See del Barrio (1985) at 249. One also should look at the *pars maxima* of Lucan *Bellum civile* 7.844 in light of Maximianus' use of the otherwise unique phrase *fastidita iacet* later in Lucan's sentence. Cf. note to 1.162. Maximianus' use of *pars* causes interpretive challenges right through the last line of elegy 6.

Tyson at 53 and Agozzino at 121 note the use of *non sum qui fueram* ("I am not who I was") at Propertius 1.12.11 and *non sum quod fueram* at Ovid *Tristia* 3.11.25. See also Bellanova (2004) at 103; Uden and Fielding (2010) at 442. Spaltenstein at 81 and Öberg at 184 cite Horace *Carmina* 4.1.3 (*non sum qualis eram*); cf. Wasyl at 122–123. Goldlust at 126 (citing Meyers [2003] at 711) characterizes this line as a "reprise" to Propertius, but the parallel does not support such a strong assertion.

The verb *periit* ("has perished") is syncopated.

1.6 Use of *langor* ("Fatigue") in the Webster text instead of the classical *languor* might reflect the shift in the language toward the Old French *langor*, but it is more likely a textual error so I emend the text accordingly. Cf. Schetter at 10; Öberg at 153. Maximianus' contemporaries, including Boethius, Cassiodorus, Dracontius, and Fortunatus all use *languor* instead of *langor*. See e.g Ennodius *Epistularum* 1.3.25 (*languoribus*); *Opuscula miscella* 5.1.10 (*languoribus*). Webster also uses the classical spelling at 5.107. In the decades after Maximianus the spelling of this word started to change, see, e.g., Gregorius Turonensis *Historiae* 10.1.7. (*nec langor mortem praevenit sed langoris moras*), although even in the eighth or ninth century the *Imitatio Maximiani* uses *languor*. See Appendix D.29. For *languor* as a term of art in Roman love elegy, see Wasyl at 124–125; Fielding (forthcoming) at 25–27. For the pairing of two nouns ending in "or," see Goldlust (2013) at 126.

Spaltenstein's (1983) objection at 82 to the standard translation of *quoque* ("too") is overstated; *quoque* may be metrical filler, but it is not exotic.

Spaltenstein (1983) at 82 makes a sound case for rejecting Schetter's substitution at 97 of *habet* for Webster's *habent* ("cling"). Cf. Öberg at 184 citing Ovid *Tristia* 3.8.24 (*corpora languor habet*), *Metamorphoses* 7.547 (*omnia languor habet*).

1.7 The term *lux* (literally "light") is a standard trope for "life." The *lux*/*luctu* wordplay, alliteration, and internal rhymes give this line an aphoristic feel. I tried to capture the paradoxical sense of *lux gravis* noted by Webster at 61–62 by using "grave" for *gravis*. For a helpful comparison of Maximianus' *in luctu* ("during grief") to the *lucibus* of Ovid *Tristia* 1.1.6, see Wasyl at 126.

The phrase *rebus . . . laetis* ("in happy times") is common. For this sense of *rebus*, see the *Oxford Latin Dictionary* (hereinafter cited as OLD) 17.

1.8 The primary meaning of *funere* ("death") is "funeral rites," but it is also a metonym for death itself. See OLD 3; cf. 6.11.

The phrase *velle mori* ("wish to die") is used by Ovid, Lucan, Seneca, and Quintilian. See Tyson at 54; Öberg at 184. Roman culture was tolerant of suicide, though it considered suicide shameful without certain justifications. Substantial physical pain of the kind described by Maximianus fits within those justifications, but this line's broad statement seems to accept the then-recent Christian view that suicide is inherently wrong. Augustine *De civitate Dei* changed the landscape by denouncing all suicides as sins, and in 533 (probably shortly before the beginning of the composition of the *Elegies*) the Church began denying Christian burial to those who committed suicide. See Brown (2001) at 21–87; Parkin (2003) at 70–73.

This line's lack of a verb stirs zeal to emend. Spaltenstein at 83 harshly criticizes the speculative Schetter (1970) emendation at 117 of *estque* for *quodque* ("any"). See also Butrica (2005) at 564. Perhaps because scribes also felt the need for a verb, at least four manuscripts have *est* after *peius* despite the metrical issues created by this addition. See Webster at 25; Schetter (1970) at 10. The simplest solution is to imply *esse*.

1.9 The phrase *mens sensusque* ("mind and senses") is common. See Spaltenstein (1983) at 83, though Tyson argues at 54 that it is distinctively Ciceronian.

Webster at 62 sees the construction *dum . . . maneret* ("while . . . stayed") as echoing tombstone inscriptions. For use of the subjunctive after *dum* in this line, see Spaltenstein (1983) at 83.

For the phrase *iuvenile decus* ("youthful handsomeness"), Öberg at 184 notes the parallel of Martial 9.17.7 (*iuvenile decus*). Cf. *Laus Pisonis* 260 (*iuvenile decus*); Q. Aurelius Symmachus *Carmina* 1.1.4.11 (*iuvenile decus*).

1.10–14 Webster and Tyson argue that these lines echo the practice of tombstones listing accomplishments of the deceased. See Tyson at 54; Webster at 62; cf. Lattimore (1962) at 285–290. Wasyl (2011) at 126–128 extends this argument in her analysis of Maximianus' language, particularly his use of hyperbole, through 1.72.

The Baehrens text, upon which Spaltenstein, Schetter and others rely, shuffles the order of these lines in a way that has neither strong manuscript support nor strong internal logic.

1.10 Webster at 62 describes *toto . . . in orbe* ("everywhere") as an "exaggeration," and Spaltenstein at 84 describes it as "remarquable." Both comments are overheated for a phrase that is substantially a synonym for *ubique* and *undique*, although it does have a hint of grandiosity about it that is entirely consistent with Maximianus' boastful description of his youth in the subsequent lines. It also echoes the *in toto . . . orbe* of Ovid *Amores* 1.15.8. Uden and Fielding cite this line of Ovid and also note *Amores* 1.3.25 (*per totum . . . orbem*). See Uden and Fielding (2010) at 444. Öberg at 184 notes Ovid *Fasti* 1.284 (*toto . . . in orbe*).

The phrase *orator . . . clarus* ("a famous speaker") parallels a much-debated phrase from Quintilian *Institutio* 8.2.3. See Varela at 314–316.

1.11 The idea of poetry as *mendacia dulcia* ("sweet deceptions") has a long history. See Tyson at 55. The same is true of *poetarum mendacia* ("deceptions of the poets"). See, e.g., Augustine *De civitate Dei* 7.18.1 (*ornatibus ea mendaciis poetarum*); Lactantius *Divinae institutiones* (*mendacium enim poetarum non in facto est*); Curtius Rufus *Historiae Alexandri Magni Macedonis* 3.1.4 (*poetarum mendacio fecit*). Öberg at 184–185 also notes the Ovidian *mendacia vatum* at *Fasti* 6.253 and *Amores* 3.6.17. There is some manuscript support for the plausible substitution of *carmina* for *dulcia*, see Schetter at 17–18, but I retain Webster's text.

1.12 Webster at 63 engages in confused speculation as to *res ficta* ("fictions"), but the phrase refers back to the poetry of the previous line. See generally Deproost (1998). Cf. Ovid *Tristia* 2.355.

The word *titulos* ("honors") is a favorite of Cassiodorus, but I cannot identify an example of *veros titulos* ("true honors") prior to Maximianus. But cf. Tacitus *De vita Iulii Agricolae* 46.2.3 (*verus honos*); Statius *Thebaid* 10.711 (*verus honos*). The *ficta*/*veros* juxtaposition reminds us of the paradoxical nature of poetry.

1.13 Webster at 63, Öberg at 185, and Schneider (2003) at 205 note a possible echo of Propertius 4.11.99 (*causa perorata est*). Tyson at 55 wrongly challenges Webster's claim at 63 that *perorata* is Ciceronian; in fact, Cicero uses *causa perorata* five times just in his *Orationes*.

The opening word of the distich, *saepe* ("often"), is the first of many examples of the rhetorical device of anaphora.

1.14 For *praemia grata* ("some welcome prizes"), cf. Luxorius *De aleatore in pretio lenocinii ludente* in *Anthologia latina* 323.5 (*An tali melius praemia grata sunt*).

The metonymy of *lingua* ("language"—literally "tongue") for speech is common in Latin poetry. See Spaltenstein at 84.

Goldlust at 126–127, relying in part on Spaltenstein at 83, misdescribes this line and the following lines as having "la forme d'une épitaphe," apparently based on their confessional content. Moreover, his dismissal of the accuracy of Maximianus' self-description as an orator does not take account of the poet's intensely rhetorical style and legal vocabulary. For a discussion of that vocabulary, see Fo (1987) at 359.

1.15 For the phrase *defectis . . . membris* ("worn out . . . in body parts"), cf. Cassianus *Collationes* 2.11.4.2 (*defectis mortificatisque iam omnibus membris*).

1.16 The phrase *portio vitae* ("much life"—literally "a share of life") first appears at Juvenal 9.127–128 (*vitae/portio*) and is rare afterward. See Webster at 63; Tyson at 56; Agozzino at 123. It also appears in Erasmus' elegy on old age, *Ad Gulielmum Copum Basiliensem artis medicae principem, Carmen de fuga vitae humanae* at 185. Michel de Montaigne quotes this line in his essay "To Philosophize Is to Learn How to Die." Montaigne at 101.

The term *senibus* ("for old men") is used mostly for men, often in comedy. Based on Maximianus' language and use of comic conventions, he knew his Plautus; the case for his knowledge of Terence is less clear.

1.17 Öberg at 185 and Agozzino at 123 note that *gratia formae* ("good looks") appears in Ovid *Metamorphoses* 7.44.

This line may echo Propertius 2.34b.59 (*nec minor his animis*). But see Günther (1997) at 72 (suggesting corruption of Propertian text). The rhetorical device of litotes, *nec minor* ("no less than"), transmits a sense of lingering swagger.

1.18 This line is almost certainly corrupt. See Spaltenstein (1983) at 87. With trepidation I emend Webster's problematic *quae vel si desit* to *quae mihi si desint* ("which, if they left me") of the Leidensis Gronovii 87 and Palatinus manuscripts. See Webster at 25. If I am wrong, Webster's *vel si . . . placent* may be an echo of

Martial 5.53.4 (*vel si non placet*). In further defense of the Webster text that I reject, the unusual phrase *vel si* appears regularly in Justinian's *Digesta* during the time period that Maximianus was writing. See 8.4.2.2, 16.3.31.1.11, 17.1.10.6.3, 29.2.20.1.8, 29.2.20.1.8, 43.12.1.15.5, 44.3.1.15.3.1. Clark suggests the speculative emendation *si desint cetera, nuda placet*. See Clark (1913) at 260.

Webster at 53 correctly rejects Petschenig's emendation of *nulla* for *multa* ("most"). Franzoi and Spinazzè at 130 does the same for Withof's (1741) substitution of *muta* for *multa*. Welsh makes a thoughtful, if not ultimately persuasive, case for the speculative emendation of *culta* for *multa* ("most"). Welsh's proposed change would also require changing *placent* ("delight") to *placet*. See Welsh, "Notes on the Text of Maximianus" Volume 15 *Exemplaria Classica* (2011) at 214–215.

There is an argument that this distich more logically belongs after lines 13–14.

1.19–1.20 Webster at 63 and Tyson at 56 argue that the phrase *fulvo pretiosior auro* ("valued more than yellow gold") is Ovidian. See also Spaltenstein at 87; *Ars amatoria* 2.299 (*pretiosior auro*); *Amores* 3.8.3; *Metamorphoses* 1.115 (*fulvo pretiosior aere*); *Metamorphoses* 8.79 (*auro pretiosior*); cf. Tibullus 1.1.1 (*fulvo auro*); but see Jerome *Commentarii in Isaiam* 6.13.33 (*pretiosior . . . auro*); *Isaias* 13.12 (*pretiosior auro*); Tertullian *Adversus Marcionem* 2.28.4 (*pretiosior auro*). Goldlust (2013) also notes Virgil *Aeneid* 10.134 (*qualis gemma micat fulvum quae dividit aurum*). See also Franzoi and Spinazzè at 130.

1.20 The best placement of the implied verb *est* ("is"), and hence the meaning of the line, is open to debate. I have compressed the verb into the comparative adjective to mimic the Latin. For Late Antique comparative adjectives, see Herman (2000) at 63–64.

Maximianus' verse often has an aphoristic quality. See Wasyl (2011) at 133–134. Ellis notes that Maximianus uses the technique of closing a line with a multisyllabic word—in this case *ingenium* ("ability")—only fourteen times, and that, when he does, he does it to create an epigrammatic effect. See Ellis, (1884a) at 14; cf. Roberts, "The Last Epic of Antiquity: Generic Continuity and Innovation in the *Vita Sancti Martini* of Venantius Fortunatus," 131 *Transactions of the American Philological Association* (2001) at 279–282.

Although the literature contains references to "epigrams" by Maximianus, all "epigrams" appear to be excerpts from the elegies. The most detailed of these references is in Thomson at 1:632–633, who indicates the "epigrams" are contained in manuscripts of Macrobius described as MSS R&F (Rome, Vatican Library Cod. Reg. 2043, eleventh century, and Florence, Biblioteca Laurenziana MS Plut. 90 sup. 25 early twelfth century).

I am exceptionally grateful to Robert Kaster, the renowned scholar on Macrobius, who did most of the following thorough detective work for me on these "epigrams." Any errors are undoubtedly mine.

Thomson's references are inaccurate; the Vatican manuscript only contains the *Saturnalia*. It begins on folio 1 and the text breaks off on folio 112, a couple of folia short of the end of the *Saturnalia* as it survives in other manuscripts.

The inaccurate reference to Florence BML Plut. 90 sup. 25 probably shows that Thompson was thinking of the *Florilegium Macrobianum*, a collection of eight brief texts that follow the *Saturnalia*. The same brief collection is found between Books 6 and 7 of the *Saturnalia* in another manuscript of Macrobius written in the second quarter of the twelfth century at Bury St. Edmunds and located now at Cambridge (Cambridge Univ. Library Ff.3.5=A.). Other, probably later, copies of the *Florilegium Macrobianum* are at fol. 50 of Vatican Ottob. Lat. 1935 and fol. 16bis (recto) and fol. 19 (recto) of Paris BNF nouv. acq. 1907.

In general, the authenticity quotient of the *Florilegium Macrobianum* is not high. It includes an epitaph attributed to Seneca, four sets of elegiac couplets attributed to Cicero, one set attributed to Lucan, and one set attributed to Ovid. Only the Ovid is authentic; they are extracts from *Epistulae ex Ponto* 1.2 and 4.3. Of the four sets attributed to Cicero, two are of unknown origin, one is taken from Claudian *Carmina minora* 1–2 and one from Ausonius *Epigrammata* 24.1–2. Amusingly, the lines attributed to Lucan are not his but are Petronius' dead-on parody of Lucan. *Satiricon* 119.1–3, 120.63–64, 65. The epitaph attributed to Seneca in this collection is in *Anthologia latina* 1.2 *carmina* 667 and is now attributed to Pseudo-Seneca.

Despite this dubious pedigree, the first four lines attributed to Maximianus track the first four lines of Maximianus' first elegy, except that the second line changes somewhat (*Cur et in hoc fesso corpora tarda venis?* to *An et in hoc fesso corpora pigra venis?*), the fifth line is the eighth line of the *Imitatio Maximiani*, and the sixth line is the fifth line of the first elegy.

In the *caveat lector* category, this manuscript's description of our elegist as a praetor perpetuates long-standing confusion between Maximianus the elegist and the soldier-statesman M. Valerius Maximianus. Cf. Maxwell (1981) at 178–179, 304. There is also potential confusion with the Maximinus whom Justinian named prefect of Italy in 542. Cf. Mastandrea (2005) at 164; Mastandrea in Franzoi and Spinazzè at 21–27. Even scholars such as Barnish and Romano have been confused by these references. Barnish (1990) at 17: "To these data can be added a note on one MS of the *Elegies*, that they were written while Maximian held the office of prefect. He may thus have reached high rank under the Byzantine empire, perhaps the city prefecture of Rome." Cf. Romano (1968–1969) at 329. Some passages in Procopius compound this confusion. Cf. Mastandrea (2005) at 163.

For a thoughtful discussion of the link between shining and nobility in the era of Theoderic which undercuts Webster's assertion at 64 that the figurative use of *micat* was rare, see Arnold (2008) at 140. Cf. 1.30.

1.21 Tyson at 55–56, Agozzino at 123, Spaltenstein (1983) at 88, Schneider (2003) at 205, and Webster at 64 cite numerous examples of *celeres sagittas* ("swift arrows") as a stock phrase of Augustan poetry.

Welsh argues that *temptare* ("try") is problematic and offers the unsupported *librare*. See Welsh (2011) at 215. That argument overstates the difficulty of the primary definition of *temptare*; one could use a word along the lines of "attack" if one were unhappy with a verb that connotes use without certain success. See

OLD 10. Franzoi and Spinazzè, Spaltenstein, and Wernsdorf (1794) use *intentare*; single manuscripts use *intemptare*, *tendere*, and *tractare*. See Franzoi at 130–131.

1.22 The phrase *praeda petita* ("the quarry . . . when hunted") is Ovidian. See, e.g., *Ars amatoria* 1.8.92 (*cito per multas praedas petita manus*); *Ars amatoria* 2.2 (*decidit in casses praeda petita meos*). Franzoi and Spinazzè at 131 note *Epistulae ex Ponto* 2.2.12 (*numina sunt telis ulla petita meis*). These echoes may seem to suggest Maximianus is speaking metaphorically, but given the gritty nature of the following lines, that interpretation is unlikely.

1.23 Webster at 64, Tyson at 57, and Öberg at 185 note that *circumdare saltus* ("to surround . . . woods") is Virgilian. See *Eclogae* 10.57; *Georgica* 1.140. Webster at 64 and Agozzino at 124 note the intriguing use of this phrase in a hunting text, Nemesianus *Cynegetica* 303.

1.24 The verb *prostravi* ("I took down") is almost always used in the third person, so Maximianus' use of it here in the first person conveys a bit of swagger. So, too, the litotes of *non sine laude* ("not without praise") suggests the pomposity of false humility.

1.25–26 Spaltenstein at 89 notes the unusual transition from the "high" activity of hunting, a traditional recreation of love elegy, to the "low" activity of wrestling in a gym, a recreation alien to Augustan love elegy. This deflating transition may subtly set the stage for Maximianus' subsequent string of amatory failures. Schneider (2003) at 205 notes other references to a gymnasium at Lucan *Bellum civile* 9.661 (*liquidaeque palaestrae*) and Prudentius *Hamartigenia* 365 (*sic Lacedaemonias oleo maduisse palaestras*). Spaltenstein (1983) at 89 and Goldlust (2013) at 128 also note Ovid *Heroides* 19.11 (*unctae . . . palaestrae*). The term *palaestra* ("gym") is associated with wrestling in a way that no English word adequately translates—it derives from the Greek verb *palalein* ("to wrestle").

1.25 For precedents for *si fors* ("if . . . by chance"), see Spaltenstein (1983) at 89. Cf. Virgil *Aeneid* 12.183. I am grateful to James Uden for persuading me that *fors* is used here in its adverbial sense. The anaphora of *si* helps to accelerate a narrative that is long for a backstory.

For *versare* I used the slangy "To hit" to capture both the verb's sense of "repeated turning" and its sense of "working." See OLD 4b, 6, 10, 13. Its meaning would change if *fors* is a noun, e.g., "luck diverted me."

1.27 For *agili cursu* ("with nimble feet") Öberg notes the parallel of Statius *Silvae* 4.3.32 (*cursus agiles*). Cf. Ammianus *Res gestae* 23.5.1 (*agili gradu*).

For metrical concern about *anteire* ("outdo"), see Altamura (1981) at 822. Webster at 27 argues that it is a case of synizesis (two syllables combining as one sound).

For *nunc* ("Sometimes") in this and the following line, see OLD 8.

1.28 I have rejected the *tragici* of the Webster text and used the *tragicos* ("tragic") proposed by Green. See Green (2000) at 448–449; but see Ellis (1884a) at 145; Spaltenstein (1983) at 90. At least three manuscripts have *tragico*, a step in the right direction, but the adjective needs to agree with *cantus*. Öberg at 185 notes a possible echo of Prudentius *Contra Symmachus* 2.647 (*tragicus cantor*). Cf.

Schetter at 17. Spaltenstein (1983) at 90 puts too much weight on this adjective in calling it a "symbole de l'activité intellectuelle" instead of recognizing the tradition of epic poetry being the favored genre for the most ambitious poets. Goldlust (2013) at 128 takes a similar position.

I follow Webster at 53, 65 and reject Ellis' proposed emendation (supported by two manuscripts) of *melo* for *melos* ("ditties" combined with *cantus*). There is some of the continuing swagger in this line.

1.29 For *augebat meritum* ("improved my worth"), cf. note to B.6.2.

The thirteenth line of a poem attributed to Alexander Neckham includes the phrase *dulcis mixtura bonorum* ("A mixture of sweet qualities"). See Thomas (2003) at 297.

1.30 Tyson at 59 notes that the pairing of *artis* and *opus* (combined as "artwork") is Ovidian. See, e.g., *Ars amatoria* 1.266, 2.214; *Fasti* 1.268; *Epistulae ex Ponto* 2.11.2. Öberg at 185 also notes Martial 6.13.2.

For *varium* ("varied"), see note to 1.32.

Altamura objects to *ut* ("just as") because he misreads it as being used in a causal sense. See Altamura (1981) at 823.

For *plus micat* ("glitters more"), cf. 1.20 (*plus micat*).

1.32 The meaning of *alterno . . . decore* ("with contrasting beauty") is open to interpretation. Lind (1988) at 320 renders it as "with alternate grace," which does not make much sense. As with *varium* ("different"), I take this phrase as a standard expression of Late Antique esthetics about combinations enhancing the whole. I am not sure that Maximianus is accurately portraying the standard rationale for this precept, which he expresses almost as an additive principle. This "additive" principle is expressed even more baldly in poems 5 and 6 of the *Appendix Maximiani*. Cf. notes to B.5.14, B.6.10. As with *varium* in the previous distich, this line may have an undercurrent of satirical self-criticism.

1.33 Webster at 64 misses the point by arguing this line's parallel with Sedulius *Carmen Paschale* 5.1 does not prove that Maximianus was a Christian. See, generally, Gärtner (2004) at 119–122. In fact, *virtutis opes* ("fine traits"—literally closer to "resources of excellence") echoes Virgil *Aeneid* 10.469 (*hoc virtutis opus*), a moving line about mortality, which is then echoed by Sedulius and others.

The noun *tolerantia* appears frequently in Augustine and Cassiodorus. The phrase *tolerantia rerum* ("fortitude in matters") may have Stoic roots. Cf. Cicero *Paradoxa Stoicorum* 4.27.4 (*tolerantia rerum*).

1.34 Maximianus may be playfully comparing himself to Caesar here. Cf. Lucan *Bellum civile* 5.578 (*sperne minas inquit pelagi*).

Maximianus may have contributed the word *insuperata* ("steadfast") to Latin and thus its descendant *insuperato* to Italian. Both *superata* and *insuperabilis* are common usages prior to Maximianus, and *insuperabilis* is a favorite word of Augustine and Cassiodorus. The term *insuperata* seems overblown given the list of activities that follows; the use of an invented (if, in fact, it is) but vaguely epic word may be another example of Maximianus using a mock-epic tone for self-deprecatory humor.

1.35 For the phrase *vertice nudato* ("with head exposed"), cf. Virgil *Aeneid* 1.12.312 (*nudato capite*). Webster at 66 notes Silius *Punica* 1.250 (*vertice nudo*). For a thoughtful discussion of the rhythm of this line and the following eight lines, see Franzoi at 131–132.

For *ventos pluviosque* ("wind and rain"), cf. Horace *Carmina* 1.17.4 (*pluviosque ventos*).

1.36 For *non mihi solstitium* ("for me no summer's heat"), cf. Ovid *Tristia* 5.10.7 (*Nec mihi solstitium*). While the primary meaning of solstitium is "solstice," it came to mean the summer solstice, and ultimately summer itself and its heat. See Goldlust (2013) at 129.

1.37 Descriptions of the Tiber are familiar features of Roman poetry. See generally Warner (1917) at 52–55. Webster at 66 and Schneider at 206 note the parallel of Persius 2.15 (*Tiberino in gurgite*), although a closer parallel is Sidonius Apollinaris *Carmen* 2.332 (*licet ingreditur Tiberini gurgitis*). Öberg at 186 notes the phrase *gelidas . . . undas* ("icy currents") appears in Ovid *Metamorphoses* 5.433. Schneider also notes Virgil *Aeneid* 10.832; Juvenal 6.523; Horace *Sermones* 2.3.291.

1.38 The term *freto* for the Tiber here is a bit unusual because it typically referred to the ocean, often choppy water. See Spaltenstein at 94; Webster at 66. I combined it with *dubio*, with its senses of "wavering" and "dangerous," as "rapids." See OLD 1, 9.

1.39–44 The dense collection of conjunctions may be a technique to build suspense for the surprising and paradoxical concluding phrase.

1.39 Agozzino notes that *requiescere somno* ("refresh . . . with sleep") also appears at Catullus 68.5.

1.40 Öberg at 186 notes that *membra fovere* ("nourish limbs") appears at Ovid *Heroides* 21.192. Cf. Lucan *Bellum civile* 4.153 (*membra fovent*).

1.41 By translating *me . . . repperit* as "sought me out," I tried to capture a hint of the "style élevé" noted by Spaltenstein (1983) at 95.

For uses of *vinosus* ("wine-soaked"), see Agozzino at 126.

1.42 Ellis objects to Webster's *multa dies* and proposes the substitution of *mulsa*. See Ellis (1884b) at 145–146. While not standard, *multa dies* is a phrase with an old and distinguished pedigree. Ennius *Annales* 287 (cited in Macrobius *Saturnalia* 6.2.16) (*multa dies in bello conficit unus*); Virgil *Aeneid* 11.425 (*multa dies uariique labor mutabilis aeui rettulit in melios*). There is no manuscript support for *mulsa*, and if Ellis' proposed emendation is correct, his rationale is surely wrong. There are precedents of the singular form of *mulsa* as "a honeyed wine" paired with *sumere*. See Petronius *Satyrica* 34.1 (*vellet mulsum sumere*); Pliny *Naturalis historia* 22.32 (*mulsa sumptum*).

Spaltenstein (1983) at 95 identifies *fecit . . . sumere* ("led to . . . drinking") as an ancient construction revived in Late Antiquity. See OLD 3; see also Goldlust (2013) at 129.

1.43–44 As the Roman gods lost ground to Christ, the wine god Bacchus retained popularity into Late Antiquity. Ausonius, a devout Christian, owned a statue of Bacchus. I have translated *pater* as "old' instead of the literal "Father" to capture the colloquial familiarity of the phrase.

Readers sometimes miss the humor of this admittedly ambiguous distich. The unhappy party is a recurring image in these elegies that satirizes the Lucretian and Horatian trope of life as a party that one should walk away from as a good and happy guest.

It is possible that the term *et* ("and") here is the shortened form of *etiam* rather than the conjunction. See OLD 6.

1.44 Medieval grammarians often quoted Maximianus to illustrate principles of rhetoric. See Lawrence-Mathers (2003) at 117–118, 153. Paradox is one of Maximianus' favorite rhetorical devices. He eliminates any doubt on that point by summarizing the difficulty of paradox in the next distich. The paradoxical phrase *vincere victus* ("vanquishes . . . vanquished") is perhaps proverbial. See Agozzino at 126.

1.45–46 This distich is a bit of a *non sequitur*. There is a hint that Maximianus might have been thinking of Boethius as a person who meets the standard of this distich, which he applies to Socrates and Cato in the next two distichs. The participle *oppositas* (collapsed with *res* into "opposites") is relatively rare and even rarer in philosophical discourse, but Boethius uses it frequently in his translation *De interpretatione*. See 2.4.2, 2.4.9, 2.4.42, 4.44.88, 5.3.83, 5.3.114, 5.3.116, 6.1.22. The *res . . . rebus* ("things") combination is an example of polyptoton.

Tyson at 64 notes that the phrase *haut facile est* ("It isn't easy") appears in Lucretius *De rerum natura* 3.328. It also appears at Juvenal 11.17 and Plautus *Mostellaria* 3.3.9–10 (*simul flare sorbereque haud facile est: ego hic esse et illic simul haud potui*) ("To blow and to swallow at the same time is not easy; I cannot at the same time be here and there"), which contains *two* paradoxes.

Tyson at 64 notes that *una duas* (reversed as "two . . . one") as a pentameter ending to a line was an Ovidian technique. See Ovid *Heroides* 7.138, 16.70, 18.126, *Fasti* 6.100. Cf. Shanzer (1988) at 259 (rejecting Ratkowitsch's [1986] argument that Maximianus echoes Fortunatus by showing they echo Ovid *Heroides* 7.138).

1.47–50 Spaltenstein (1983) at 98, Goldlust (2013) at 129–130, and Öberg at 185 note that *certamine*, *socratem*, and *promeruisse* may echo Boethius *Consolatio philosophiae* 1.3.6 (*magnum saepe certamen cum stultitiae temeritate certavimus eodemque superstite praeceptor eius Socrates iniustae victoriam mortis me adstante promeruit*). Wasyl (2011) at 130 notes the more pertinent parallel of Horace *Carmina* 3.21.9–12.

1.48 Some commentators doubt the accuracy of *socratem* ("Socrates"), largely based on metrical concerns, and offer a variety of emendations. See Ellis (1884b) at 146. Cf. Boethius *De interpretatione* 1.2.116, 1.2.117, 1.3.43, 1.4.24, 1.4.29, 1.4.42, 1.4.43, 2.2.87, 2.2.171, 3.2.6, 3.2.135, 3.2.138, 3.2.139, 3.2.140; Augustine *De civitate Dei* 8.4.3; Plato *Apology* 36d 399. Webster at 66, Green at 449, and Wasyl (2011) at 130 all see *socratem* and *catonem* in line 49 as echoing Horace *Carmina* 3.21.9–12. For an overview of Maximianus' prosody (an understudied topic), see Lekusch (1896) at 257–262; see also Altamura (1981) at 822; Cupaiuolo (1997) in D'Allessandro et al. at 381–391.

The noun *palmam* ("a palm") refers to the prize for victors in competitions.

1.49 There is customary uncertainty here as to which of the Catos and which of their proverbs Maximianus intends to cite. See Franzoi at 133. While it is not clear which incident Maximianus is describing, a good guess would be the triumph awarded to Cato the Elder in 194 BC for leading a brutally successful campaign in Spain. The epithet *rigidus* ("stern") is standard for any Cato. See Webster at 66–67. Boethius also uses this epithet for Cato. See *Consolatio philosophiae* 2.7.2.15.

For a critique of Smolak's proposed emendation of *caluisse* for *valuisse* ("had the power"), see Gärtner (2004) at 123.

1.50 Tyson notes that *in vitium cadunt* ("count toward guilt") is the only time Maximianus uses the accusative after *in*, and also notes that one manuscript has *vitio*. For "in," see OLD 22. From the context it seems as if this line should strike a familiar chord, but it doesn't. Webster fails at 67 to make a persuasive identification. Indeed, except for *in vitium cadit* in Prudentius *Peristephanon* 10.989 (as noted by Spaltenstein at 99 and Öberg at 186), it is difficult to find a phrase in poetry that is close. The shorter phrase *in vitium*, however, appears three times in Horace *Ars poetica* and has legal overtones; it appears regularly in Justinian *Institutiones*. Cf. Fo (1987) at 351, 359. It is used with *cadere* in *Institutiones* 2.6 (*quippe ea res in furti vitium non ceciderit*), a section which details that an heir's right to stolen property turns on the heir's state of mind at the time of acquisition. The terms *res* and *facta* also have strong legal associations (*mens rea* is still a contemporary legal phrase for "the intent to commit a crime"), and I believe that the best take on *cadunt* is the definition in OLD 16 (note its pairing there with *in* followed by the accusative). For *res* as "acts," see OLD 7.

Maximianus appears to be expressing in this line the view that an act is not inherently moral or immoral but depends on intent and context. Cf. Juvenal 10.69 (*sed quo cedit sub crimine?*). He might be remembering a famous passage in Horace *Sermones* 1.2.31–35 in which Horace mocks Cato for commending a man leaving a brothel for good judgment in not luring a Roman wife into adultery, but the connection to the previous lines is unclear.

1.51 Spaltenstein (1983) at 99 and Guardalben (1993) at 117 reject Schetter's arguments for Baehrens' *adversa* for *ad utrasque* and *ferebam* for *ferebar*. See Schetter (1970) at 81–83; Franzoi and Spinazzè at 133. I side with Schetter on *ferebam* ("I'd argue") but not on *adversa*. Students of rhetoric were trained to argue both sides of an argument, and *ad utrasque* better fits with the sense of the previous three distichs. It is also Ciceronian. See, e.g., *In Verrem* 2.5.6 (*ad utram partem*); *De inventione* 2.147 (*ad utram*); cf. Boethius *De interpretatione* 1.2.11 (*ad utrasque*); Caesar *De bello Gallico* 7.89 (*ad utramque*).

1.52 Öberg at 186 notes a parallel between *tristia cuncta* ("depressed, they all") and Venantius Fortunatus *Carmina* 3.13.34 (*gaudia restituens tristia cuncta fugas*).

Roger Green brought to my attention Pseudo-Ausonius *Septem sapientem sententiae* 6.3 (*tristia cuncta exsuperas*).

1.53 Professing love for poverty (usually by a poet who is not poor) is a cliché of Augustan poetry, particularly elegy. It is likely that this line embraces this paradoxical pose. A son trained in grammar and rhetoric in the late fifth century almost certainly came from an affluent household.

1.54 The grandiloquent phrase *rerum dominus* ("the lord of goods") appears in the work of Cicero, Ovid, and others, but its most likely source is Virgil *Aeneid* 1.282 (*Romanos rerum dominos gentemque togatam*). Cf. Tyson at 67–68; Webster at 68. Lucan is possible as well. Cf. *Bellum civile* 5.698–699 (*non rector ut orbis / nec dominus rerum*), 6.595 (*vel dominus rerum vel tanti funeris heres*). An unlikely, but more contemporary, possibility is Ennodius *Epistulae* 9.11.9 (*rerum dominus*).

Virgil's phrase is usually translated "lords of the world," but Maximianus appears to be playing off that image with a diminished definition of *res* in order to create a paradox in the line.

For *nil cupiendo* ("by wanting nothing"), cf. Horace *Carmina* 3.16.15 (*Nil cupientium*). Goldlust (2013) at 130 argues for a broader influence of Horace in this distich. Alfonsi makes a weak case for the influence of Tibullus 1.1.5 and 1.1.25. See Alfonsi (1942) at 89. Altamura sees a metrical issue in *cupiendo*. See (1981) at 822.

1.55 For *subdis* ("you overcome"), cf. Augustine *Enarrationes in Psalmos* 17.48 (*subdis populos sub me Deus*); *Sermones* 1.154.12 (*subdis in Deo*); Cassiodorus *Expositio in psalterium* 1.17.54 (*subdis populos sub me*). Cf. Boethius *Consolatio philosophiae* 1.5.41 (*summos gaudent subdere reges*). Uden and Fielding see this line, as well as lines 257 and 261–262, as an image of military defeat reflecting "the widespread destruction wrought to the western half of the empire in the mid-sixth century by Justinian's 'reconquest.'" See Uden and Fielding (2010) at 444–445. Tyson at 68 notes that the phrase *tu me sola* ("Only you . . . me") is a standard form of address to a lover in elegy and argues that Maximianus is being ironic using it to address old age. Cf. Tibullus 3.19.3; Propertius 1.11.23, 2.7.19; Ovid *Ars amatoria* 1.42, *Remedia amoris* 464.

Franzoi and Spinazzè at 134 see echoes of Virgil *Aeneid* 12.934 (*miserere senectae*) in *miserandus senectus* ("miserable old age").

This line and the following three lines may belong after 1.8 or elsewhere.

1.56 This line creates a contrast with 1.43–44.

1.57 Webster argues that *fatiscunt* ("cracks") echoes Prudentius *Cathemerinon* 10.96, a proposition about which I am skeptical. There are multiple plausible ways to translate the verbs in this line; I render them in a way consistent with the Uden and Fielding "ruin" trope.

1.58 Schetter (1970) and Green would substitute *quaeque* for *teque* (collapsed into "and you're consumed") in this line. As tempting as that recommendation is, I retain Webster's *teque*.

1.59 This distich is a jarring non sequitur, but see note to 1.55.

The phrase *his ornatus meritis* ("Equipped with these endowments") is novel and ambiguous.

Some commentators read too much into the phrase *provincia tota* ("the whole province"). See, e.g, Webster at 68.

1.60 For *natis* as "daughters," see Agozzino at 130.

1.61 For the phrase *resolute . . . collo* ("with . . . neck unyoked"), Goldlust (2013) at 131 notes parallels at Propertius 3.15.11–12 and Tibullus 1.2.92. Cf. note to 1.55.

Scholars of classical Latin tend to believe, often strongly, that the term *magis* here means "indeed" or "rather," but in Late Antiquity *magis* is often used to make an adverb comparative. See Herman at 63–64.

1.62 Webster at 68 calls *vincula grata pati* ("bore the welcome chains") "another of the hackneyed erotic paradoxes." In fact, this phrase is a novel twist in that it refers to the welcome chains of marriage rather than the welcome chains of romantic adventure that fueled Augustan love elegy. Cf. Tibullus 2.2.18 (*flavaque coniugio vincula portet amor*); Propertius 3.15.8 (*collo dulcia vincla meo*). For contemporaneous uses, see, e.g., Cassiodorus *Variae* 8.1.3–6; Arator *De actibus Apostolica* 1.1070–1076; cf. Vitiello (2014) at 225.

1.63 This line shows Maximianus' familiarity with the physically, politically, and morally diminished city of Rome, a bit of evidence that offers some slight support for the hypothesis that the author of these elegies is the same Maximianus asked by Theoderic to lead the restoration of Rome. See Appendix A; see generally Sinnigen "Administrative Shifts of Competence Under Theoderic," 21 *Traditio* (1965) at 456–467; Johnson, "Toward a History of Theoderic's Building Program," 42 *Dumbarton Oaks Papers* (1988) at 77.

Ellis has an odd theory that *venali* ("for sale") is a pun on Maximianus' "real" name. Ellis (1884b) at 146. Despite his theory, he also offers *vernali* as a substitute. This bit of erudition would destroy the sense of the line and is only supported by one manuscript. Cf. Öberg at 155. For support of *venali* as "for sale," see Schetter at 144. My advisors divided bitterly on the question of *whose* flesh is for sale here; I interpret it as the female flesh, and perhaps the male flesh, of the seamier parts of Rome, not as a reference to the sale of Maximianus' own flesh. But see Arcaz Pozo (2011) at 69. To view Maximianus as "on the market" in this way, while philologically plausible, would discount the fact that such conduct by adult males, whether the actual sale of sexual services by an adult male, was widely considered shameful by Romans. See generally McGinn (2004). Moreover, it is hard to reconcile the view that Maximianus was "for sale" with his high self-image and declarations of a *casto pectore* ("pure soul") in 1.74 and a *viduo . . . toro* ("wifeless bed") in 1.76. Welsh concurs that *venali* ("for sale") as applied to Maximianus is problematic, but looks to emend it to the speculative *geniali*. See Welsh (2011) at 215–216. Goldlust's (2013) suggestion of an echo of Sallust *Bellum Iugurthinum* 35 (*urbem venalem*) is unlikely.

For the phrase *per mediam . . . Romam* ("through central Rome") Öberg at 186 notes the parallel of Ovid *Metamorphoses* 14.745 (*mediam per urbem*); cf. Prudentius *Contra Symmachum* 2.1.581 (*per mediam spoliorum fercula Romam*).

1.64 With its use of *cuncta* ("by all"), this line slyly incorporates both girls who were for hire and those who were not. For this euphemistic use of *virginibus* ("the girls"), see Adams (1982) at 94.

1.65–66 Webster at 69 notes the unusual interlocked alliteration of this distich. For Maximianus' use of alliteration and assonance, see Alfonsi (1941–1942) at 347. For Ovidian echoes, see Franzoi and Spinazzè at 135.

1.66 For modern readers *erubuit* ("would blush") has connotations of Victorian modesty. During the classical and Late Antique eras, blushing conveyed a sense of sexual arousal. Goldlust (2013) at 131 notes that this verb is also transitive in Propertius 3.14.20 (*nec fratres erebuisse deos*).

1.67–68 Ellis doubts the accuracy of this distich based on objections to the "jingle" caused by three gerunds. Ellis (1884b) at 147. Baehrens (probably at least in part to address this same concern) substitutes *effugiis* for *effugiens*. Aside from a fussy preference for classical Latin, there is no reason to doubt the integrity of these lines. See Webster at 69; Guardalben (1993) at 117; Goldlust (2103) at 131. Franzoi and Spinazzè at 135 notes a similar "jingle" in Fortunatus *Carmina* 2.7.18 (*effugiens . . . volens*). Shanzer eviscerates Ratkowitsch's (1986) argument that this line echoes Fortunatus and shows instead that it echoes Boethius *Consolatio philosophiae* 2.5.29. Shanzer (1988) at 259–260.

Spaltenstein (1983) at 104 notes that the coquettish girl wanting to be seen appears with somewhat parallel language in both Virgil *Eclogae* 3.64–65 and Horace *Carmina* 1.9.21.

Webster at 69 correctly notes that Milton echoes the same idea with similar language, although Webster's citation is incorrect. See *Elegia quinta. In adventus veris* 129–130 (*Jamque latet, latiansque cupit male tecta videri / Et fugit, et fugiens pervelit ipsa capi*).

1.69 Spaltenstein (1983) at 105 notes that the phrase *sed magis* ("instead") goes back to the preclassical *Epigrammata* 1.3 of Lutatius. Cf. Horace *Carmina* 2.13.30–31 (*sed magis / pugnas et exactos tyrannos*); Livy *Ab urbe condita* 3.39.1 (*Sed magis oboedienter ventum in curiam esse*).

1.71 Wasyl (2011) at 120–121 notes that *formosus* ("beautiful") was a familiar adjective of love elegy, but one invariably reserved for women, and from that observation concludes, probably soundly, that Maximianus is portraying himself as a "dandy." Such a use is not without at least one precedent; Roger Green pointed out to me that Virgil *Eclogae* 2.1 describes a male as *formosum*. See generally Spaltenstein (1983) at 104; cf. *Eclogae* 5.86.

1.72 For the rights and responsibilities of a *sponsus* ("suitor") under Gothic law, see Reynolds (1994) at 89–93. Ellis takes Maximianus to task for the "barbarism" of *sponsus generalis*, but he overreads *sponsus generalis* by rendering it as a nonexistent term of art, "universal suitor." See Ellis (1884a) at 12. Spaltenstein at 106 is similarly confused; the term *generalis* ("standard") here is mundane. Despite Ellis' claim that "*generalis* in this meaning is found in Cicero, but only became common in the decline of the Empire," Maximianus uses it here in the sense of "usual" or "typical." See OLD 1a; cf. note to 5.110.

1.73 Franzoi and Spinazzè at 135 argue that *natura pudicum* ("nature . . . chaste") is Ovidian based on *Tristia* 3.385 (*natura pudicos*).

1.74 The phrase *casto pectore* ("in my virgin soul") appears to be Senecan in origin. Cf. *Phaedra* 130 (*casto pectore*); Franzoi and Spinazzè at 135. Later Christian writers often, but not always, used the phrase *casto corpore*. See, e.g., Sedulius *Carmen Paschale* 2.245 (*pectore casto*); Orientius *Commonitorum* 1.600 (*casto seruatus pectore pacis amor*); Augustine *Sermones* 11.49.1 (*pectore casto*). One of my advisors suggests this phrase involves sexual wordplay with *durus*, which I translate as "steadfast" but often means "hard." For *pectore* as "soul," see OLD 4.

1.76 The phrase *viduo frigidus . . . toro* ("in a frigid, wifeless bed") was common in elegies. See, e.g., Ovid *Amores* 3.5.42 (*frigidus in viduo destituere toro*). See Consolino (1997) at 373; cf. Ovid *Heroides* 1.10.16, 1.18.106; Propertius 2.9.16; Lucan *Bellum civile* 5.806. Fielding (forthcoming) at 4 also notes *Amores* 2.10.17 and Propertius 2.9.16.

For criticism of Schetter's (1970) interpretation and Öberg's translation of this distich, see Gärtner (2004) at 124–125.

1.77 For useful discussions of the prosody of this line and the manuscript variants, see Consolino (2009) at 191–192; Franzoi and Spinazzè at 135–136.

1.77–80 The repeated phrase *omnis mihi* ("each . . . to me") is another example of anaphora. The rhetorical and aphoristic qualities of this passage intensify with the additional anaphora of *horrebam* ("shuddered") in line 79 and *non mihi* ("for me") in line 80. For anaphora as a feature of legal and official Latin, see generally Adams (2013) at 492.

Wasyl (2011) at 121 argues that the list of qualities of an ideal woman in this line and the next twenty lines echoes and responds to Ovid *Amores* 2.4 and 3.263–288. Fielding argues that they play off of Ovid *Remedia amoris* 325–330. See Fielding (forthcoming) at 32–33.

1.78 Tyson at 74 notes that *coniugio digna* ("deserved . . . wife") is common in Augustan poetry. See, e.g., Propertius 3.12.16; Ovid *Metamorphoses* 8.131, 8.704–705.

1.80 With the *brevis . . . longa* ("short . . . tall") pairing Maximianus may be having fun with the famous Latin version of Hippocrates' aphorism ("*Ars longa, vita brevis*"). Agozzino at 132 sees inspiration from Ovid *Amores* 2.4.33–36 and Franzoi at 136 sees other Ovidian resonances.

1.81 Spaltenstein at 109 sees nonexistent tension between this distich and its predecessor. The opposite is true—dismissal of extremes leads to "satisfaction" in the middle. Franzoi and Spinazzè at 136 note use of an infinitive after *dilexi* ("I loved") is a rare Late Antique usage.

Spaltenstein (1983) at 109 misreads *ludere* ("to frolic") as "un poétisme gallant" instead of a verb of earthy fun.

1.82 Webster at 70, Green at 449, and Lind at 321 see an allusion to the Aristotelian "golden mean" in this line; they overread *mediis . . . rebus* ("midrange things") as "high" when it is primarily "low." The term *res* often had, as it does here, a sexual connotation similar to the Shakespearean "thing." See Adams (1982) at 62; OLD 8c. There is also a sexual connotation to *mediis*. See Adams at 46–47. Spaltenstein (1983) at 109 notes the potential sexuality of this line but misses the joke.

The verb *inest* ("is in") is not as "habituel en cet emploi" as Spaltenstein (1983) suggests at 109, but is a favorite of Pliny, Cicero, and Boethius. It also strengthens the sexual suggestion of the distich.

1.83 Spaltenstein (1983) at 110 suggests that *lascivia* ("lasciviousness") is personified here, but there were no "seven deadly sins" at the time of these elegies, and personification of *lascivia* did not become common until the late medieval era. Prudentius inspired much medieval personification with his *Psychomachia* but did not personify *lascivia.*

1.84 The noun *mater* ("mother") is as much a way of saying "source" as a personification. The phrase *mater amoris* ("Love's mother") originally referred to Venus—see, e.g., Ovid *Ars amatoria* 1.30, *Amores* 3.1.43—then became a Christian term for the Virgin Mary. To the extent that this phrase is a personification here, it is a diffuse one.

For *habet* as "rules," see OLD 6.

1.85 I concur with Spaltenstein's (1983) observation at 110 that *macra* ("scrawny") is pejorative here. See also Agozzino at 133.

1.86 For *officium* ("function"), see OLD 4 at 163. The noun *carnis* ("with meat"), from which the adjective *carnea* ("carnal") is derived, originally meant "meat," but by Late Antiquity it frequently meant "human flesh." Cf. Herman at 103–104. Its adjectival form is uncommon, and, to the best of my knowledge, appears no earlier than the works of Tertullian; earlier writers used *carnosus.* Franzoi and Spinazzè at 163 nots the paronomasia of *carnis . . . carnea.* There is no perfect way in English to capture both the meaning and the wordplay of this line.

1.87 Tyson notes at 77 that *in amplexu* ("in an embrace") is a favorite phrase of Ovid. See *Amores* 3.8.12; *Epistulae ex Ponto* 1.9.19; cf. *Heroides* 5.102 (*in amplexus*); *Ars amatoria* 3.732 (*in amplexus*); *Fasti* 2.180 (*in amplexus*), 4.171(*in amplexum*).

The infinitive *stringere* ("be caressed"), which could be either active or passive, poses a dilemma. Depending on your view of the line, it could mean "hold tightly," "hold lightly," or "strip." Tyson argues that *stringere corpus* playfully echoes Virgil *Aeneid* 10.331 (*stringentia corpus*); Virgil's phrase is part of a description of a deflected spear grazing a body.

Goldlust (1983) at 133 sees lines beginning at Martial 11.100.1 as the model for this line and the following lines, but provides no rationale.

1.89 Pink on pale skin is a cliché of beauty for Augustan poets for whom blushing is a sign of sexual arousal.

1.90 The verb *vernarent* ("blossomed") is rare. But see Martial 2.61.1 (*cum tibi vernarent dubia lanugine malae*). It also appears often in the writings of Ambrose. See, e.g., *Hexaemeron* 3.9.42 (*vernarent*); *De fide ad Gratianum Augustum* 5.10.128 (*vernaret*); *In Psalmum David CXVIII exposito* 6.15 (*vernaret*). Spaltenstein (1983) at 112 stumbles in his discussion of this image; he calls it "difficile" and claims "on ne peut pas concevoir concrètement l'image chez MAXIM." In fact, it is a lovely and skilled metaphor that embraces vitality, modesty, and beauty. Webster at 70 notes that Petschenig also missed the lyricism of this line. Mann (1973) at 178 displays her understanding of Maximianus' craftsmanship: "The use of the subjunctive to indicate the hypothetical existence of the perfect girl, and of the past tense in speaking of the individual features of feminine beauty which once brought him pleasure, flavor the whole description with a mood of nostalgia and elusiveness." Öberg at 187 notes an intriguing parallel with Dracontius *Romulea* 6.8–9 (*candor ruborque / qui vernat in ore puellis*). Altamura (1981) at 820–821 notes the parallel of Virgil *Georgica* 1.430 (*suffuderit ore ruborem*); cf. Ennodius *Carmina* 2.10.7 (*candorem roseo perfundat doctor ab ore*). Fielding suggests that this image evokes Flora, the Italian goddess of flowers, who speaks to Ovid at *Fasti* 5.194 using the verb *vernas*. See Fielding (forthcoming) at 33–35.

1.91 The verb *vindicat* ("demands") is a legally flavored term associated with a legal demand or claim.

1.92 Cyprus was the home of one of the cults of Venus, hence her alternative name "Cypris," sometimes rendered as "the Cyprian."

1.93–97 Webster sees many unsupportable associations in these lines but misses the parallel to Virgil *Aeneid* 8.659–661(*aurea caesaries ollis atque aurea vestis / virgatis lucent sagulis tum lactea colla / auro innectuntur*). Cf. *Aeneid* 10.222; Faral (1913) at 105; Tyson at 93. Öberg notes that the phrase *lactea cervix* ("milky neck") also echoes Virgil *Aeneid* 10.137. Cf. Franzoi and Spinazzè at 137–138.

A poem in the *Carmina Burana*, probably by Peter of Blois (ca. 1135–ca. 1203), echoes lines 93–97, particularly *tumentia labra* ("sultry . . . lips"). See Walsh (1993) at 27–28. Cf. Jerome *Proverbia* 26.23 (*labia tumentia*). For *tumentia* as "sultry," see OLD 3.For an overheated discussion of the influence of these two distichs on later medieval literature, see Brewer, "The Ideal of Feminine Beauty in Medieval Literature" 50, no. 3 *Modern Language Review* (1955) at 257–262.

1.94 For my choice of the rare *decere* ("to fit") of the Reginensis 2080 manuscript over Webster's problematic *sedere*, cf. Lemaire (1826) at 205–206. At least six manuscripts also support *placere* here. See Öberg at 156. Plautus pairs *decere* with *magis* twice. See *Captivi* 2.2.71 (*decere videatur magis*), *Rudens* 2.3.77 (*magis decere*); cf. Pliny *Epistulae* 1.18.12.3 (*magis decuit*). Maximianus also uses *decere* eight lines later in this elegy. Cf. 1.102.

Webster at 72 argues that *vultibus ingenuis* ("with modest looks") echoes Juvenal 11.154 (*ingenui vultus*).

1.95 Webster at 72 defends the repetition of *nigra* ("black") in this line from criticism by Baehrens and Petschenig in part by noting the parallel to Horace *Carmina* 1.32.11 (*Lycum nigris oculis nigroque*). Cf. Horace *Ars poetica* 37 (*spectandum nigris oculis nigroque capillo*). Maximianus' preference for dark-haired beauties instead of the blondes traditionally prized in elegy may stem from pride in his Etruscan heritage, which is revealed at 5.5. But see C.1.7; cf. Sullivan (1976) at 80. Öberg at 187 notes *lumina nigra* ("black eyes") at Propertius 2.12.23 and 4.3.14. Blonde hair was understandably associated with people from northern regions, and perhaps particularly the Ostrogoths. For a discussion of the variant *clara*, which appears in three manuscripts, for *nigra*, see Schneider (2003) at 207–208; Webster at 53.

For *frons libera* ("a confident expression"), cf. Cassiodorus *Variae* 12.2.4; Ambrose *Hexaemeron* 6.9.58; Paulinus Petricordiae *Vita Sancti Martini* 2.51. The adjective *libera* could mean "licentious," but that would seem to undercut the sentiment of the previous distich. It could mean something like "carefree," which assumes the *docta puella* of the elegiac tradition—a confident young freedwoman independent of the responsibilities of a slave or wife. Prada (1919), Schetter (1970), Oberg, and Schneider (2003) would emend *libera* to the *clara* of three manuscripts. See Franzoi and Spinazzè at 138.

For metrical concerns about *supercilia* ("brows"), see Altamura (1981) at 822.

1.96 As formulaic as *urere* ("inflamed") is in Augustan elegy, the phrase *urebant animam* ("inflamed my soul") appears not to have been a cliché. But cf. Ennodius *Panegyricus regi Theoderico* 12.4 (*urebant animum*); 5.63 (*animum . . . uri*).

1.97–98 Tyson at 80 argues that the paradoxical *labra quae gustata* ("lips, / which, being tasted") echoes Cicero. *Pro Caelio* 28 (*labris gustassent*); *De natura deorum* 1.20 (*labris gustasse*). Goldlust (2013) at 133 sees echoes of Catullus and Ovid, which strike me as equally unlikely, but he makes a better case for the possible influence of Ennodius *Epithalamium dictum Maximo V.S.* 23 (*flamma labellis*) on this distich's *flammea . . . labra* ("scarlet lips").

1.98 *The Court of Love*, a Middle English poem once attributed to Chaucer but now believed to have been written later, cites both this line and its author: "For yf the basse ben full, there is delite / Maximyan truly thus doth be write" (797–798).

For the dating of this poem, see Forni (2001) at 157–158. Reception of Maximianus was more substantial in Britain than in the rest of Europe, but there has been little scholarship on the topic. There are some recent and useful obervations about reception in Arcaz Pozo (2011) at 29–34.

Webster at 72–73 argues that the term *basia* ("kisses") is more "ordinary" than "literary" speech. It does not appear in Ovid or Tibullus but appears regularly in Catullus, Juvenal, and Martial. Descendants of the term survive in many Romance languages. Altamura argues that *basia . . . darent* ("gave . . . kisses") may echo Petronius *Satyricon* 110.3 (*basium dedit*).

1.99 For *pretiosius aurum* ("gold . . . more precious"), cf. 1.19 (*pretiosior auro*).

Öberg notes that *tereti collo* ("on a silky neck") appears at Ovid *Metamorphoses* 10.113. Cf. Statius *Achilleid* 1.609; Calpurnius Siculus *Eclogae* 6.38.

1.100 The phrase *meo iudicio* ("in my view") has a rhetorical and legal flavor. It is a favorite of Cicero. See, e.g., Cicero *Epistulae ad familiares* 9.21, 188.3. Öberg at 187 notes that Ovid uses it at *Heroides* 17.108 and *Fasti* 1.332. Amory (1997) at 44 argues that Theoderic's advisors borrowed legal terms from Roman law, particularly the terminology of obligation—words such as *civilitas, utilitas, libertas,* and *devotion*—to add legitimacy to their Ostrogothic regime.

1.101 This line's self-referential declaration that an old man going over details of the past is shameful (although it doesn't stop Maximianus from doing it) offers slight support for the argument that Maximianus used *Nugae* as his title, as discussed in the note on the title.

Webster at 73 notes that *turpe seni* ("old men . . . is shameful") probably echoes Ovid *Amores* 1.9.4 (*turpe senex miles turpe senilis amor*). See also Öberg at 187; Wasyl (2011) at 122. Franzoi at 138–139 notes other possible Ovidian inspirations.

Goldlust (2013) at 133 sees *singula . . . referre* ("Each....rehash") as an echo of Ovid *Amores* 1.5.23 (*singula . . . referam*). See also Agozzino at 136. Webster at 73 observes that this line from Ovid and Martial 11.8.11 both used *singula* to break up a litany.

1.102 The phrase *crimen habet* ("keeps its verdict") appears regularly in Ovid except in *Metamorphoses.* See *Amores* 2.5.6 (*habent*); *Ars amatoria* 1.586 (*habet*), 2.634 (*habet*), 3.454 (*habent*); *Fasti* 1.445 (*habetis*), 2.162 (*habet*), 3.782; *Heroides* 18.144 (*habet*); *Tristia* 2.265 (*habebit*), 2.498 (*habent*), 4.285 (*habebo*). Cf. Juvenal 8.141, 13.210; Propertius 2.32.2. Like much of Maximianus' language, the phrase has a legal and commercial flavor. See Hollis at 127; note to 6.4.

For *decuit* ("occurred"), see note to 1.94.

1.103–104 Montaigne cites these lines (attributing them to Gallus) in his essay "All Things Have Their Season." Montaigne at 798.

Franzoi and Spinazzè at 139 note possible Senecan influences for the polyptoton of *diversos diversa* ("Diverse . . . diverse").

1.103–110 Jacob Handl put these lines to music in *The Moralia of 1596.* Skei (1965) at 29–32.

1.105 The internal rhyme of *levitate/gravitate* ("folly . . . sternness") would have horrified Augustan sensibilities; I could not mimic it. This pair of nouns has a heaviness/lightness juxtaposition, but it is also legalistic—the contrast of being free of rules instead of weighed down by their application. Franzoi and Spinazzè at 139 see Ciceronian influence for *levitate* that I do not see.

1.106 Boano views this line as echoed in Corippus *Iohannis* 7.34. See Boano (1949) at 201.

1.107 I try to mimic this line's unusual alliteration. Ellis (1884b) at 147 overstates his case when he argues that *clarior* ("more famous") "must be wrong" and that it is "almost certain" it should be *carior.* Cf. Webster at 29; Schneider at 208. Ellis would also trade *hunc* for *haec,* which would change the meaning of the line by switching the gender of the subject. Ellis lacks manuscript authority for his proposed emendations and ignores the fact that the phrase in most of the manuscripts is a logical and balanced, if belabored, *exemplum* for the proposition asserted in 1.103.

Webster at 73 has a useful note on the rhetorical flourishes of this line.

1.110 Tyson at 84 notes that Propertius closes three lines in a similar manner: 1.2.12 (*currere lympha vias*), 2.1.34 (*currere rostra via*), 3.1.14 (*currere lata via*).

For *certa . . . via* ("a certain route"), cf. Cicero *Philippicae* 11.4 (*via et certa neque longa*); Cassiodorus *Expositio in psalterium* 3.118.8 (*qui certa via*).

Without explanation Goldlust (2013) at 134 rejects the *quaeque* (combined with *nec* as "and no one") of Webster and Baehrens for *quemque*, which does appear in one manuscript but is syntactically problematic.

1.111 Webster at 74, Franzoi and Spinazzè at 139–140, and Öberg at 187 note the similarity of Martial 11.69.7 (*non mihi longa dies nec inutilis abstulit aetas*). The adjective *inutile* ("futile") may have had some hint of "impotence." See Gowers (2012) at 267.

1.112 Tyson at 85, Agozzino at 137, and Öberg at 187 note that the phrase *sit mihi posse mori* ("let me die") is Ovidian. Cf. *Ars amatoria* 2.28, *Tristia* 1.1.34.

This line introduces a discussion of old age that thematically parallels much of Juvenal 10.188–288.

1.113 Ellis vigorously objects to *condicio* ("contract") on metrical grounds and proposes *contritio* ("grief") despite the lack of manuscript support. See Ellis (1884b) at 147; cf. Altamura (1981) at 822. However, *condicio* has legal connotations consistent with Maximianus' vocabulary, and the phrase *condicio vitae* ("life's…contract") is Ciceronian. See *Pro Balbo* 18 (*lex vitae et condicio*), *De officiis* 3.85 (*vitae ea condicio sit*), *Tusculanae disputationes* 4.62 (*condicio lexque vitae*); cf. Seneca *Epistulae* 107.2 (*uitae condicio*), *Consolatio ad Marcum* 6.18.8 (*condicionem uitae nossent*), *De ira* 2.10.6 (*condicionem humanae uitae*); see Tyson at 85.

1.114 The phrase *humano arbitrio* ("human will") is rare in the classical era. But see Quintilian *Declamationes maiores* 279.5; Pliny *Naturalis historia* 29.53. See Tyson at 86. It is more popular in Late Antiquity and the medieval era, perhaps due to its use by Augustine. See, e.g., *Epistulae* 194.2.3; but see Webster at 74 ("*arbitrio humana* has theological tang, but this is a mere accident").

For sexual connotations of the verb *subiacere* ("acquiesce") in elegy, see Kennedy (1993) at 32. It also has legal connotations.

1.115 Boano views this line as echoed in Corippus *Iohannis* 7.178. See Boano (1949) at 201.

1.115–116 My sweet/retreat internal rhyme tries to mimic the sound of *optata/praecipitata* in this couplet. Öberg at 187 notes the parallel to the famous *dulce . . . mori* of Horace *Carmina* 3.2.13.

1.116 The Ovidian participle *praecipitata* ("all in a rush") is somewhat uncommon. See *Metamorphoses* 11.556, 7.760; *Tristia* 1.3.47, 3.11.24; *Heroides* 10.14. It is a favorite of Cassiodorus. Cf. *Expositio in psalterium* 1.7.22, 2.77.17, 3.105, 3.113.8, 3.118.100; *Variae* 0.2.

I have substituted the *et* ("and") of the Leidensis Gronovii 87 manuscript for Webster's *at*.

1.117 There is some manuscript support for *perfunctum* instead of *defunctum* ("dead"), see Webster at 29, but that emendation would just be a less compelling way of saying the same thing. Welsh argues for the speculative *defectum*, but I see *defunctum* as both the overwhelming choice of the manuscript tradition and a logical extension of the "living dead" motif noted by many scholars. See, e.g., Welsh (2011) at 216–217.

Ellis (1884b) at 148 strenuously argues for dropping *in*; I retain it because it is not clear what problem the emendation would solve; manuscripts vary widely. See also Welsh (2011) at 216–217. Writers of the early medieval period use *in* after *defunctum*. See, e.g., Hrabanus Maurus (*defunctum in ecclesia*) *Martyrologium* 6.17. Augustine and Livy also used *in* after *mortuum*, the more common synonym for *defunctum*. See Augustine *De trinitate* 4.7.11.1 (*mortuum in carne*), *Enarrationes in Psalmos* 56.4 (*mortuum in cruce*), 127.2 (*mortuum in lecto*), *Sermones* 10.10.1 (*mortuum in sinu*); Livy *Ab urbe condita* 26.23 (*mortuum in Sicilia*), 42.16 (*mortuum in Asiam*).

1.118 Öberg at 187 argues *inire vias* ("enter . . . roads") echoes Ovid *Remedia amoris* 578 (*ignotas cogor inire vias*). Franzoi and Spinazzè at 140 note possible Senecan influence. Cf. *Oetaeus* 1119 (*via Tartari*). I follow Webster's *tartareas vias* ("hellish roads"), although some manuscripts reverse the words. See Ellis (1884b) at 148.

1.119 The first five words of this line are an example of the rhetorical technique of asyndeton, the dropping of one or more expected conjunctions. Franzoi and Spinazzè at 141 stretch by seeing an echo of Propertius 2.34.83 (*minor . . . minor*).

On metrical grounds Ellis objects to *caligant* ("are fogging") and proposes *vacillant*. See Ellis (1884b) at 148. There is no manuscript support for this emendation, and it would make the poetry less compelling. Altamura concurs that there is a metrical issue here but does not indicate that he supports an emendation as a result. See Altamura (1981) at 822.

1.121 Tyson at 87 and Webster at 75 note that the phrase *grata voluptas* ("pleasure gratifying") is Ovidian. See *Ars amatoria* 1.347, 2.687.

1.122 While this statement is a description of decrepit old age, it could also be construed as a description of death itself with no afterlife.

1.123 Webster compares this line to Ovid *Tristia* 1.5.13 (*quam subeant animo meritorum oblivia nostro*). Fielding makes a broader comparison of these lines to *Tristia* 4.1–90. See Fielding (forthcoming) at 28–30.

For *lethaea . . . oblivia* ("Lethean amnesia"), cf. Lucan *Bellum civile* 3.28 (*lethaeae . . . oblivia*); Silius *Punica* 1.236 (*oblivia . . . Lethes*).

1.125 This line has been rendered inconsistently by translators. The noun *opus* ("for work") probably refers to Maximianus' own poetry, see Spaltenstein (1983) at 123. The verb *consurgit* ("rise") was a term with legal undertones, as in "rising for a closing argument." For a discussion of parallel uses of *opus surgit* and *opus consurgit* in Ovid, Lucan, and Propertius, see Masters (1992) at 33. Franzoi and Spinazzè at 140 note Manilius *Astronomica* 2.782 (*consurgit opus*). There may be some punning about impotency in this line with "not rising" and "flesh languishing." See Tyson at 88 for *languet* as a term of art in elegy; see also Adams (1982) at 156–157.

1.126 Webster at 75 and Öberg at 188 note the parallel to Ovid *Tristia* 4.1.4 (*mens intenta suis ne foret usque malis*). There is a nearly even split in the manuscripts between *astupet* ("is benumbed") and *obstupet*; I retain Webster's *astupet* based on its slightly more common representation in the manuscripts and its slightly better sense in context. See Webster at 29, 75. Cf. Ovid *Tristia* 1.2.32 (*stupet ipsa malis*).

I reject Webster's *illa* for the *ipsa* ("own") included in four manuscripts, in part because it brings it closer to *Tristia* 1.2.32. Cf. Spaltenstein (1983) at 123. It also makes better sense and echoes Ovid *Metamorphoses* 3.418 (*adstupet ipse mihi*). Cf. Ellis (1884b) at 148, Fo (1986–1987) at 128; but see Schneider (2003) at 208, Schetter (1970) at 128, and Tandoi (1973) at 142. Use of both *ipsa* and *illa* increased in Late Antiquity. See Herman (2000) at 68.

1.127 Webster at 75, Agozzino at 140, and Öberg at 188 note the parallel to Virgil *Eclogae* 1.77 (*carmina nulla canam*). There may be a slight echo of Catullus' haunting 65.12 (*carmina morte canam*).

1.128 Spaltenstein (1983) at 124 asserts that "*vera* est étrange." While it is true that the phrase *vera gratia* ("true charm") did not become popular until after Maximianus, the phrase was a favorite of Augustine. See, e.g., *In Ioannis evangelium* 124.87.3 (*hoc est vera gratia*), *De dono persuerantiae* 20.53 (*ut posit uera Dei gratia*), *Contra duas epistulas Pelagianorum* 2.6.12 (*Dei uero gratia*).

1.129 Recourse to *blanda poemata* ("fawning poems")—both panegyrics and love poems—is common for the ambitious, the fearful, and the hormonal. See James (2004) at 247; cf. Appendix B.1–4.

Spaltenstein at 124 inexplicably declares this straightforward list of foregone physical and mental pleasures to be "inexplicable."

The noun *fora* ("courts") is not completely clear here. The distich refers back to his description of his youth writing poems and litigating, so it seems to me that *fora* in context is more likely to mean a place related to his legal pursuits and less likely to mean "marketplaces" or "public squares." See OLD 5, 6.

1.130 Ellis argues for *aut* over Webster's *haut* and dismisses Baehrens' *haud*. See Ellis (1884b) at 148. The majority of the manuscripts have *aut*, but I retain *haut* (incorporated into "don't") because it makes the most sense in context. Cf. Öberg at 157, Schetter (1970) at 34–35, Goldlust (2013) at 135.

Ellis sneeringly dismisses Bröring's use of the Eton manuscript's *iura* in this line over the Bodleian *dura*. See Ellis (1894) at 235, although he seems to have accepted it a decade earlier at Ellis (1884b) at 148. I follow Webster at 30 and accept the *iura* of the Eton manuscript. Ellis' substitution provides a less satisfactory reading of this line in part because *iura* appears to be another instance of Maximianus using the phraseology, perhaps the more jargony phraseology, of the courts. The phrase *litibus . . . iura* ("lawsuits"—literally "disputes at law") is not redundant because *litibus* does not necessarily mean a legal dispute. Even its more legally colored cousin *litigatus* sometimes added the specificity of *iure*. See, e.g., Augustine *Sermones* 1.52.9 (*iura litigatorum*).

The term *commoda* ("awards") is a supple term used regularly by Ovid, but it also has Stoic associations. See generally Roller (2001) at 70; Morgan (1909) at 166–170. In this line it seems to have a more limited legal meaning. See Post (2015) at 362–363, 423. Boethius does not use *commoda* in his writings, but Cassiodorus does, often in a legal sense. See, e.g., *Variae* 1.3.4 (*civilia iura custodiens publica privataque commoda*); *Variae* 2.26.4 (*commoda non habet actionis*).

Ellis' defense of the Bodleian manuscript requires *dura* to modify *commoda* instead of *litibus*. While, with some effort the line makes sense in isolation, it does not add the expected third item to the distich's list of foregone youthful pleasures and it is unclear what a difficult award or benefit would mean in this context. Lastly, I am unable to identify another instance of *dura* modifying *commoda*. But see Schneider (2003) at 209, Schetter (1970) at 33–35, and Tandoi at 142.

1.131 For *species* ("looks") as a classical term for beauty, see Spaltenstein at 125; Webster at 75.

For this line Franzoi and Spinazzè at 142 suggest unpersuasive echoes of Virgil, Claudian, and Paulinus Petricordiae.

1.132 Webster and Spaltenstein disagree sharply with Giardelli's contention that *formae* ("appearance") is dative. See Webster at 75–76; Spaltenstein (1983) at 125; Giardelli (1899) at 8.

1.134 For the adjective *exsanguis* ("bloodless"), Öberg at 188 notes the echo of Ovid *Tristia* 3.1.55 (*exsanguis . . . color*). This image is the first of many "living dead" descriptions. See Goldlust at 135.

1.135 Öberg at 188 notes that Corippus *Iohannis* 6.321 (*nerui cutis aret*) echoes this line.

1.136 Tyson at 90 notes that the phrase *uncae . . . manus* ("clawlike hands") echoes Virgil's description of the Harpies at *Aeneid* 3.216–217 (*uncaeque manus*). Webster at 76 notes an echo of Virgil *Georgica* 2.365–366 (*uncis . . . manibus*).

Webster at 76 suggests that the adjective *scabida* ("itchy") originates in this line, but it does not. The term is rare in Maximianus' era, probably because it was considered a word for common conversation, not for literature. The earliest example I have been able to identify is Tertullian *De anima* 38.2 (*exinde scabida etiam in ceteras culpas et deliquendi non naturales*). Schetter (1970) at 23, Agozzino at 141 and Spaltenstein (1983) at 126 argue for *scabrida*, a variant that appears in the Florentinus and Britannicus Reg. 15, A.7 manuscripts, but that choice is even more obscure and there is no compelling reason to adopt it. But see Fortunatus *Vita Sancta Martini* 4.18 (*Quam nitor scabridis indignus carpere verba*). Goldlust (2013) at 135 defends *scabida* despite noting the metrical issue it creates. See also Altamura (1981) at 822; but see Meyers (2003) at 701; cf. note to 1.245.

1.137 Spaltenstein (1983) at 127 notes that the phrase *fonte perenni* ("with a never-ending stream") appears in Ovid *Heroides* 8.64 (*fonte perenne*) and *Amores* 3.9.25 (*fonte perenni*). Webster at 76 calls it a "commonplace" and notes its presence not only in Ovid but in Prudentius and Sedulius as well.

1.138 Tyson notes at 91 that *deplangunt* ("bemoan") is rare but appears at Ovid *Metamorphoses* 4.546 (*deplanxere*), 14.580 (*deplangitur*) and Seneca *Hercules Oetaeus* 1851 (*deplanxit*). Cf. Jerome *Epistulae* 4.108.2 (*deplangunt*).

1.139 Ellis rightly raises the issue of whether Maximianus used the rare word *cilium* to mean "brows" instead of the standard "eyelids" here. See Ellis (1884b) at 148–149. Cf. Pliny *Naturalis historia* 11.157 (*cilium*); Martianus Capella *De nuptis Philologiae et Mercurii* 2.132 (*ciliorum*); Isidorus *Etymologiae* 11.1.36 (*ciliorum*).

1.140 Tyson at 91 notes that *desuper incumbens* ("harasses . . . from above") echoes Statius *Achilleid* 2.151.

Goldlust (2013) at 135 sees in this line what I consider to be a debatable hint of Juvenal 9.12–13 (*horrida siccae / silva comae*).

1.141 One has to wonder whether Maximianus' *conduntur in antro* ("they are shrouded . . . in some . . . cave") is playing with Boethius' *caveae clauditur antro* from *Consolatio philosophiae* 3.2.2.15, or perhaps more directly the metaphor of the cave from Plato's *Republic*.

Webster at 76 is rightly critical of Ellis for wanting to substitute *condantur* for *conduntur* ("are shrouded") without any manuscript support, but Ellis' concern about the verb seeming to demand the subjunctive tense is reasonable. See Ellis (1884b) at 5.

1.142 Some manuscripts have *seu* or *vel* for *heu* ("Alas"). Webster at 30; see also Ellis (1884b) at 149. Goldlust (2013) at 136 supports the Baehrens conjecture of *ceu*.

Öberg at 188 notes the parallel between this line and Ovid *Epistulae ex Ponto* 2.8.22 (*torvaque nescioquid forma minantis habet*).

Lewis and Short (1879) note that *nescio* ("something") can be used as a noun meaning "the unknown."

1.144 The wordplay of *hominem/humana* emphasizes the paradox of a human being not being human.

The phrase *ratione caret* ("lacks his faculties") is a staple of medical-legal terminology in the medieval era, though it is rare in the classical era. But see Ovid *Amores* 1.10.25 (*ratione carentes*), *Fasti* 3.119 (*ratione carentes*). The phrase later appeared in Marcus Aurelius *Meditations* 9.9 (*quae ratione carent*) and 10.33 (*ratione carente*) as well as Caelius Aelianus *De natura animalium* 17.1.26–27 (*quae ratione carent*). In Maximianus' time it is still rare, but it appears in Boethius *Consolatio philosophiae* 4.4.1.41 (*malos vero odisse ratione caret*) and Justinian *Institutiones* 4.9 (*quae ratione carent*).

1.145 Although there are no linguistic parallels, Horace also describes double vision (caused by excessive wine) at *Sermones* 2.1.24–25.

1.146 Öberg at 188 notes that *nota mihi* ("familiar") appears at Ovid *Heroides* 17.40.

1.147 Öberg at 188 notes that *claram lucem* ("a brilliant light") appears at Virgil *Aeneid* 2.569. Cf. Seneca *Epistulae* 94.20 (*claram lucem*); Orosius *Historiae* 4.13.12 (*lucem claram*). Agozzino at 143 notes that the image may be drawn from Plautus.

1.148 In context the best rendering of *serena* is "clear" but there is wordplay here too—another definition of the term is "cloudless."

1.149 The phrase *caeca caligine* ("deep darkness") is popular among Roman poets. See, e.g., Lucretius *De rerum natura* 3.304, 4.458; Virgil *Aeneid* 3.203, 8.253;

Ovid *Metamorphoses* 1.70; Catullus 64.207. For this definition of *caeca*, see OLD 5. Altamura sees a metrical issue with *caligine*. See Altamura (1981) at 822.

Some manuscripts have *nocte* or *luce* for *morte* in this line. Webster at 30; see also Ellis (1884b) at 149. Schneider (2003) at 209 follows Spaltenstein (1983) and Schadd and Schröder by arguing for *nocte*. Cf. Goldlust (2013) at 136. Context strongly supports my use of *nocte* ("night").

Spaltenstein (1983) at 130 misreads this line by describing *dies* ("Day") as a rare metaphor. By changing a verb for "seizing" from the active to the passive, Maximianus seems to be playing on Horace's famed command of *carpe diem*.

1.151 Webster at 77 and Spaltenstein (1983) at 130 note that the first half of this line echoes Virgil *Aeneid* 4.107 (*quis talia demens*). Tyson at 94 and Schneider (2003) at 209 argue that the second half of this line echoes Virgil *Georgica* 2.315 ("*Nec tibi tam prudens quisquam persuadeat auctor*"). Shanzer (1988) at 261 cites with qualified approval, but without explanation, the suggestion of Ratkowitsch (1986) suggestion that the *auctor* ("expert") mentioned here is the Cicero of *De senectute*. Ratkowitsch and Shanzer might be right; Maximianus could be satirizing Cicero's generally positive view of old age with a *reductio ad absurdum* argument.

Another alternative is that Maximianus is satirizing a Christian writer, such as Boethius, Augustine, or Jerome, for viewing old age as a desirable state because it brings a righteous man closer to heaven. The difficulty with this interpretation is that the reference doesn't include enough information to make the allusion clear. Finally, it is possible that it is a generic reference and that this couplet is just Maximianus' way of saying that his proposition is self-evident. Goldlust at 136 declares the line incoherent.

1.152 Ellis defends Withof's emendation of *ipse* for *esse* ("to be") despite the lack of manuscript support. See Ellis (1884b) at 149–150. Guardalben (1993) at 118 correctly rejects Baehrens' *ecce* for *esse*. See also Goldlust (2013) at 136.

1.153–154 Webster at 78, Spaltenstein (1983) at 131, Agozzino at 143–144, and Öberg at 188 note the echo of Virgil *Georgica* 3.67 (*subeunt morbi tristisque senectus*). The melodic repetition of *iam* ("first . . . then") and *subeunt* ("encroach . . . encroach") is an example of anaphora. Tyson at 95–96 misidentifies Maximianus' repetition of *iam* as "a poetic tradition" shared with Virgil and mistranslates the second *iam* in the line as a second "now." In fact, *iam . . . iam* here is a pedestrian way of saying *first . . . then* or *now . . . then*. See OLD 1d. The rhetorical flourishes of this line also include asyndeton, the dropping of one or more expected conjunctions.

For *discrimina mille* ("uncounted risks"), see Pseudo-Ausonius *Periochae Iliadis* 1.2 (*mille . . . discrimina*). The number *mille* typically meant "a great many." See OLD 1b, 2a. Boano views this line as echoed in Corippus *In laudem Iustini* 2.170. See Boano (1949) at 201.

1.154 Ellis' defense of the Bodleian *duplices* for *dulces* ("sweets") on the hypothesis of "a second banquet" or "a double ration sometimes given as a reward to soldiers" is silly, even with Horace *Carmina* 3.8.6 (*dulcis epulae*). See Ellis (1884b) at 150.

In this line Gärtner sees a debatable but intriguing echo of Ovid *Amores* 2.20 (*dulcis ut esca nocet*). See Gärtner (2009b) at 132. Cf. 1.161–162 *infra* (*dulcis . . . esca*).

Disturbingly for contemporary readers, but not for most Romans, the term *deliciaeque* ("and pleasures") also means "an object of pederastic desire." See Laes, "Desperately Different? *Delicia* Children in the Roman Household" in Balch and Osiek (2003) at 298–326. See generally Laes; see also Adams (1982) at 196–197. It also means "erotic verse."

1.155 Öberg at 188 and Franzoi and Spinazzè at 144 note the parallel between *animum suspendere* ("to give up fondness") and Ovid *Metamorphoses* 7.308. For *animum* as "fondness," see OLD 8, 9.

1.156 The phrase *ut vivamus vivere destitimus* ("and we stop living so that we might live") is another example of paradox. Webster at 78 is mistaken in claiming that *vivere* is in "the technical sense of the erotic poetry." Cf. Boethius *De interpretatione* 2.2.162 (*ut si vivente Socrate dicat Socrates non vivit*).

1.157 Despite the lack of manuscript support, Schetter (19700 at 87, with tentative support from Spaltenstein (1983) at 132, argues for emendation of *et me quem dudum non ulla adversa nocebant* based primarily on the parallel of Virgil *Aeneid* 2.726 (*et me quem dudum non ulla injecta movebant*). Webster at 78 anticipates and rightly rejects this argument.

Gärtner notes a parallel between *nulla adversa nocebant* ("no adversaries harmed") and Sedulius *Carmen Paschale* 4.159 (*Nulla . . . adversa nocebit*). See Gärtner (2009b) at 132. Webster at 54 rejects Heege's (1893) emendation of *iam* ("now") for *non*.

1.157–158 The long/wrong rhyme is an attempt to imitate *nocebant/gravant*.

There may be a hint of a political subtext in *regimur* ("I'm ruled by") and *gravant* ("oppress").

1.159–160 Maximianus is using both paradox and chiasmus twice here.

1.160 The verb *praestat* ("It's best") has some legal flavor. See OLD 5.

Ellis (1884b) at 150 argues for substituting the Bodleian 38 *abstineas* for *abstineam* ("I fast") on the grounds of the harshness of the elision, although he acknowledges three precedents in Catullus. Webster at 78 defends *abstineam* by noting the hiatus makes the combination less harsh. See also Altamura (1981) at 822.

1.161 I see no strong precedent for *contraria redditur* ("the opposite returns"), but I suspect that it is the first reference in classical literature to acid reflux; it is also possible that the phrase refers to vomit. Gärtner notes a linguistic parallel to Manilius *Astronomica* 1.400 (*contraria redditur*), though the sense of the phrase in that context is quite different. See Gärtner (2009b) at 133. Gärtner also notes a possible inspiration for *quae modo profuerat* ("that served well once") in Rutilius Numantius *De reditu suo* 1.324 (*quae modo profuerant*).

1.162 The verb *iacet* ("one throws away") causes considerable debate. Webster at 78 correctly rejects the argument of Giardelli at 16 that it means "is," but Webster offers no definition. Spaltenstein (1983) at 134 suggests it should be the equivalent of "to be neglected or abandoned." Webster at 78 notes that the phrase *fastidita iacet* ("repelled, one throws away") appears at Lucan *Bellum civile* 7.845.

1.163 The phrase *munera bacchi* ("gifts of wine") is common. See, e.g., Ovid *Ars amatoria* 1.565.

Agozzino incorrectly refers to this line as "proverbiale." Schneider (20030 at 209 notes that Baehrens and Fels (2000) follow the emendation of Withof at 315 of *Cereris* for *Veneris*, which is supported by five manuscripts. Cf. Öberg at 158. It might balance a symbol for mead with a symbol for wine, but on balance I agree with Guardalben (1993) at 118 that this complaint does not sound authentic focused on two types of alcohol. Cf. Franzoi and Spinazzè at 145. However, it does make sense as a metonym for food and so I reluctantly follow Withof. See OLD 1b, 2b.

1.164 The noun *damna* ("losses") is another legally flavored term. Cf. Gärtner (2009b) at 135–136.

1.165 Öberg at 188 notes that *per horas* ("in time") appears at Ovid *Epistulae ex Ponto* 3.5.9. The phrase is a favorite of Manilius. See *Astronomica* 3.306, 3.387, 3.397, 3.449, 3.521; cf. Justinian *Digesta Iustiniani* 38.1.3.11; Servius *In Vergilii Aeneidos libros* 3.512.1.

Gärtner notes that the phrase *iacens natura* ("nature lying") appears at Dracontius *Carmen de Deo* 2.95 (*natura iacens*). See Gärtner (2009b) at 133; see also OLD.

1.166 Webster at 78 and Öberg at 188 note that this line echoes Ovid *Ars amatoria* 2.114 (*fit minor et spatio carpitur ipsa suo*).

1.167 Öberg at 188 and Schneider at 59 note the parallel between *non . . . medicamina prosunt* ("treatments . . . do not help") and Fortunatus *Carmina* 6.5.159 (*nulla . . . medicamina prosunt*).

1.168 The phrase *ferre opes* ("do the job") is common from the classical era through Late Antiquity. While it appears in "high" literature, it is also common in colloquial language, such as the plays of Plautus. See, e.g., Plautus *Bacchides* 638. For syntactical agreement I have emended Webster and adopted the *solebant opes* ("tends . . . the jobs") of the Florentinus manuscript.

1.169–170 For an interpretation based on *materia* as "flesh," see Uden and Fielding (2010) at 449. My take is slightly different; I believe that the word is used in the technical sense of an herbal treatment as in such texts as Pedanius Discorides *De materia medica*.

This distich is maddeningly opaque, but it appears from the wordplay of *pereunt/parantur* in the first line and the *magis/damnis/suis* rhymes in the second (imitated with are/far) that Maximianus is trying to give it an aphoristic, and perhaps sardonic, quality. The noun *urna* ("urn") may be a reference to a funerary urn, which would suggest that the *damnis* ("losses") are human ash. Cf. note to 1.164. However, there appears to be no precedent for using *damnis* in that sense and the logic of the line is hard to discern. I have considered the possibility that *urna* is the equivalent of a chamber pot (usually called a *matella*), but there is not much support for that idea either. It is possible that the gist of the line is that the doctors' balms and herbal treatments do no good and end up with the patient's ashes in a funerary urn. Cf. Schneider (2008) at 1–24; but see Gärtner (2009b) at 131–144 (particularly at 137 arguing for a metaphorical link to the *vas* in Lucretius *De rerum natura* 3.936). It is possible that the line refers to the urn in which a physician prepared his medications. It is also possible that the line is corrupt, but I concur with Guardalben at 118 in rejecting Baehrens' conjecture of *orba* for *urna*.

The term *magis* ("much") in this line is problematic. See Ellis (1884b) at 151; Webster at 78. I reject the suggestion that *magis* could be "platter" here. See Green (2000) at 449. Classicists tend to find use of *magis* as an intensifier for a comparative adjective to be unappealing, but it was common in Late Antiquity. See Herman (2000) at 63–64.

Ellis' proposed substitutions of *donis* for *damnis* ("losses") and *strictior* for *tristior* ("sadder") without manuscript support are unpersuasive. Ellis (1884b) at 151. The use of *damnis* in a low sense following *damna* in a high sense in line 164 may add to a sense of increasing degradation in this passage.

1.171 The trope of *fulcire ruinam* ("to brace a . . . ruin") appears often as far back as Lucretius; in *Epistulae* 58 Seneca compares old age to a tottering building. Bellanova (2004) at 108 argues for Ovidian inspiration, an argument strengthened by Ovid *Tristia* 1.6.5 (*fulta ruina est*). Webster notes that Corippus may echo Maximianus' *fulcire ruina* in *Iohannis* 1.51 (*tantam cupiens fulcire ruinam*). Cf. Boano (1949) at 201. Uden and Fielding (2010) argue that Maximianus is "clearly spoofing" the "ruin" motif they discuss at 447–450. Montaigne quotes these lines in his essay "On Experience." See Montaigne at 1237.

This line arguably lends slight support to the idea that the Maximianus who wrote these elegies is the same Maximianus asked by Cassiodorus in the name of Theoderic to preserve collapsing buildings in Rome. See Appendix A; cf. Bjornlie (2009) at 163–164.

The phrase *non secus* ("Not unlike") is a favorite of Virgil. See Spaltenstein at 136–137.

1.173 The idiomatic phrase *longa dies* ("time's passage") is a common one in "high" and "low" Latin. Addition of the word *donec* before *longa dies* may be Virgilian, cf. Virgil *Aeneid* 6.745, but Tyson at 99 overreads by suggesting the phrase has "epic grandeur." Cf. note to 2.17.

Spaltenstein (1983) at 137–138 and Öberg at 188 note that *compage soluta* ("broken into pieces" in line 174) also appears in Lucan *Bellum civile* 1.72. Cf. Claudian *De raptu Proserpinae* 1.1.115; Persius 3.58; Statius *Thebaid* 8.31; Augustine *Sermones* 21.179.2.

1.174 Webster points out at 79 that *auxilium* ("the help" in line 173) can have architectural connotations. The comparison of the body to a collapsing house is a Lucretian metaphor. Cf. *De rerum natura* 3.774–775.

1.175 The phrase *spectacula rerum* ("public shows") echoes Virgil *Georgica* 4.3 (*admiranda tibi levium spectacula rerum*). See McGill (2005) at 64–65. It probably refers to gladiator combat, animal fights, and chariot racing that Honorius and

Valentinian III tried to outlaw in the late fourth and early fifth centuries, a ban which Theoderic later lifted to effusive praise by Ennodius, Cassiodorus, and the author of the *Anonymus Valesianus*. Vitiello (2014) at 81 notes that "Boethius was particularly grandiose in organizing circus games and triumphant parades." As the Ostrogothic Empire crumbled, these games ended, primarily due to cost, thus Maximianus' complaint tends to support a date for this text toward the end of Ostrogothic rule. Justinian did not ban public shows; his Hippodrome in Constantinople seated one hundred thousand spectators.

Spaltenstein (1983) at 175 correctly rejects Schetter's argument at 139 that this line and the five that follow "sont interpolés."

1.176 The phrase *dissimulare licet* ("One cannot hide") is Ovidian. See, e.g., *Heroides* 9.122; *Tristia* 4.9.32, 4.9.304.

This line's lament about hiding pains probably refers to the strategic distraction of the *spectacula rerum* of the previous line.

1.177–178 Schneider at 210 notes that Schetter (1970) at 139 and Spaltenstein (1983) at 139 accept the Baehrens *cultus* over *vultus* ("looks"). Cf. Guardalben (1993) at 118. Ellis concurs with this emendation, which was originally Ommeren's. See Ellis (1884b) at 152. Nonetheless, I believe that Webster's *vultus* makes more sense, avoids redundancy, and has the advantage of being used in most of the manuscripts. See Öberg at 159. For *vultus . . . vesteque* ("clothes and . . . looks") Franzoi and Spinazzè at 146 notes a parallel with Prudentius *Psychomachia* 553 (*vultuque et veste*) and a potentially significant echo in Corippus *In laudem Iustini minor* 4.330 (*vultuque et veste*). See also Juvenal 14.110 (*vultuque et veste*).

This distich again demonstrates Maximianus' love of paradox. See note to 1.44. Some manuscripts have *senem* or *sene* for Webster's *seni* ("the old"). Webster at 31; Ellis (1884b) at 151–152. This repetition of *turpe seni* ("It shames the old"—*esse* is implied) is an example of "serpentine verse." See note to 3.5–6. See also Goldlust at 137 (rejecting Baehrens' speculative *quin sine maestitia vivere turpe seni*).

1.179–180 The term *crimen* has legal connotations and could be translated as "crime,""guilt," or "stigma." It also has religious connotations and could be translated as "sin." Maximianus has an appreciation for law and not for religion, but one must recall he is describing what others say. Moreover, songs and jokes were generally not illegal, so it seems the better choice here is to pick the more neutral "vice." Öberg at 189 notes *crimen habent* ("display their vice") at Propertius 2.32.11 and Ovid *Amores* 2.5.6. Cf. OLD 19a for *habent*. For more extensive references, see note to 1.102. Agozzino at 148 makes a weak case that these lines "dipende da" Horace *Epistulae* 2.55–57. Maximianus again uses anaphora with *crimen* and paradox to give this distich an aphoristic feel.

Montaigne quotes line 180 in his essay "On Some Lines of Virgil." Montaigne at 994.

Maximianus may be tweaking Roman moralists with *convivia cantus* ("the feasts, the songs"). Cf. Cicero *Pro Caelio* 35.11 (*convivia . . . cantus*); Seneca *Epistulae morales ad Lucilium* (*convivia cantusque*).

1.181 Wasyl (2011) persuasively argues at 131 that this line is part of a pattern of Maximianus echoing Horace (specifically here *Epodes* 1.5.12 et seq.), albeit with more depressing overtones. Cf. Ratkowitsch (1986) at 45.

1.182 The phrase *largus opum* ("great wealth") borders on cliché. See, e.g., Martial 4.73.7, 5.25.4; Virgil *Aeneid* 11.338; Horace *Carmina* 4.1.18.

1.183 The phrase *partis . . . rebus* ("purchased assets") is rare but appears in Ovid *Heroides* 1.94. The term *partis* is not the plural of the noun *pars*, but the past participle of *pario*. See Knox (1995) at 107; OLD 5c.

1.184 The term *violare* ("harming them") has connotations of violating a law or trust as well as the connotation of raping. Öberg at 189 notes that *violare nefas* ("harming them . . . wrong") appears at Juvenal 15.9. Cf. Servius *In Vergiliis Aenidos libros* 3.80.9.

1.185 For the story of Tantalus, see Homer *Odyssey* 11.582–592; cf. Horace *Sermones* 1.1.68; Ovid *Amores* 3.7.49–52; Virgil *Aeneid* 6.585–603. For *vicinas undas* ("nearby streams"), cf. Propertius 4.8.58 (*vicinas aquas*).

Webster at 80 notes that the phrase *non aliter* ("As when"—literally "not otherwise") is similar to *non secus*, see note to 1.171, in that it is an elevated way of introducing a comparison.

1.187 Maximianus emphasizes his diminished state with the phrase *custos rerum . . . mearum* ("watchman of my wealth"). Horace uses *custode rerum Caesare* to describe a benevolent leader of everything that mattered in Rome. See *Carmina* 4.15.17. By inserting *mearum* into Horace's phrase Maximianus lowers *rerum* from the lofty to the granular, thus diminishing *custos*, and ultimately himself. Cf. Wasyl at 131. Webster at 80 notes that Corippus uses the phrase *rerum custos* in *In laudem Iustini* 1.55.

1.189 For *auricomis* ("golden leaves"), cf. Virgil *Aeneid* 6.141; Silius *Punica* 3.608; Valerius Flaccus *Argonautica* 4.92; see also Tyson at 104.

Spaltenstein at 142 correctly rejects Schetter's substitution at 75 of *pendentia* for Webster's *dependens* ("draped") as well as Baehrens' *se tendens*, although there is substantial manuscript support for Schetter's position. See also Schneider (2003) at 210; Guardalben (1993) at 118; Goldlust (2013) at 138.

1.190 The *draco* ("snake") here is Ladon, a hundred-headed snake who guarded the apples of the Hesperides but lost them to Hercules. Maximianus' most likely source is Ovid *Metamorphoses* 4.637 et seq., although Ladon is also mentioned by Propertius and Seneca.

Goldlust (2013) at 138 correctly notes the echo of Virgil *Georgica* 2.82 (*non suo poma*) as well as the pairing of *pervigil* and *draco* in Ovid. See *Metamorphoses* 7.149 (*pervigilem . . . draconem*), *Heroides* 6.15 (*pervigilem draconem*).

1.191–192 For the phrase *super omnia* ("above all else"), see *super* at OLD 11. Webster at 81 notes this phrase in Virgil *Aeneid* 8.303 and Ovid *Metamorphoses* 6.526, 8.677.

Tyson at 104 sees a pun in *torquent* ("torture"), which also means "twist," as in the motion of Ladon in the previous line.

Tyson at 105 argues that anaphora with *hinc* ("so") occurs in epic, not elegy.

Öberg at 189 notes a parallel between *hinc sollicitum* and Horace *Carmina* 1.23.6 (*hinc sollicitus*).

Agozzino at 150 notes that *non requies . . . datur ulla* ("rest is never given") echoes Virgil *Aeneid* 6.600 (*nec . . . requies datur ulla*).

1.193–194 Tyson at 105–106 notes that Ovid uses this type of anaphora by repeating *semper* ("always") three times in consecutive lines at *Ars amatoria* 1.401–403. Spaltenstein (1983) at 143 misreads the text by adopting acrobatic and inconsistent definitions for *semper*.

1.194 Maximianus again turns to paradox, this time to capture the oddness of the passage of time.

1.195 Tyson at 106 notes that *tremulus* ("shaking") was a traditional epithet for the old that appears at Tibullus 1.2.90–91, Ovid *Metamorphoses*14.143, and Juvenal 6.622. Cf. Juvenal 16.56 (*tremulus captat pater*). Agozzino at 150 notes Plautus *Curculio* 160 (*anus tremula*).

1.197 Webster at 81 notes chiasmus in this line.

Alfonsi (misciting the lines in Maximianus) sees a nonexistent connection between this distich and Horace *Ars poetica* 172–175. Alfonsi (1942) at 89.

1.198 For *sapit* ("he . . . thinks") used to mock another difficult character, cf. Juvenal 5.170 (*ille sapit*).

1.199 The term *peritum* ("skillful") here is the adjective, not the past participle of *perire*.

1.200 Maximianus uses paradox again, this time to make his satirical point. The clarity of the paradox supports Webster's retention of *desipit* ("acts . . . foolish") over the *despicit* of five manuscripts.

1.201 Some manuscripts substitute *nobis* or *nolit* for *nolis* ('you do not want"). See Öberg at 160; see also Ellis (1884b) at 152. Baehrens substituted *notis* without any manuscript support, thereby eliminating Maximianus' joke, a substitution which Spaltenstein (1983) defends without a compelling rationale at 145 but which Gagliardi rightly calls "una vera banalizzazione." See Gagliardi (1988) at 36. Webster at 54 notes that *licet nolis* appears in the same line location at Lucan *Bellum civile* 2.512 and Martial 9.0.2. See also Boano (1949) at 212–213.

Webster at 54 and Guardalben (1993) at 118 properly reject Baehrens' emendation of *multa* ("much" in line 202) for *stulta*.

1.202 A number of manuscripts substitute *horrent* or *narrat* for *horret* ("he . . . shakes"). See OLD 4; see also Webster at 32; Ellis (1884b) at 152; Guardalben (1993) at 118. Webster at 81 defends Ellis' defense of "he becomes disgusting," which Spaltenstein (1983) at 145 states is "possible."

Use of the noun *alloquium* ("speech") is rare among classical authors. But see Ovid *Tristia* 1.372, 1.546. Ambrose, Cassiodorus, and other writers of Late Antiquity use it regularly.

1.203 Note the anaphora of *deficit . . . deficit* ("fades . . . fade").

1.205 Heege at 14 notes that *clamosis vocibus implet* ("he fills up . . . with shouted words") echoes Virgil *Aeneid* 11.274 (*lacrimosis vocibus implent*).

1.206 The phrase *nil satis est* ("Nothing's enough") is surprisingly rare prior to

Maximianus. It appears in a conversation in Horace and was probably colloquial. See Horace *Sermones* 1.1.62.

1.207 The wordplay of *arridet de se ridentibus* ("he mocks his being mocked") is probably Senecan. Cf. *De ira* 2.2.5 (*adridemus ridentibus*); *De clementia* 2.6.4 (*adridere ridentibus*). Maximianus may have also been inspired by Horace's even more playful *ut ridentibus adrident ita flentibus adsunt* with its unusual three rhymes. *Ars poetica* 101. For a thoughtful analysis of this possibility, see Wasyl at 132; cf. Agozzino at 152; Franzoi at 149.

1.209 Ellis argues that *his partibus* ("throughout these limbs") should be translated as "by these degrees." See Ellis (1884b) at 152.

The phrase *primitiae mortis* ("first fruits of death") is striking. Romans typically use the term *primitiae* in its literal sense, although Virgil uses it metaphorically with *primitiae iuvenis miserae*. Virgil *Aeneid* 11.156. Maximianus' use of the "first fruits" trope to death is unexpected and powerful; the phrase occurs again with a different sense in Crashaw's *Christus Circumcisus ad Patrem* 1 (*Has en primitias nostrae pater accipe mortis*). Although *primitiae* has its roots in rites of the Roman gods, Christian writers such as Jerome, Ambrose, and Augustine used it more regularly than classical writers. Cassiodorus used *primitiae* in a sense similar to *primitiae mortis*. See *Variae* 1.14.39 (*post resurrectionem a mortuis quorum primitiae factus est Dominus noster Iesus*). Altamura has metrical doubts about *mortis*. See Altamura (1981) at 822.

1.210 Webster at 82 rightly rejects Ellis' assertion that *ima petit* ("searches for the depths") is Macrobian and cites a number of earlier precedents. For *ima* as a noun, see OLD 1d. Goldlust at 139 comes to a similar view of *ima* and cites Ovid *Metamorphoses* 10.47 (*qui regit ima*) for support.

The adjective *pigris* ("sluggish") is often used to describe old age, see Tyson at 107, but not to modify *gressibus* ("steps").

Spaltenstein (1983) notes that *aetas/defluit* ("age creeps") echoes Juvenal 7.32 (*sed defluit aetas*).

1.211–212 The phrase *gressus euntis* ("one's gait") echoes Virgil *Aeneid* 5.649 (*gressus eunti*). Cotton Mather, in his 1702 book *Magnalia Christi Americana*, quotes these lines without attribution. Reiner Smolinski, a leading Mather scholar, explained to me that in this period people used *catenae*, such as Aquinas' *Catena Aurea*, or any of the *Polyantheas*, such as those of Wheare, Alsted, Heidfeld, and Lange, to lift quotations. Professor Smolinski noted Kenneth B. Murdock's suggestion that Mather probably used Johan Heidfeld's *Sphinx Theologico-Philosophica* (Herborn, 1621) or Joseph Lange's *Florilegii magni seu Polyantheae* (Leyden, 1648). See Mather (1977) at 227 (ll. 47–48), 375 (annotation on 94:67), 446 (annotation on 227:47–48).

The anaphora with *non* ("not . . . not . . . not . . . no") punctuates the transition from an abstract list of problems to a more visceral list.

Both Tyson at 108 and Webster at 82 note that the phrase *quae fuit ante manet* ("stays the same it was before") is a favorite of Ovid. See, e.g., *Fasti* 6.265; *Amores* 3.3.2; *Tristia* 4.576, 5.88.

1.213 Boano views this line as echoed in Corippus *Iohannis* 2.135. See Boano (1949) at 201.

1.215 There is a fairly even split in the manuscripts between *ipsi* and *ipsa* ("themselves" in line 216). See Öberg at 110.

1.216 There is one manuscript that supports Baehrens' emendation of *diminui* ("diminished") for *deminui*, an emendation defended without much rationale by Spaltenstein (1983) at 148. See Öberg at 160. While rare, *diminui* is a verb used by Cicero, Lucretius, Ovid, Plautus, Seneca, and Tacitus.

1.217 Webster's assertion at 82 that this line is "apparently a common description of old age" is inaccurate; one citation to Sedulius *Carmen Paschale* 3.199 does not support such a broad pronouncement.

James Uden suggests that this reference to an old man peering down suggests that he is animal-like due to the ancient distinction between human beings, who look up at the sky, and beasts that look down at the ground. Cf. Ovid *Metamorphoses* 1.84–86.

1.218 This line probably does not echo *Genesis* 3.19. But see Agozzino at 154–155. The Vulgate version is *donec revertaris in terram de qua sumptus* ("until thou return to the earth out of which thou wast taken"). Similar sentiments, however, abound in Roman verse. Webster has a helpful, though excessive, note on this line at 82–84.

1.219 This line refers to the riddle of the Sphinx. Her question is, "What walks on four feet in the morning, two at noon, and three at night?" The penalty for a wrong answer is becoming her next meal. Oedipus answers correctly with "Man," and thereby causes the Sphinx's death. Maximianus' source is unclear.

Webster at 84 incorrectly responds to Ellis' argument that the Bodleian *rursus* should be substituted for *prorsus* ("even") by arguing that the best sense of *prorsus* is "next" or "after that" instead of the awkward "perfect" offered by Ellis. See Ellis (1884b) at 152; OLD; see also Boano (1949) at 213. Cf. OLD 3.

Webster at 84 incorrectly suggests "Ausonius . . . seems to be first to introduce *quadrupes*." Among classical and Late Antique texts, it appears most often in the *Digesta Iustiniani*, but it also appears in Virgil, Ovid, and many other authors.

1.220 See notes to 1.224–225.

1.221 This line and the following fifteen lines are cited by George Lyman Kittredge as a source for Chaucer's *Pardoner's Tale*, in the first scholarly article documenting Maximianus' influence on Chaucer. Kittredge (1888) at 84–85. See also Nitecki, "The Convention of the Old Man's Lament in the *Pardoner's Tale*," 16, no. 1 *Chaucer Review* (1981) at 76–84. Maximianus also inspired *Le regret de Maximian* (Appendix D) and other Middle English works.

1.222 Webster at 84 notes that *redit ad nihilum* ("returns to nothing") is Lucretian. Cf. *De rerum natura* 1.248 (*redit ad nihilum*), 1.541 (*ad nihilum redissent*), 1.673 (*redeant ad nilum*), 1.797 (*redeant ad nilum*).

For the phrase *quod ante fuit nihil* ("what was nothing once"), cf. Quintilian *Institutio* 10.2.5 (*quod fuit ante nihil*); Lucretius *De rerum natura*.2.999 (*quod fuit ante*); 3.521 (*continuo hoc mors est illius quod fuit ante*). Kittredge (1888) at 84 argues that this entire line is a close translation of a line from Euripides. Franzoi and Spinazzè at 150–151 stretch in finding an echo of Prudentius *Contra Symmachus* 2.131 (*pro nihil in nihilum quia sunt reditura*).

1.223 In the "turnabout is fair play" category, Pseudo-Ovid echoes Maximianus' *ruitura senectus* ("a failing old man") at *De vetula* 2.708. Gärtner notes *ventura senectus* at Statius *Thebaid* 7.304. Gärtner (2009a) at 505.

Spaltenstein (1983) at 151 notes that Corippus at *Iohannis* 1.364 echoes *hinc est quod*, a phrase that was rare until later in the medieval period. But see Macrobius *Saturnalia* 1.2 (*hinc est quod*). I compress the literal "Hence it is that" to the more colloquial "It's why."

Webster at 84 sees an echo of Seneca *Hercules furens* 662 (*iners senectus adiuvat baculo gradum*). For other possible Senecan influences, cf. *De Clementia* 2.6.3.11 (*baculo senectum*), *Oetaeus* 657 (*baculo senili*).

1.224 The phrase *pulsat humum* ("keeps pounding . . . earth") is Ovidian. Cf. *Tristia* 1.9.30 (*pulsat humum*), *Metamorphoses* 5.84 (*humum moribundo vertice pulsat*), *Fasti* 6.330 (*pulsat humum*). Agozzino also notes Horace *Carmina* 1.37.2 (*pulsanda tellus*). Note the repetition of *humum* from line 220. Maximianus' comparison of the sounds of a banging staff to the rhythms of poetry is another example of his wry humor.

Spaltenstein (1983) at 152 misses the point of this line when he equates *pigram* ("stubborn") with "indolent." The sense here may be that the earth does not respond to the beating, making *senectus* ("old age") frustrated, pathetic, and even comic in a dark way.

1.225 The term *vestigia* ("footsteps") suggests the common wordplay on *pedes*, which means both a metrical foot and a body's foot. Maximianus may also be playing on *numerosa* ("many"), which can mean "rhythmic," much like *certo*. Cf. James (2004) at 249.

1.227 The phrase *miserere laborum* ("Pity struggles") echoes a dramatic scene in Virgil *Aeneid* 2.143–144 (*oro miserere laborum / tantorum miserere animi non digna ferentis*).

The term *genetrix* ("Mother") often refers to Venus but generally means something on the spectrum from "mother" to "creator." Wasyl at 124 compares this prayer to similar prayer-like passages in Ovid, particularly in *Tristia*. See Uden and Fielding (2010) at 449 (equating *genetrix* with "Mother Earth"); Gärtner (2009a) at 505–508.

1.227–234 Spaltenstein (1983) at 152–153 persuasively dismisses Schetter's argument at 29–33 for a line order represented in a few manuscripts.

1.228 For a discussion of the phrase *gremio fovere tuo* ("warm . . . upon your lap") and Augustine's frequent use of *fovere*, see O'Connell (1994) at 95–97. Cf. 1.40 (*membra fovere*). In these and the following lines Webster at 85 sees echoes of the language of tombstones. See also Ramírez de Verger (1986) at 188. Webster at 85 also notes the possible inspiration of Lucretius *De rerum natura* 1.251 (*in gremium matris*). Goldlust (2013) at 140 notes the parallel of Seneca *Oedipus* 746–747 (*genetrixque suo reddi gremio / . . . vidit alumnos*).

For *fessa* ("weak"), cf. 1.2 (*fesso*); Ovid *Metamorphoses* 7.163 (*iam proprior leto fessusque senilibus annis*), 13.66 (*vulnere tardus equi fessusque senilibus annis*). The term could also mean "weary."

1.229–230 The wordplay of *horrent* ("dread") with *horrendos* ("so dreadful"), combined with the internal rhymes, mimics some effects of anaphora.

1.231 For the phrase *nil mihi cum superis* ("With no one left for me"), cf. Lucan *Bellum civile* 5.762 (*nil mihi de fatis superisque relictum est*), I follow Spaltenstein (1983) at 153 and the scholarly consensus. They rely on OLD 2 for *superis* as "mortals" or "the living," but the phrase could mean "the gods." Cf. OLD 3.

Spaltenstein (1983) at 154 incorrectly suggests that *munerae vitae* ("life's gifts") "semble unique." The phrase is a favorite of Christian writers. See, e.g., Juvencus *Evangelia* 2.229, 2.769, 4.346; Paulinus of Nola *Carmina* 32.227; Marius Victor *Alethia* 1.344; Sedulius *Carmen Paschale* 5.290; Dracontius *De laude dei* 2.579, 3.467; Arator *De actibus apostolorum* 1.591, 1.845. A classical example is Martial 3.6.5 (*magna licet dederit iucundae munera vitae*). Cf. Pseudo-Virgil *Culex* 414 (*funeris officium vitae pro munere reddit*). Green also makes a thoughtful suggestion about the possible influence of Ausonius. See Green (2000) at 449; cf. Ausonius *Versus Paschales prosidici* 11 (*finem animae donas aeternae munere vitae*). Gärtner notes the phrase at Ausonius *Epigrammata* 13.5. See Gärtner (2009a) at 505.

1.232 Scholars tend to overlook what seems to be a statement of implied exile. Although this posture may be an Ovidian affectation, it is likely that Maximianus was composing this line around 537–539 AD when Romans were fleeing their homes due to the advance of Justinian's forces. On the other hand, it could also be a dramatic statement that life is exile from the dust of the Earth. Franzoi and Spinazzè at 151–152 see this line as echoing Propertius 3.7.25 (*reddite corpus humo*).

1.233 For *miseros variis . . . poenis* ("assorted punishments for wretched men"), cf. Orentius *Commonitorium* 2.513 (*et miseros poenis variis*). Franzoi and Spinazzè at 152 suggest that *quid miseros variis prodest* echoes Propertius 1.9.9 (*quid miseros . . . prodest*).

Webster at 33 rejects *suspendere* and *expendere* for *extendere* ("add"). But see Ellis (1884b) at 152–153; Schetter (1970) at 30; Schneider (2003) at 212. With some trepidation, I stand by Webster.

1.234 For the sentimental *materni pectoris* ("mother's heart"), cf. Ovid *Amores* 1.13.34 (*materni . . . pectoris*).

1.235 Webster at 86 notes the "semi-humorous" intent of *trunco* ("tree trunk" in line 236), a bulkier version of *baculus,* the expected walking stick or staff. The tapping sounds or stuttering suggested by the onomatopoeia of *titubantes* ("swaying") and five other *t*-sounds in this line may have added to the humor of recitations. The promotion of the walking stick to a log may be meant to remind the reader of the doomed props and braces used for decrepit buildings in 1.171–172. Heege at 22 notes that this line may echo Ovid *Metamorphoses* 4.26–27 (*senex ferula titubantes ebrius artus / sustinet*); Franzoi at 152 stretches to find an echo in Prudentius *Contra Symmachus* 2.994–995. My translation's wordplay with "limbs" and "tree trunk" mimics the original Latin.

1.237 Maximianus' *misero quid funere differt* ("how does he differ from a wretched corpse?") echoes Ovid again. See *Epistulae ex Ponto* 2.3.3 (*quid enim status hic a funere differt*); see also Bellanova (2004) at 113–114. Webster at 86 notes the use of *funere* for "corpse" is classical. See also Stevenson (2008) at 81. Spaltenstein (1983) at 156 argues that *differt* with the ablative was rare and generally not used until Late Antiquity. Goldlust (2013) at 141 notes the return of the "living dead" motif.

1.238 For a discussion of textual variants for *adtracti* ("withered") and a silly argument for *adtacti*, see Ellis (1884b) at 153. See Öberg at 161; cf. Apuleius *Metamorphoses* 10.28.26 (*mulieris adtractis*).

1.239 Webster at 86 correctly notes the use of paradox in this line.

For Ellis' support of Webster's *iaceam vivamque* ("I rest, and live") over other manuscript versions, see Ellis (1894) at 153. But see Guardalben (1993) at 119 (supporting the *iaceat vivatque* of Spaltenstein); cf. Boano (1949) at 238–240. Spaltenstein (1983) at 156 interprets the line more accurately than Webster at 86; *iaceam* is not being used in the sense of dying, but is more likely simply "resting" or "lying down" here.

It is unclear whether *magis* should be translated as "instead" or "more." With advice from Aaron Pelttari, I leaned toward "instead" based on word placement and context.

1.240 The preposition *sub* is problematic and the distich is opaque. See Webster at 86 ("*sub* means 'anywhere near'"); see also Spaltenstein (1983) at 156; Schetter (1970) at 35–37. Clark is harshly critical of Webster's use of the Eton text's *sub vitali*. See Clark (1913) at 260; see also Welsh (2011) at 217. Ellis, with some reluctance, supports the reading of the Eton text, see Ellis (1894) at 234, without explicitly renouncing his earlier proposed *subdivali* for *sub vitali*, *rogo* for *loco*, and *non putet* for *computet*. See Ellis (1884b) at 153. I accept the *me putet* ("think I") of Schetter (1970) at 35–37 and Schneider (2003) at 212, which is supported by six manuscripts and without which it is difficult to identify a supportable reading. See also Welsh (2011) at 217 (arguing for *me . . . computet*).

I reluctantly adopt the speculative emendation of *suo* ("his") for *sub* because I scoured tens of thousands of lines looking for another *sub loco* and did not find it; *suo loco* ("for his part") is common, particularly in Justinian *Corpus civilis iuris*, and it makes some sense. Moreover, the OLD notes for *locus* that it is often accompanied by *suus* when used in the sense of "the position properly or habitually used by a person or thing." OLD 5a. It would be an easy mistake for a scribe to make and would have been an early one. But see Guardalben at 119.

1.241 For *urimur aestu* ("we're scorched by heat"), see Ovid *Metamorphoses* 7.815 (*urimur aestus*); cf Ovid *Metamorphoses* 3.543 (*perurimur aestu*); see also Goldlust (2013) at 141.

The phrase *totum quod vivimus* ("All that we're living through") is a postclassical phrase. See, e.g., Quintilian *Declamationes maiores* 8.17; Tertullian *De testi-*

monio animae 1.5. It does not appear in Boethius but appears four times in Cassiodorus and over fifty times in works by Augustine. Roger Green noted for me the parallel of Ausonius' elegiac Epigram 20 to his wife (*vivamus quod vixamus*). Ausonius' line probably echoes Catullus 5 (*vivamus mea Lesbia*). See generally Sklenár, "Ausonius' Elegiac Wife: Epigram 20 and the Traditions of Latin Love Poetry," 101, no. 1 *The Classical Journal* (2005) at 51–62.

For *poena* ("pain") in Late Antique Latin, see Herman (2000) at 28.

1.242 Enk (1946) at 74 and Franzoi and Spinazzè at 153 note that *et aura nocet* ("clouds punish") echoes Propertius 2.4.12 (*et aura nocet*).

1.245 For *tussis anhela* ("a raspy cough"), Webster at 86 and Franzoi and Spinazzè at 153 note an echo of Virgil *Georgica* 3.497 (*tussis anhela*). In discussion Roger Green suggested this line subtly refers back to the previous one; itching (caused by allergies?) is associated with the spring and coughing with the fall.

For a metrical issue with *scabies* ("itching"), see Altamura (1981) at 822.

1.246 For *aegra senectus* ("sick old age") Webster notes that the phrase occurs in Ovid *Metamorphoses* 14.143; Prudentius *Contra Symmachus* 2.322; and Lactantius *De ave phoenice* 15. He is incorrect about *Contra Symmachus*; the words do appear in lines 322 and 323, but not as a phrase. Altamura sees a metrical issue with *senectus*. See Altamura (1981) at 822.

For *habet* as "involves," see OLD 4b, 14.

1.247 Spaltenstein (1983) at 158 overstates the rareness of *reor* ("I believe") in Late Antiquity.

1.249 I have followed the *ipse* ("even") of most manuscripts over Webster's *ipsa*.

1.252 Spaltenstein (1983) at 159 correctly rejects the proposed substitution by Schetter (2003) at 76 of *heu* for *in* ("in"), although Schetter's proposal is supported by at least nine manuscripts.

Franzoi and Spinazzè at 153 note an unlikely possible echo of *turbidus . . . horret* ("confused, it horrifies") in Valerius Flaccus *Argonautica* 3.252 (*turbatus horret*).

1.253 For *fulcra* as "couch" see Webster at 87. Ellis dismisses "the ordinary reading" of *fulcra* and declares there "can be little doubt that *filtra* is the right word." The ordinary meaning of *filtra* would be "filter." Ellis himself acknowledges that there is no proof that *filtra* had even entered the language by the mid sixth century. There still isn't, although eight of the manuscripts do have *filtra*. See Schetter at 22; Öberg at 163; but see Ellis (1901) at 370. Altamura provides some additional support for *fulcra* by noting the use of *fulcro* by Propertius at 2.13.21 and 4.7.3. See Altamura (1981) at 821; see also Agozzino at 161.

The phrase *duris . . . cautibus* ("rough . . . rocks") is Virgilian. See *Aeneid* 4.366; *Eclogae* 8.44.

1.254 Webster at 87 and Spaltenstein (1983) at 159 note that the words that close Ovid *Heroides* 21.170 (*pallia pondus habent*) also close this line.

1.255 For *per mediam . . . noctem* ("in the middle of the night"), cf. Juvenal 5.54 (*per mediam . . . noctem*); Horace *Sermones* 1.5.83 (*ad mediam . . . noctem*), 1.10.33 (*post mediam . . . noctem*).

1.256 Suffering to avoid suffering is another paradox.

1.257 Webster at 87 notes the paradox of being conquered by feebleness. See note to 1.55 for more on military defeat as a metaphor for old age. The backdrop for this line may be Justinian's invasion of Italy.

1.258 In classical Latin and the *Digesta Iustiniani* the phrase *hac parte* ("into this role") tends to be preceded by a preposition, but I suspect that Seneca *Phoenissae* 181 (*Hac parte mortem perage coepi mori*) influences this line. Franzoi and Spinazzè at 154 note the echo of Ovid *Amores* 1.4.32 (*hac ego parte*).

1.259 Ellis (1884b) at 154 proposes an exchange of Ovidian terms with *vincula* for *viscera* ("organs").While both readings have challenges, and *vincula* would add an interesting Boethian echo, only one manuscript supports Ellis' emendation. See Öberg at 162. With some reluctance, I adopt Spaltenstein's (1983) argument at 259 for *naturae* as "body." In this distich Maximianus returns to the trope of the aging body as a collapsing structure at 1.173–174—including returning to *omnis* and *solvo*.

1.260 I have had a number of useful exchanges abut this line with Aaron Poochigian and Robert Maltby, who persuaded me to use the definition of *nutat* found in OLD 4 ("totters").

I disagree with Roger Green's suggestion that *opus* ("structure") has a sexual connotation here, although I agree with his suggestion that the same word has a sexual connotation later in the *Elegies* at 5.84. See Green (2000) at 449.

1.261 For the adjective *incurva* ("bent") in Late Antiquity used in connection with old age, see Sedulius *Carmen Paschale* 3.200 (*non senio tremebunda gemens incurva caducis*); Jerome *Commentarii in Isaiam* 7.19.26 (*incurvo senes*); Augustine *Sermones* 1.86.9 (*senex incurvus*), *In Ioannis evangelium* 124.38.10 (*corpore fessi et incurva senis mortuae sunt vires*); Orientius *Commonitorium* 2.235 (*incurvos quarulos*). Webster at 88 notes that *incurva* occurs in a list of infirmities of the old in Terence *Eunuchus* 2.3.45. Cf. Statius *Thebaid* 4.419 (*incurva senecta*); Ammianus *Res gestae* 24.1.10 (*senex incurvus*); Cicero *In Verrem* 2.2.87.4 (*senilis incurva*).

Mastandrea notes a strong parallel between this line and Boethius *Consolatio philosophiae* 1.1.7–10, particularly line 9 (*venit enim properata malis inopina senectus*). See Mastandrea (2005) at 161; see also Boano (1949) at 200. Boano also notes an echo of line in the *Carmina* 14.1 of Eugene of Toledo, the second poet (after Corippus) known to echo Maximianus.

1.262 For *cedere* ("to yield") as a military and political metaphor for defeat of the body by old age, see note to 1.55.

1.263 Except for Propertius 2.26b.9, the phrase *per longum* ("for long") was not part of classical literary diction, and it may be a shortened version of other phrases. See, e.g., Ovid *Ars amatoria* 3.780 (*per longum annum*), *Metamorphoses* 15.353 (*per longum aevum*); Pliny *Naturalis historia* (*per longum tempus*). The first popularizer of the phrase appears to be Silius. See *Punica* 1.469, 2.465, 10.206, 13.462, 15.785, 17.473. It appears later in works of Christian theologians. See, e.g., Augustine *Confessiones* 3.12.7.1; Jerome *Commentarii in Ezechielem* 14.46.36,

14.46.42, *Ezechiel* 46.22, *Exodus* 27.11; Orosius *Historiae* 1.2.34, 1.2.64, 1.2.76, 1.2.90. It does not appear in Boethius but does appear once in Cassiodorus. See Cassiodorus *De orthographia* 24.

Altamura sees a metrical issue with *ergo* ("thus"). See Altamura (1981) at 822.

1.265 This distich has intense alliteration, internal rhyme, and anaphora unknown in the Augustan era.

1.266 There is debate about whether *hic* ("here") in this line should be *sic*, *ac*, *quam*, or *bis*. See Webster at 34; Öberg at 163; Ellis (1901) at 370; Spaltenstein (19830 at 163. Schneider (2003) at 213 follows Spaltenstein, Schadd, and Guardalben in embracing *sic* over *hic*. I believe that *hic* here echos the *hic iacet* of grave memorials.

Maximianus' use of *sensus* ("senses") as the direct object of *sepelire* ("bury") is quite striking. The verb *sepelire* typically takes a concrete direct object, such as a dead person. Webster at 88 and Guardalben (1993) at 119 are right in rejecting Baehrens' speculative emendation of *conspelire* for *sepelire*, an emendation which fosters fallacious arguments for Maximianus' Christianity of the type articulated by Manitius and Heege.

1.267–268 The dissolution of the world and the moral neutrality of nature are Lucretian sentiments that echo 1.173–174 and 1.259; use of *solvere* and words for "all" link all three sections.

The phrase *naturae . . . iussa* ("the laws of nature") is uncommon until centuries after Maximianus, but similar phrases are common. See generally Horsley, "The Law of Nature in Philo and Cicero" 71, nos. 1–2 *Harvard Theological Review* (1978) at 35–59. The verb *queror* ("I . . . protest") has a legal flavor and sets the stage for *iussa* in the next line.

1.269 The phrase *longaevo tempore* ("in the course of time") is one of Late Antiquity. Cf. Gregorius Turonensis *Historiae* 10.29.11. Boano views this line as echoed in Corippus *In laudem Iustini* 4.198. See Boano (1949) at 201.

1.270 Use of the classical *pulcer* ("fine") instead of the *pulcher* perferred for the subsequent five centuries may reflect the influence of Cicero's rejection of his era's tendency to add aspiration to words. See generally Ramage, "Cicero on Extra-Roman Speech," 92 *Transactions and Proceedings of the American Philological Association* (1961) at 481–494. On the other hand, one has to consider the variability caused by medieval scribes, and *pulcher* is used in some manuscripts. See Öberg at 163.

Webster at 88, without a coherent rationale, waters down the definition of *turpis* ("repulsive") and argues that it means "past the prime of youth and love" and that it "conveys neither moral reprehension, nor aesthetic distaste, but implies physical disability." In fact, this line contrasts *turpis* with *pulcer*, so in context that Maximianus uses *turpis* in its primary sense of a strongly negative esthetic response. See OLD 1, 2.

The trope of the aging horse has a long and distinguished pedigree in Roman literature. Perhaps the most significant example is Cicero's citation at *De senectute* 14 of two lines from Ennius (*Sicut fortis equus spatio qui saepe supremo / Vicit*

Olimpia nunc senio confectus quiescit). Cf. Ovid *Metamorphoses* 13.848 (*turpis equus*); Horace *Epistulae* 1.8–9; Tibullus 1.4.31–32.

1.271 For a defense of *fracta diu* ("Long broken down") against the substitution of *die* for *diu* by Petschenig, see Ellis, "*Maximiani Elegiae. Ad fidem codicis Etonensis recensuit et emenduit M. Petschenig* (review)" 970 *The Academy* (December 6, 1890). In addition to the use of *fracta diu* by Manilius noted by Ellis, more likely inspiration occurs in Cicero's *De oratore* 3.62 (*diu fracta*) and Claudian *De consulatu Stilichonis* 3.125 (*fracta diu*).

Roman writers regularly pair lions and tigers, as we do today. See Spaltenstein at 164. Spaltenstein suggests, wrongly, that *rabidi* ("angry") could apply to *diu* instead of *leonis*; Ellis rightly criticizes Bröring for this same suggestion. See Ellis (1894) at 234; cf. Sidonius Apollinaris *Carmina propempticon* 55 (*rabidi leonis*).

1.272 Ellis criticizes Petschenig for including *aspera* instead of *caspia* (or the Bodleian variant *caspida*, another rare term that means "Caspian") by arguing that most manuscripts have *caspia*. See Ellis (1901) at 370. Spaltenstein (1983) at 164–165 seems unaware of the textual issue in this line. Schneider (2003) at 213 notes that Baehrens, Agozzino, and Guardalben all follow Ellis, but Schadd also follows the *aspera* of Webster and Petschenig. After helpful conversations with Michael Roberts and Roger Green, I accept *caspia*. Cf. Claudian *De raptu Proserpinae* 3.105 (*caspia tigris*); see generally Guardalben (1993) at 119. Caspian tigers frequently fought as entertainment for Romans. Sadly, they became extinct, perhaps as late as the 1990s.

Webster and Spaltenstein (1983) overread this distich. Webster at 89 cites Dracontius *Carmina* prof 1.7 and declares that "*lenta . . . tigris* is the impossible." Spaltenstein at 165 declares it "en effet paradoxal." In fact, this distich is an unremarkable comment on the leveling effect of time—in effect, an extension of the previous distich's description of the beautiful horse becoming repulsive.

For metrical issues with this line, see Altamura (1981) at 822.

1.273 Spaltenstein (1983) notes that erosion of rock is a familiar trope in love elegy and cites Tibullus 1.4.18 along with Ovid *Amores* 1.15.31–32 and *Epistulae ex Ponto* 4.8.49.

1.274 Spaltenstein at 165 states that the noun *opus* ("work") "désigne sans doute un édifice." In fact, there is not only doubt, but a better reading. Despite the recurring ruin motif, we should not assume that Maximianus is restricting his observation to edifices; the broad noun he uses can cover a range of human efforts, including literature, and the aphoristic quality of the line along with its double negative verb construction indicate that Maximianus intends to make a sweeping statement.

A possible linguistic echo of *tempore cedat* ("yield with time") in this line is Horace's Lucretian-inspired trope of the guest leaving the party. Cf. Horace *Sermones* 1.1.118–119 (*exacto contentus tempore vita / cedat uti conviva satur*). Maximianus puts a grimmer spin on this trope at the ends of elegies 5 and 6.

1.275–276 This distich sets the groundwork for the more explicit discussion of the ruin theme used in the following distich. The noun *casus* ("woes") connotes "fall" or "ruins." Cf. note to 1.279–280.

Enk at 74 notes a parallel between *venturos melius praevertere* ("better to forestall . . . coming") and Propertius 3.11.5 (*venturam melius praesagit*). Franzoi at 155 notes a parallel between *praevertere casus* ("forestall . . . woes") and Paulinus of Nola *Carmina* 10.326 (*praevertere casus*).

1.277 For *ruina* ("ruin") as "one of the characteristic motifs of the poem," see generally Uden and Fielding (2010) at 447–450.

1.277–278 These lines are quoted in Michel de Montaigne's essay "On Physiognomy." See Montaigne at 1190.

1.279–280 This distich is obscure. The gist seems to be that an old man cannot even recall everything that weighs him down, but it could be that he is referring to the emotional difficulty of sharing what depresses him. For *casus* ("woes"), cf. note to 1.275.

Guardalben (1993) at 119 rightly rejects Baehrens' emendation of *ac* for *at* ("But").

1.280 Franzoi and Spinazzè at 156 correctly reject Spaltenstein's definition at 167 of *commemorasse* ("recalling") as "raconter."

1.281 There appear to be no other literary uses of the phrase *violentaque damna* ("heavy losses") and I suspect that the phrase is commercial and legal. I am grateful to my former collaborator, Robert Maltby, for bringing to my attention a citation which tends to support that hypothesis, Justinian *Codex Iustinianus* 47.8.2 (*vim: et sine vi si quid callide admissum est, aeque continebitur. "Damni" praetor inquit: omnia ergo damna continent et clandestina. sed non puto clandestina, sed ea, quae violentia permixta sunt.*). Spaltenstein (1983) at 167 objects to the word *damna* in this phrase ("mais *damna* ne s'applique á rien dans ces vers"), but he misses both that it is a general statement and that ruin is a recurring theme of these elegies.

1.282 The phrase *praebet opem* ("offered . . . help") is common in medieval literature but does not seem to appear earlier than this line. The next earliest use I can find is Fortunatus *De Cariberetho rege* 10 (*praebet opem*). The verb *praebet* has legal connotations, perhaps in the sense of "tendered" an offer or a proposition. See Vidén (1984) at 107.

1.283 I follow Lemaire at 227 and emend Webster's *ipse* to *ipsi* ("themselves") because in context it should agree with *pueri*.

1.283–284 In content, though not in specific words, Maximianus seems to be echoing Tibullus 1.4.75–84, particularly 83–84, perhaps without as much erotic tension. Spaltenstein at 168 underestimates the force of *dominum* ("master") by equating it with "Monsieur." It may indicate that Maximianus ran a household with many servants. See Sessa (2012) at 53–62.

1.285 The anaphora of *irrident . . . irrident* ("mock . . . mock") in these closing lines may have some flavor of a litigator's closing summation.

1.287 A blind person observing is another paradox.

1.289 Spaltenstein (1983) at 170 notes that the makarismos, *felix qui* ("happy is the man who . . ."), is also found in Virgil, Lucan, and Prudentius. Schneider at 213 notes *Anthologia latina.* II 1.779.9. Altamura (1981) at 821 notes Virgil *Georgica* 2.490.

1.292 *Summo culmine* ("the highest peak") is a Virgilian phrase appearing at *Aeneid* 7.512 (*culmine summo*) and *Georgica* 1.402 (*culmine summo*). Cf. McBrine (2008) at 27.

Barnish argues for *missa* instead of *mersa* ("the plunge"—literally "having plunged") in this line. See Barnish (1990) at 23. See also Schneider (2003) at 213–214 (noting that Schadd and Fels use *mersa*, and that Agostino and Guardalben use *missa*). Barnish also sees parallels between this distich and Boethius *Consolatio philosophiae* 2.4.4–6. Id.

Elegy 2

2.1–2 Both Martial and Gallus called their love interests "Lycoris." We have no extrinsic evidence about Maximianus' Lycoris or his other love interests, if they existed at all. Szövérffy badly misses the point of Maximianus' description of Lycoris by dismissing it as "a generic antifeminist satire" with "the rather overdrawn picture of a lecherous, libidinous, selfish woman who abandons loyalty and faith." Szövérffy (1968) at 362. Just the opposite is true. Maximianus' description of Lycoris is fairly charitable considering she was his long-term *coniunx*. Indeed, as this elegy progresses, Lycoris remains the vital and attractive person as Maximianus degenerates into the pathetic *senex* of Roman comedy. This pattern sets the stage for the subsequent elegies; in each one Maximianus paints the female figure from somewhat to very charitably as he himself becomes progressively more ridiculous, a pattern which culminates with his extreme humiliation during the Greek girl's lament in elegy 5. In short, Szövérffy rightly sees Maximianus as a satirist, but entirely misses the point that Maximianus is satirizing himself—or as Barnish aptly puts it, "Maximian . . . shows wit, but small pleasure in his play: it is a savage exercise in Swiftian despair." Barnish (1990) at 32.

I have used the *lichoris* of most of the manuscripts rather than the implicitly updated *Lycoris* of Webster.

For discussion of Prada's argument that these lines are the start of a second book, see Franzoi (2011) at 161.

For *res* as "world," see OLD 4.

2.3 The adjective *indivisi* ("together") is rare and generally not used in this sense until Late Antiquity. See Spaltenstein (1983) at 173.

For *multos annos* ("the many years"), cf. Juvenal 10.188.

2.4 Schneider (2003) at 214 notes that Spaltenstein, Schadd, and Guardalben follow Webster's Ovidian *pavefacta* ("dismayed"), as I have, but Agozzino and Fels follow Baehrens' conjecture of *labefacta*. Goldlust (2013) at 144 also follows Webster. Cf. Ovid *Metamorphoses* 9.314, 15.878, 15.636. There is also some manuscript support for *stupefacta*. See Ellis (1884b) at 154. Welsh suggests the intriguing *tubefacta*, but his argument relies too heavily on the premise that *pavefacta* necessarily involves fear. See Welsh (2011) at 218.

For *respuit* ("kissed off"), which also means "spit" or "spew," cf. Ovid *Remedia amoris* 124–125. It starts an unpleasant string of verbs. Cf. 2.12 (*expuit*); 2.15 (*fundit*).

One scholar wrongly believes that he can tell that this description is an "indicio probable de que la situación descrita es más product de la imagination que de la realidad." Ramírez de Verger (1986) at 190.

2.5 Spaltenstein (1983) at 173 misses the meaning of this line when he asserts it is "donc incohérent." The implication is that the young men she is chasing are not her first, exactly what one would expect from a *docta puella* of love elegy.

2.5–6 Burton's *Anatomy of Melancholy* quotes these lines. Burton (2001) at 267. One can't help wondering whether Maximianus' use of *imbellem* ("gutless") to describe a *senem* ("an old man") hints at his own sense of helplessness as the forces of Justinian advanced through Italy toward Ravenna. Goldlust (2013) at 145 argues that *imbellem* is used in the sense of "improper au combat amoreux" and cites Martial 7.58.5 (*deseris imbelles thalamus mollemque maritum*) and Juvenal 6.366 (*eunuchi imbelles*). Agozzino at 176 notes Virgil *Aeneid* 2.544 (*imbelle sine ictu*). Cf. Appendix C.3 (*inbellis*).

Webster at 90 blunders when he dismisses as "mere nonsense" Manitius' point that *decrepitumque senem* ("weak old man") may echo Plautus *Asinaria* 862 "for the collocation must have been common." In fact, the combination is rare, but Plautus uses it other places as well, thereby increasing the likelihood that Manitius was right. See *Mercator* 291 (*senex . . . decrepitus*), 314 (*decrepitus senex*); see also *Casina* 559 (*decrepitum . . . virum*), *Epidicus* 666 (*vetulos decrepitos*); cf. Apuleius *Apologia* 70.8 (*decrepito seni*); Seneca *Dialogi* 10.11.1.2 (*decrepiti senes*).

2.7 The phrase *transactae . . . vitae* ("transpired life") may be an import from Christian writers of the fourth and fifth centuries. Cf. Augustine *De Trinitate* 14.2.4 (*Tunc ergo etsi vitae huius mortalis transactae meminerimus*); Pseudo-Ambrose *In epistolas beati Pauli* (*transacta hac vita*). It may also be drawn from Apuleius *Metamorphoses* 11.21.27 (*transactis vitae*) or, with its sense of a life "that is spent" it may be another of Maximianus' commercial/legal imports into poetry. Cf. OLD 3; Justinian *Codex Iustinianae* 1.16.229 (*Transacta finitave*).

I have joined Ellis, Guardalben, Goldlust, and Webster in accepting *volet* ("wishes") over Wernsdorf's *valet* and Ommeren's *solet*. See Ellis (1884b) at 154; Guardalben (1993) at 119; cf. Schneider (2003) at 214; Öberg at 164.

Franzoi and Spinazzè at 33–35 rely on variant readings for *nec meminisse solet transactae dulcia vitae*, a version which better supports Spinazzè's theory that this line is echoed in the *Ad Sethum* (*Quid meminisse iuvat transactae gaudia vitae*), a text debatably attributed to Saint Columbanus. As for the assertion that this line constitutes "l'indizio più precoce della conoscenza del testo massimiano," ibid. at 159, the attribution of *Ad Sethem* to Columbanus is controversial and many scholars date the text significantly after the works of Corippus and Eugene of Toledo. See, e.g., Herren, "Some Quantitative Poems Attributed to Columbanus" in Marenbon at 99–112. Moreover, the phrase *dulcia vitae* may derive, directly or indirectly, from Lucretius. See *De rerum natura* 6.4 (*dulcia vita*). Although Franzoi places too much weight on Spinazzè's argument, this type of research on reception is long overdue and offers hope for improving our understanding of this text.

2.8 The verb *reddidit* ("left") has legal and commercial connotations. Cf. note to 1.161.

From the context here and in line 6, *senem* ("an old man") is not just descriptive but derogatory. Indeed, these lines appear to mark the transition from the extended backstory of elegy 1 to the satire of elegies 2–5. Maximianus' repeated use of Plautan language reinforces his wrestling with the absurdity of becoming a *senex amator*, a stock character of comedy. See generally Ryder, "*Senex Amator* in Plautus" 31, no. 2 *Greece and Rome* (1984) at 181–189.

Goldlust (2013) at 145 sees paradox and clumsy zeugma in this line.

2.9–10 The terms *causas* ("claims"), *vitio* ("fault"), and *iudicet* ("judge") all have a heavy legal flavor appropriate for Lycoris' metaphorical role as prosecutor. Franzoi and Spinazzè at 158 note that *ingrata ac perfida* echoes Juvenal 9.82 (*ingrate ac perfide*). I translate *spretum* ("rejection") in this same vein, although I am unaware of any legal connotation for *spretum*.

Ellis (1884b) at 154 would embrace the variants *ipse* for *esse*, *respretu* for *et spretum*, and *iudicer* for *iudicet*, none of which I find persuasive. Schneider (2003) at 214 notes Baehrens and Fels would substitute *indicet* for *iudicet*, which I also find unpersuasive. Schetter (1970) at 47–49 and Guardalben (1993) at 119 defend *spretus* for *spretum* and *iudicer* for *iudicet*. Cf. Öberg at 164; Franzoi and Spinazzè at 159. Ellis (1884b) at 54 defends *iudicet* over *me indicet* by noting that Maximianus does not use elision in the pentameter lines elsewhere in the text.

2.11 Schneider (2003) at 11 notes that Baehrens and Fels substitute *ductum* for *dudum* ("not long ago"). Welsh suggests *denum*, which has no support in the manuscripts and muddies an otherwise lucid passage. His argument relies in part on a parallel to *Halieutica* 34–37, a text occasionally misattributed to Ovid based on one comment by Pliny the Elder. Aside from the scholarly consensus that this attribution is spurious, I know of no evidence that *Halieutica* was available to Romans during Maximianus' era, much less that Maximianus read it. See Welsh (2011) at 218.

Note the repetition of *praeteriens* ("passing by") at 2.24.

2.12 The verb *expuit* ("she spat") is rare in Late Antiquity but hardly the *hapax* suggested by Spaltenstein (1983) at 175–176. See, e.g., Augustine *In Ioannis evangelium* 124.44.2, 124.44.7; Tertullian *Apologeticus adversus gentes* 50.5. It also occurs in the classical era. See, e.g., Catullus 64.155; Pliny *Naturalis historia* 16.45. Spitting and covering oneself with clothes are traditional Roman ways of warding off evil. Welsh argues for an echo of Pseudo-Ovid *Haleutica* 37, an argument that I reject. See Welsh (2011) at 218. Cf. note to 2.11.

For the participle *obductis* ("covered up"), cf. Propertius 3.16.5 (*obductis*); Ovid *Metamorphoses* 2.325 (*obductos*), 12.542–544 (*obductos*).

2.13 For *dilexi* ("I liked") and *amavit* ("Did he love"), cf. Catullus 72.

2.14 The phrase *oscula blanda* ("tender kisses") is Ovidian. See *Amores* 2.6.56;

3.7.55–56. Fo notes the parallel between *oscula blanda dedi* and 2.18 of the *Appendix Maximiani* (*oscula blanda dabis*). See "Fo (1984–1985) at 183.

For *nefas* ("Damn it!") as an interjection, see Webster at 91; OLD 3c. Indeclinable nouns such as *nefas* are called *aptota*.

2.15 The dual senses of *fundit* ("spews") in this line befuddle readers. Though the term's primary meaning is "to pour forth," it also described verbal emissions inspired by the Muses or other inspiration. What is being spewed are the *words* "past love," not actual past love. Since Maximianus is often criticized for being derivative, note that this line is disgustingly inventive.

2.16 While I am confident that "curses" is the best translation of *dira*, it lacks associations that *dira* would have had for Maximianus. Etymologically, it is probably a contraction of *dei ira* ("wrath of a god") and would have conjured memories of Virgil *Aeneid* 3.256, where Jupiter sends a small owl to pester Turnus and signal his imminent death. But see Spaltenstein (1983) at 177 ("*Dira* signifie ici 'injures'").

2.17 See note to 1.173 regarding *longa dies* ("long life"). Given the verb, Agozzino at 178 is right to draw attention to the parallel of Juvenal 10.265 (*longa dies igitur quid contulit*).

The Ellis/Baehrens emendation of *non* for *nunc* ("now") has support in four manuscripts, but distorts the sense of the distich. See Ellis (1884b) at 155; Öberg at 165.

2.18 For *prodere* ("to screw") as "betray" and "thrust forward," see OLD 7, 8. It could be translated in other ways, including "reveal."

2.19 The earliest use of *nonne fuit melius* ("Wouldn't it have been better") seems to be Prudentius *Hamartigenia* 462 (*nonne fuit melius saevum Memphitidis aulae*); cf. Virgil *Eclogae* 2.14 (*nonne fuit satius*); Propertius 1.17.15 (*nonne fuit levius*); 2.15.11 (*nonne fuit satius*).

For *fungi* as "to have died," see OLD 2b, c. I assume it is shorthand for a phrase that would have *morte* or *via* after it. Cf. Agozzino at 178.

A more literal translation of *tali . . . tempore* ("right then") would be "at such a time."

2.22 The phrase *meritis . . . criminibus* ("with merited indictments") appears to be another import from the courts.

Spaltenstein (1983) at 178 argues that this line is "sans doute un des seuls véritables oxymores de ce texte." For other oxymorons in this text, see Altamura (1981) at 823.

2.23 There is a thoughtful discussion of the inherently paradoxical *nihil est quod* ("that . . . is nothing") in Fowler, "Latin Adjectival Clauses with the Subjunctive," 12, no. 22 *Classical Weekly* (1918) at 172–175. The phrase may be a Lucretian echo—it appears four times in Book 1 of *De rerum natura* at 1.430, 1.652, 1.1001, and 1.1070.

Franzoi and Spinazzè at 161 note that *totum quod viximus* ("All that we lived") exactly echoes Seneca *Phaedra* 776.

2.24 The simple but striking phrase *summa hora* ("at the final hour") feels familiar but does not appear to have antecedents. Webster at 91 notes that *suprema* would be the adjective expected where Maximianus used *summa*.

For *praeteriens* ("passing time"), cf. 2.11.

2.25–26 Wasyl (2011) at 136 rightly cites these and the next lines to reject Szövérffy's flimsy argument that Maximianus is a misogynist.

2.25 Guardalben (1993) correctly rejects Baehrens' *dumque* for *atque* ("and"). Goldlust (2013) at 146 suggests consideration of Meyers' oral suggestion of *atque eidem* for *dumque tamen* ("and yet, as"), a variant in several manuscripts, a view that I find unpersuasive. Gärtner argues for *at quamquam* as the first two words of this line. See Gärtner (2004) at 130.

2.26 These *notis* ("marks") are probably the bruises common in old age. The adjective *caeruleis* ("deep blue") is often associated with the ocean, and thus can mean dark blue or greenish blue, either of which is apt for bruises. Such marks may have been even more chilling for Maximianus' readers because their color evoked Virgil's description of a dragon's back. See *Aeneid* 5.87 (*caeruleae cui terga notae*); cf. Claudian *Panegyricus dictus Probino et Olybrio* at 215 (*caerulis infecta notis*).

Schetter (1970) at 77–79 argues for *caeruleus* over *caeruleis*, and a number of the manuscripts support that position, but I believe that the adjective modifies *notis*, and so I retain the Webster text here.

Schetter also argues for *inficit* over *infecit*, a variant present in many manuscripts, as well as *ora* over *hora* ("time"). For a defense of Schetter's version of this line, see Gärtner (2004); see also Öberg at 165. Ellis (1884b) at 156 assesses variants in this distich and also embraces *ora* over *hora*. Cf. Lucan *Bellum civile* 5.214 (*inficit ora*); Ovid *Metamorphoses* 3.76 (*ore niger Stygio vitiatas inficit umbras*); Prudentius *Cathemerinon* 10.98 (*color albidus inficit ora*); Tibullus 3.4.32 (*inficitur . . . ore*); Öberg at 165. Altamura notes the possible influence of Horace *Epodi* 7.15 (*ora inficit*). See Altamura (1981) at 821; Franzoi and Spinazzè at 161.

2.27 Ellis argues for Baehrens' *perstat* instead of *praestat* ("she stands out"), but I retain Webster's version based on sense and the weight of the manuscripts. See Ellis (1884b) at 156; cf. Spaltenstein (1983) at 180; Schneider (2003) at 214; Öberg at 165; Goldlust (2013) at 146; but see Agozzino at 180–181.

2.28 Spaltenstein at 180 sees a nonexistent double meaning in *despicit* ("resents"). He does, however, rightly criticize Baehrens for defending the variant *secum* for *mecum* ("with me"). See also Guardalben (1993) at 120.

2.29 For *fateor* ("I concede") as a parenthetical, see Webster at 91; Spaltenstein (1983) at 181.

2.30 The term *monimenta* ("a trace") is a variant of *monumenta*, which can mean memorial, tomb, reminder, or history. This line is perhaps further evidence for the argument made by Uden and Fielding (2010) at 439–460 that these elegies are colored not just by the decay of the human body but by the collapse of the empire and its physical structures. Note that Cassiodorus' letter to Maximianus instructs the author to do what he can to restore the collapsing glories of Rome's architecture. See Appendix A; see also Bjornlie (2009) at 164–165. No one word in English can capture the subtlety of Maximianus' metaphor here, which makes the physical collapse of Lycoris more striking and ghostly by comparing it to the ruined buildings all around. The term's hint of a tomb makes his comparison all the more apt.

Wernsdorf is right in seeing in this line an echo of Horace *Carmina* 4.13.28, but Webster at 91 stretches to add Horace *Carmina* 2.1.7.

Spaltenstein (1983) at 181 properly rejects Baehrens' conjecture of *micat* for *manet* ("stays").

2.31 For debate over the gender of *pulcris* ("the beautiful"), see Spaltenstein (1983) at 182. Spaltenstein sees this line as paradoxical, when it is not; Maximianus is merely noting an exception to a general rule.

2.32 Spaltenstein compares this use of *veteris* ("bygone") to Ovid *Metamorphoses* 1.237 (*fit lupus et veteris servat vestigia formae*).

2.33 There is a creepy quality to the trope of this line (*reliquiis* often has the sense of physical remains); in some bizarre way it seems akin to Maximianus' recurring "living dead" imagery.

2.34 Significant manuscripts and Webster include *set*, but the majority of manuscripts have *et* ("and"). See Webster at 37, 55. It appears to be a scribal error importing the word from the same position in 2.39, so I have used *et*.

I join Goldlust (2013) in rejecting Baehrens' emendation of *nunc* ("still") to *non*.

2.35 Guardalben (1993) at 119 rightly rejects the Baehrens emendation of *artus* for *actus* ("exploits"). I concur with Goldlust (2013) at 147 that *actus* ("exploits") encompasses both sexual and nonsexual exploits and that Spaltenstein (1983) at 182 unduly limits the term.

2.35–37 My translation does not mimic the end rhyme of these lines.

2.36 Webster correctly observes parallels in language, but not meaning, with Ovid *Remedia amoris* 12 (*praeteritum . . . opus*). See Webster at 92 (note the typographical error confusing line 39 with line 36). For nuances in the interpretation of *opus* ("accomplishments"), see Fielding (forthcoming) at 8–9.

2.37 Schneider (2003) at 215 notes that Schadd and Baehrens follow the conjecture of Withof at 321 of substituting *at* for *et* ("and"). But see Guardalben (1993) at 120. Some manuscripts have *set*, the same opening word of 2.39. From context it appears that in the Webster text the similar opening words of 2.37 and 2.39 have been reversed, and I have made the corresponding changes in my text.

2.38 For a sound rejection of Schetter's (1970) acrobatic emendation at 39 of *nemo qui me amplectitur* for Webster's *nullius amplexus* ("nobody . . . sex"), see Spaltenstein (1983) at 183, Guardalben (19930 at 120; cf. Schneider (2003) at 215, Webster at 92. Ellis would insert *ad* before *amplexus*. See Ellis (1884b) at 156.

For *quod memoretur* ("memory" or literally "what is recalled"), cf. note to 2.44. Boano correctly argues for *quod* instead of the *quos* of four manuscripts. See Boano (1949) at 214.

Agozzino at 183 unpersuasively defends Baehrens' speculative *notos* for *nullius*. For a metrical issue with *nullius*, see Altamura (1981) at 822. Two of the manuscripts have the appealing *nullus*, although one follows it with *ad* and one with *in*.

The phrase *in amplexu* was much more common than *ad amplexu*, and Statius used *nullus in amplexu*. See Statius *Thebaid* 5.73. Accordingly, I reluctantly use the *nullus* ("nothing") of the Palatinus 1573 manuscript, but use *in amplexu* ("of an embrace") instead of *amplexum* because most of Maximianus' sources, including Ovid, used *amplexu* in similar syntax. Regardless of emendations, this distich is challenging and obscure.

2.39 For *post omnia* ("after everything"), cf. Horace *Sermones* 1.86; Juvenal 8.97; Statius *Thebaid* 11.330–331. Cf. note to 2.41.

It is hard to judge whether *set* here is a throwback or a scribal error. Cf. notes to 2.34; 2.37.

2.40 A literal version of this line would be along the lines of: "I had as many good things then as the many losses I now lament."

2.41 The *omnia/omnia/omnes/omnia* combination in lines 2.39 and 2.41 is an unusual example of polyptoton not easily imitated in English.

2.42 This line is a paradox which restates a tenet of Augustan love elegy. See, e.g., Ovid *Amores* 1.7.38 (*forti victa puella viro est*). Enk at 74 notes the parallel to Propertius 3.11.16 (*vicit victorem candida forma virum*).Webster at 92 suggests that this line and the following lines are "philosophic fooling, in Ausonius' style." Agozzino at 183 misses the point and heritage of this paradox by futilely defending Baehrens' clunking emendation of *iuncta* for *victa* ("won"). While this aphoristic line can be read in several ways, it seems to flash some wry humor that expresses sympathy for women.

2.43 This bleak sentiment, driven home by the comparison denying the existence of a human soul, reflects Maximianus' dour form of Lucretianism.

Guardalben (1993) at 120 rightly defends Webster's *manebunt* ("will remain") over Baehrens' *valebunt*. See also Goldlust (2013) at 147; but see Agozzino at 184.

Altamura sees a metrical issue with *ergo* ("thus"). See Altamura (1981) at 822.

2.44 The phrase *quod memoretur* ("will be what's recalled") echoes the *quod memoretur* of 2.38. Webster at 37 reads *quod* differently and renders this line as a question.

2.45 Amid manuscript disagreement documented by Webster at 37 and Schetter (1970) at 24–27, Schneider (2003) at 215 rejects Webster, then follows Schetter (1970) at 24 and Schadd in adopting *fugiant* for *fugiunt* ("avoid"). I follow Guardalben at 120 in retaining the Webster text.

2.45–50 Spaltenstein (1983) at 187 and Agozzino at 184 note the parallels between these lines and Theoderic's message to a Maximianus and an Andreas (perhaps the same Andreas promoted many years later to department head in *Variae* 11.21) at Cassiodorus *Variae* 1.21 (*Aves ipsae per aera vagantes proprios nidos amant: erratiles ferae ad cubilia dumosa festinant: voluptosi pisces campos liquidos transeuntes cauernas suas studiosa indagatione perquirunt cunctaque animalia ubi se norunt refugere, longissima cupiunt aetate constare*). These parallels (and other parallels noted below) suggest that Maximianus carefully read the *Variae*, which improves the odds that the letter to Maximianus in Appendix A is a memorandum to our elegist.

2.45 Guardalben (1993) at 120 and Schetter (1970) at 24 reject Baehrens' *at* in favor of Webster's *cum* ("while").

2.47 Schneider (2003) at 215 notes that Schetter (1970) at 24, Schadd, and Guardalben (1970) at 120 have *umbra* (also in at least three of the manuscripts) for Webster's *umbram* ("in shade"). Cf. Franzoi and Spinazzè at 163; Spaltenstein (1983) at 187; Goldlust (2013) at 148. The verb *requiescere* ("to rest") often takes the ablative. See OLD 2 and 3. Accordingly, I emend the Webster text consistent with comments by Schetter et al.

Guardalben (1993) at 120 accepts Webster's *decubuit* ("he has lain") over Baehrens' *consuerit*. Cf. Goldlust (2013) at 148.

2.49–52 The four consecutive end rhymes here, which I cannot duplicate, are unusual in sixth-century Latin poetry even though poets of this era use more end rhyme than their predecessors.

2.51–52 Franzoi and Spinazzè at 95 reject the tradition of rendering this distich as a question, but it seems to me that this sudden address to the reader doesn't work as a declarative sentence because, ironically perhaps, Maximianus doesn't know enough to make an affirmative statement. Either way it is cryptic, and it has crossed my mind that it may be an ironic self-deprecatory comment on his adventures—personal or professional—discussed in elegy 5.

2.52 The noun *hospitia* ("accomodations") could mean either "physical lodgings," "hospitality," or "sponsorship" (as in the financial and political support rich Romans gave to poets and others). For a thoughtful overview of *hospitia*, see Nicol, "Hospitality among the Romans" in Peachin at 422–437.

The phrase *non manifesta* ("unclear") is Ovidian. See Ovid *Metamorphoses* 1.404, 15.579.

2.53 The phrase *certis rebus* ("sure things") has roots in law, rhetoric, and Lucretius. See, e.g., Lucretius *De rerum natura* 1.813, 4.218, 6.924; Gaius *Institutionem epitome* 1.147; Justinian *Digesta Iustiniani* 36.1.30.2, 36.158.2; Cicero *In Verrem* 1.37.8, Cicero *Rhetorica ad Herennium* 2.39.4.

2.54 For *eventus varios* ("uncertain outcomes"), cf. Pliny *Naturalis historia praefatio* 12 (*eventus varios*); Ammianus *Res gestae* 21.16.14 (*eventus variante*); Caesar *De bello Gallico* 2.22.1.1 (*eventus varii*).

2.55 Agozzino at 185 cites *grandaevus* ("ancient") as an example of elevated poetic language.

2.56 Maximianus' use of the phrase *animos conciliare solet* ("tends to bring together minds") may reflect reading of Cicero. See generally Fantham, "Ciceronian *Conciliare* and Aristotelian Ethos," 27, no. 3 *Phoenix* (1973). See *De officiis* 2.7 (*conciliare animos humanum*); cf. Avianus *Fabulae* 32.10 (*animis conciliare tuis*). The intimacy of this aphoristic direct address suggests that Maximianus recited, or intended to recite, his elegies to a select number of contemporaries. Agozzino at 186 sees an unlikely connection to Horace *Epistulae* 1.10.4–5.

2.57–58 Webster at 93 veers off the rails when he claims that this distich is "very evidently Ausonian," which it is not, and that his declared parallel "makes it pretty certain that Elegy II is no more autobiographical or personal than I."

2.59 For more information on *colonis* in Late Antiquity as "tenant farmers," see Sessa (2012) at 46–47.

Franzoi and Spinazzè at 164 note that *reverentia prisca* ("The old respect") parallels Claudian *Carmina minora* 30.139 (*reverentia . . . prisca*).

2.60 Spaltenstein (1983) at 190 rightly mocks Webster's suggestion at 93 that the polyptoton of *milite miles* ("soldier . . . soldier") has "a hint of 'Love's warfare.'" Webster's misreading reveals the risk of reading each line of Maximianus as if it were lifelessly encased in the classical love elegy tradition. Despite this warning, for Ovid's use of military metaphors to describe romantic conquest, see Murgatroyd, "*Militia amoris* and the Roman Elegist," 34 *Latomus* (1975) at 77–79; Cahoon, "The Bed as Battlefield; Erotic Conquest and Militiary Metaphors in Ovid's *Amores*," 118 *Transactions of the American Philological Society* (1988) at 293–307. This image of the aging soldier loving the youthful soldier may foreshadow Maximianus loving the singer Candida at 4.26; both descriptions rely on declarations that include *amat* ("loves").

2.61 There is no manuscript or other support for Baehrens (followed by Fels) emending *cessisse* ("that's been retired") to *cessasse*. See Schneider (2003) at 216; Öberg at 166; Guardalben (1993) at 120.

2.63 I follow Webster as well as Spaltenstein (1983) at 191, Guardalben (1993) at 120, and Schetter (1970) at 24 in using *non* ("not") instead of Baehrens' *nec*; *nec* is used in six manuscripts. See also Öberg at 166; Franzoi and Spinazzè at 165.

The noun *floris* ("blossoming") is often used metaphorically. See OLD 3. Maximianus may be undercutting this grandiose self-assessment in the following line if you accept Webster's *media dicta* (which might best be translated as "plain-spoken").

2.64 Webster at 93 notes a metrical objection to *media*, but retains it over other alternatives. On the advice of Michael Roberts, I have used the metrically superior *mea facta* ("my works") of the Leidensis Lipsii 36 and Britannicus Reg. 15, A.7 manuscripts for *media dicta*. Schneider (2003) at 216, Schetter (1970) at 41, and Goldlust (2013) at 148 all follow Webster's *dicta*. Schneider notes that Fo (1987) at 113 and Guardalben (1993) at 120 substitute *facta* (as do Franzoi and Spinazzè at 165), and that Öberg and Fels use Baehrens' *fata*. Welsh also makes a plausible case for the speculative *ficta*. See Welsh (2011) at 219.

2.65 Ellis argues that elision in Maximianus is rare and generally confined to words with a short *e*, *que*, *atque*, or syllables that precede *est*. This line is one of three that Ellis cites as having unusual elision. Ellis (1884a) at 14. Cf. 3.66, 5.99.

Webster at 93 notes that Dracontius 8.236 and Corippus *Iohannis* 7.202 also close with *veneranda senectus* (combined with *est* as "respect old age").

2.66 The verb *nosti* ("you knew") is the syncopated form of *novisti*.

2.67 The verb *condemnet* ("would condemn") was primarily a legal term, although Cicero uses it regularly.

For *in alterius . . . crimine* ("another's . . . for its wrongdoing"), cf. Gratian *De vera et falsa penitentia* D.6.1.3 (*in alterius crimine*).

2.68 Webster at 93 notes that *claudere . . . iter* ("to block the path") is an Ovidian trope. See *Metamorphoses* 8.549, *Epistulae ex Ponto* 1.1.6, *Fasti* 1.272, *Tristia* 3.6.16.

For a thoughtful discussion of minor variants in this line, see Schetter (1970) at 41–43.

2.69 For the verb *dedignaris* ("you refuse") Altamura suggests an echo of Ovid *Epistulae ex Ponto* 1.7.33 (*dedignatus amicum*). See Altamura (1981) at 821.

The sentiment that naming someone fondly is a kind act may have been inspired by Horace *Sermones* 1.3.43–66. Fielding (forthcoming) at 9–10 notes a more specific parallel with Lygdamus' first elegy. See Tibullus 3.1.23 (*haec tibi vir quondam nunc frater*). See also Consolino (1997) at 392.

2.70 I reject Ellis' argument for substituting the *affectus* of the Bodleian and Britannicus Reg. 15, A. 7 manuscripts for *affectum* ("affection"). See Ellis (1884b) at 156–157.

2.71 For *pietas* as "duty," see Nathan at (2000) 26.

Wasyl and Fo both criticize this distich as disjointed, an objection that understimates the theatrical flavor of this exit. See Fo (1986–1987) at 96: Wasyl (2011) at 135.

2.73 For more on *lacrimis* ("with . . . tears") among elegiac lovers, see generally James, "Her Time to Cry: The Politics of Weeping in Roman Love Elegy," 133, no. 1 *Transactions of the American Philological Society* (2003) at 99–122.

The idiom *quantum fas* ("as much as proper") can have either a religious or secular sense. Given the nonreligious tone of the elegies, I do not want to import the religious sense into the line. Cf. Rufinus *Historia ecclesiastica* 1.2.7 (*quantum fas erat deum hominibus*).

For a discussion of the syntax of this line and how it relates to *longos . . . annos* ("long years"), see Gärtner (2004) at 133; Schneider (2003) at 198. I imitate this internal rhyme in my translation.

2.74 I translate *quod doleat* (literally "what hurts") as "pain."

Elegy 3

3.1 The phrase *operae pretium* ("worthwhile"—literally closer to "the price of the work") is an idiom and a bit of a poetic cliché. See Webster at 95; OLD 2b. Spaltenstein (1983) at 195–196 notes the phrase goes as far back as Ennius *Annales* 465 *(audire est operae pretium)*, which tends to undercut Uden's argument that *operae* here functions as a sexual pun. See Uden (2009) at 219; cf. Horace *Sermones* 1.2.37 (*operae pretium*).

For a discussion of parallelism between the opening of this elegy and elegy 4, see Franzoi (2011) at 162.

3.2 For *pauca referre* ("say a bit"), cf. Virgil *Aeneid* 4.333, 8154, 10.17; Ovid *Fasti* 2.104, 3.8.28.

3.3–4 The phrase *rerum vertigine* ("by change"—literally "by a turn in things") may echo Lucan *Bellum civile* 8.16–17 (*vertigine rerum / attoniti*). Fielding (forthcoming) at 10 also notes Lucretius *De rerum natura* 8.16–17 (*vertigine rerum /*

attoniti). Cf. Lucan (ed. Postgate, 1917) at 37–38; Ammianus *Res gestae* 31.19 (*in ipsa vertigine pereuntium rerum*).

The phrase *fractam mentem* ("a mind undone") may be Senecan. Cf. *De consolatione ad Polybium* 5 (*si fractam ducis sui mentem viderint*).

The phrase *mentem . . . erigat* ("uplift a mind") has strong Christian overtones. See, e.g., Augustine *Sermones* 4.352.2 (*erigant mentes*); Ennodius *Dictio* 8.1.18 (*erigere mens*). Although Uden reasonably translates *erigat* as "excite" and Lind (1988) at 328 mistranslates it as "clear," it was originally a construction term (an area of expertise for Maximianus if we believe he is the addressee of the letter from Cassiodorus in Appendix A). See Uden (2009) at 219. In this context and in some of the later religious uses, it retains some hint of building something up, and here its meaning is closest to "raise" or "lift up." Ennodius also uses it in his long poem celebrating the marriage of Maximus. See *Epthalamium dictum Maximo V.S.* at 7 (*Erigitur genio tellus tumefacta marito*).

3.5 It is traditional for elegists to identify a beloved with a pseudonym, often the metrical equivalent of her real name. In the previous elegy Maximianus called the object of his affections "Lycoris," a name for a lover used by Gallus and Catullus. Given that Aquilina maintains her virginity despite her best intentions to do otherwise, Maximianus may draw the name from the late third-century virgin martyr, Saint Aquilina, who was tortured and then beheaded at the age of twelve. Uden argues, probably correctly, that Maximianus is blending—with subversive intent—the *puella* of Augustan elegy with the virgin martyr of Late Antique popular hagiography. See Uden (2009) at 207–222.

Maximianus' sources are unclear, though Uden notes similarities between elegy 3 and Prudentius *Peristephanon,* Damasus *Epigrammata*, and the *Passio Agnetis* often attributed to Ambrose. Uden (2009) at 211. Saint Aquilina was known for a church dedicated to her in Constantinople, which was destroyed in the Nika Riots of 532. This event would have been recent history for Maximianus, and the selection of the name "Aquilina" may hint at anxiety about civil disorder. Franzoi and Spinazzè at 168 note that "Aquilina" derives from *aquilus*, a color between black and brown, which contrasts with the pseudonym in the next elegy of *Candida*, which means "white" or "shining."

3.5–6 The repetition of *captus amore tuo* ("seduced by love for you") at the beginning and the end of the distich is an example of "serpentine verse" (sometimes known as ophite verse), a much-reviled technique used occasionally in classical times. See, e.g., Ovid *Amores* 1.9.1–2. To the consternation of future scholars, it became popular in Late Antiquity.

The phrase *demens . . . ferebar* ("I went mad"—literally "I was borne off out of my mind") may echo Virgil *Aeneid* 2.588 (*furiata mente ferebar*).

The adjective *pallidus* ("pale") is a standard way of describing the lovesick. See generally Franzoi and Spinazzè at 169.

3.8 The term *rusticitate* ("awkwardess") is derived from *rus* ("country") and has a strong suggestion of country/city class divisions. This mention of *rusticitate* may be another indication that Maximianus grew up outside of Rome before he took to roaming *mediam Romam* for young women. Cf. 1.62–63. Goldlust (2013) at 150 notes Ovid's use of the term to describe someone inexperienced in amorous adventures. Cf. Ovid *Heroides* 17.188; *Ars amatoria* 1.670.

3.9 Franzoi and Spinazzè at 169 note that *nec minus ille meo* ("She . . . not any less . . . than me") echoes Ovid *Epistulae ex Ponto* 4.9.14 (*nec minus ille meus*). He also criticizes Schneider (2003), who uses Webster's *meo* instead of *mei*, perhaps because he views the phrase as litotes when it is more of a comparison. Franzoi and Spinazzè at 169–170.

3.11 Maximianus' elegies are thoroughly infused with the work of Ovid but show few or no traces of Propertius or Tibullus. More than a century ago B. O. Foster argued that this line echoes Propertius 3.11 and, in addition, that five lines of elegy 5 also echo Propertius. See Foster, "Propertius III 24," 30,, no. 1 *American Journal of Philology* (1909) at 60. (Maximianus 5.20/Propertius 1.18.17, Maximianus 5.23/Propertius 3.19.3, Maximianus 5.25/Propertius 3.8.25, Maximianus 5.41/Propertius 3.8.19, Maximianus 53–58/Propertius 1.9.33–34). Foster's comparisons are unpersuasive; Enk at 74 lists more persuasive parallels. The most strenuous effort to show influences of Propertius is Altamura (1981) at 821; see also Merone (1950) at 336; Uden (2012) at 459–460.

For *carmina*, rare in this usage, as "carding combs" (carding combs were used in weaving), see Webster at 96. Some commentators prefer the variant reading *stamina*, which is a slightly different version of the same image. See Boano (1949) at 215. Spaltenstein (1983) at 199 and Ellis (1884b) at 157 cite Claudian *In Eutropium* 2.458 (*quam bene texentum laudabas carmina tutus*) as support for *carmina*. Others would translate *carmina* as "poems" or "songs." See, e.g., Lind at 328; but see Relihan (2007) at 149; Goldlust (2011) at 63 (translating *carmina* as "*carde*"). If the carding comb image is correct, it reinforces the parallel between Aquilina and Penelope, who used her weaving to fend off suitors while waiting for Odysseus to return.

The missing conjunction in this line is another example of the rhetorical device of asyndeton. Cf. note to 1.119.

3.13 For *viam* as "method," see OLD 6–10.

For *caecum . . . ignem* ("hidden fire"), see Virgil *Aeneid* 4.2 (*caeco . . . igni*). Guardalben (1993) at 120–121 and Schetter (1970) at 83 accept Webster's *qua caecum* ("that . . . hidden") over Baehrens' *qua caecum*. Spaltenstein (1983) at 199 concurs with Schetter. Cf. Franzoi and Spinazzè 92014) (2009) at 402. For intriguing but unlikely sources for *pasceret ignem* ("would feed the . . . fire"), see Franzoi and Spinazzè at 170.

Heege at 14 notes that *nec reperire viam* ("she found no method") echoes Virgil *Aeneid* 5.807 (*nec reperire viam*).

3.14 The phrase *alternis notis* ("with two-way signals") describes elegiac lovers communicating surreptitiously through techniques such as a *nutis amantis* ("a lover's nod"). See, e.g., Tibullus 1.8.1–2. For a more detailed description, see Ovid *Amores* 1.4.13–28. In essence, Maximianus is saying he does not know *how* to be an elegiac lover despite Aquilina's amorous intentions. Fielding makes a persuasive case that this line and following lines allude to the Pyramus and Thisbe section of

Ovid *Metamorphoses* at 4.55–166. See Fielding (forthcoming) at 40–50; cf. Tibullus 1.2.22 (*verba notis*); Kleywegt (2005) at 256 (arguing *reddere verba* can mean either "respond" or just "communicate").

3.15 Webster at 96 notes that this line may echo Virgil *Eclogae* 2.5 (*studio iactabant inani*).

3.16 Spaltenstein (1983) at 200 misreads *anxia* ("anxious") by equating it with "*amoreux*," a reading that makes this line banal and ignores the anxieties of the scene.

3.17 The noun *pedagogus* ("Her tutor"), usually a slave who accompanied children to school, was the Late Antique version of the classical *paedagogus*. The *paedagogus* is a regular character in Greek and Roman comedy who typically succeeds in protecting the morality of his charges less well than Aquilina's tutor does in elegy 3. For a metrical issue, see Altamura (1981) at 822.

Schneider (2003) at 217 notes that Petschenig, Prada, Schadd, and Öberg defend Webster's *agit* ("chased") over the *adit* preferred by Guardalben, Franzoi, and Baehrens. There is also manuscript support for *alit*. See Öberg at 168. Once one accepts *agit*, it does not provide much precision—one could argue that the tutor did anything from fending him off with an evil eye to striking him. For metrical concern about *agit*, see Altamura (1981). Michael Roberts has suggested to me the possibility of wordplay with *agit* and *pedagogus*.

3.19 For *nutusque* ("and nods"), cf. Ovid *Amores* 3.11.23 (*nutus*), 1.4.17 (*nutusque*); *Ars amatoria* 1.138 (*nutus*), *Metamorphoses* (*nutu signisque loquuntur*).

Ellis argues for the *prensabant* of the Florentinus and Britannicus Add. 21, 213 manuscripts over *pensabant* ("they scrutinized"). See Ellis (1884b) at 157.

3.20 Guardalben (1993) at 121 follows Spaltenstein (1983) in accepting Baehrens' *calor* over Webster's *color* ("coloring"). See also Franzoi (2009) at 403. I have hesitantly rejected their emendation.

I have accepted the *dicere* ("to signal") of three manuscripts over Webster's *ducere*.

3.21 For *dum licuit* as "When possible," see Spaltenstein (1983) at 202.

Franzoi and Spinazzè at 172 note that *compressimus ambo* ("we both stifled") seems to anticipate the climactic *discedimus ambo* ("Both . . . we split up") of 3.93.

3.23 For criticism of the meter of *verecundia* ("modesty"), see Kaster (1988) at 61, 207; Sandys (1906) at 448; Ellis (1884a) at 14; Nisard (1863) at 610. Such concerns provoked Ellis to suggest the unintelligible emendation *iracundia*. See Ellis (1884b) at 157.

Blushing for the Romans was a sign of desire, not modesty. See Adams (1982) at 54–55. For the significance of *frontem* ("face"), see Spaltenstein (1983) at 202. See also Schneider (2003) at 217 on Quintilian *Institutio oratoria* 2.4.16 (*frons inverecunda*). For Ennodius' use of the term, see note to 5.55.

3.24 Spaltenstein (1983) at 203 notes that *penitus . . . recepta* ("deep hidden") also occurs at Ovid *Fasti* 5.403. See also Franzoi (2009) at 403.

Franzoi notes a precedent for the combination of *valet* with a passive infinitive in Prudentius *Peristephanon* 10.314. Franzoi (2009) at 403.

3.26 For *superciliis luminibusque* ("with eyebrows and our eyes"), cf. Cicero *Orationes pro Roscio comoedo* 20 (*oculi supercilia*); Augustine *In Ioannis evangelium* 124.23.9 (*superciliis oculis*); Ambrose *Hexaemeron* 6.9.59 (*superciliis oculi*). Maximianus uses the less common noun *lumen* rather than the more common and more clinical *oculus*. This preference may not be purely poetic because Romans typically believed, based on Greek science, that light from the eyes combines with light from an object to create vision. This concept is clear in the opening two words (*lux oculis*) of the second poem of the *Appendix Maximiani* (see Appendix B.2).

3.28 Webster at 97 argues—unconvincingly—that the sense of this line combined with its internal rhyme echoes Tibullus 1.1.20 (*illa pedem nullo ponere posse sono*) and that it is the best evidence of Tibullus providing a model for Maximianus. Spaltenstein (1983) at 204 and Franzoi and Spinazzè at 172 make similar arguments.

Schneider (2003) at 217 defends Webster's *tota* over the *muta* ("without a sound") conjectured by Baehrens and defended by Fels, Guardalben, and Agozzino. I have followed Baehrens.

3.29–30 Uden (2009) at 210 notes that Aquilina's mother intended to cure *vulnera*, the metaphorical wounds of elegy, with *vulneribus*, actual physical wounds. See generally Adams (1982) at 152. *Vulnera vulneribus* ("the wounds with wounds") is an example of polyptoton and antanaclasis. Webster at 97 is vague and arrogant in his dismissal of this line as "another instance of Ausonian trifling."

There are two intriguing parallels for *sensit* in *furtivum sensit amorem* ("sensed our secret love"). See Claudian *De raptu Proserpinae* 2.1.274 (*et primi suspiria sensit amoris*); Propertius 1.15.17 (*Hypsipyle nullos post illos sensit amores*). Altamura (1981) at 821 notes Virgil *Aeneid* 4.171 (*furtivum . . . amorem*).

3.31 Ellis (1884b) at 158 notes *caedis* at Ovid *Amores* 1.7.27 and states that *caedibus* ("slaps") is "unexampled." In fact, classical writers such as Livy, Silius, Statius, and Tacitus use *caedibus* frequently, as do such later Christian writers as Augustine, Cassiodorus, Damasus, Orosius, and Prudentius. Spaltenstein (1983) at 205 mistranslates *caedibus* as "mouvements de va-et-vient." I interpret *caedibus* as mock-heroic with a tone similar to the Greek girl's lament in Elegy V.

3.33 For *concipiunt* as "ignite" see OLD 1b.

3.34 Enk at 74 notes that *saevit amore dolor* ("anguish . . . with love is raging") echoes Propertius 2.8.36 (*saevit amore dolor*).

3.35 The phrase *per totum* ("around") is the Late Antique version of *ex totum*.

I have followed Spaltenstein (1983) at 206 and Goldlust (2013) at 153 (arguing that *visceribus*, despite being plural, should be translated as *Coeur*). For *anhelis* as a modifier of *visceribus*, cf. Cassiodorus *De anima* 12.18 (*non aestus anhelum corpus exurit*). For possible associations with martyrologies and a well-reasoned rejection of Spaltenstein's interpretation of *anhelis* as "whistling," see Uden (2009) at 213.

Baehrens and Ellis conjecture *tum* for *tunc* ("then"). See Ellis (1884b) at 158.

3.36 The term *emptum* ("purchase") at first seems oddly transactional here, although Uden cites *Corinthians* 7.23 ("You were bought with a price") and other sources to place it in the Christian tradition of bodily sacrifice. Uden (2009) at 214; see also Grensted at 5–6, 32–55. His point is strengthened by the following line, which evokes the wounds of Christ displayed after he emerged from his tomb, and the bloodstained relics of Christ's shroud. Uden also notes that St. Eulalia similarly takes pride in her wounds in Prudentius *Peristephanon* 3, an author Maximianus appears to have parodied sacrilegiously in elegy 5. See note to 5.37–38.

3.37 I use Uden's thoughtful "stained" for *turpesque*. Uden (2009) at 210. Cf. Traina (1987) at 54–57, (1988) at 122.

Uden also sees a connection between *memorare* ("recollect") and the *memoria* of Late Antiquity, which are shrines to martyrs. Uden (2009) at 219. Franzoi and Spinazzè at 175 argue that *nec memorare pudet* ("She's shameless . . . recollect") echoes the *nec memorare pudet* of Statius *Thebaid* 9.423.

I cannot find another use of *revolvere* ("to roll back") with *vestes* ("clothing"). In the sixth century the verb is most associated with the rolling back of the boulder outside the tomb of Jesus. Perhaps due to this novelty, there is a surprising amount of disagreement over the seemingly noncontroversial *vestes* ("clothing"). Guardalben (1993) at 121 accepts the conjecture of Traina of *restes* over the Baehrens conjecture of *caedes*. See Traina (1988) at 54–57.See also Goldlust (2013) at 153–154. For support of Webster's *vestes*, see Ellis (1884a) at 12. Some of my readers have been ardent in their support of the Baehrens conjecture, but I think that reading is hard to reconcile with the verb *revolvere* and neglects the significance of bloodstained clothing in Christian martyrologies, which I believe Maximianus is satirizing. Aquilina's blows here are probably not from Maximianus given the innocence of their relationship, but from her mother, hence her "martyrdom" is humorously inflated.

3.40 The noun *pretium* ("return") retains some of the commercial flavor of *emptum*. See note to 3.36. It may echo Augustine or other Christian writers. See, e.g., Augustine *Sermones* 1.70.4 (*quod emptum est pretio sanguinis Christi*). Franzoi and Spinazzè at 174 note the parallel of *pretium dulce* ("the sweet return") with Ovid *Amores* 2.8.21 (*pretium . . . dulce*).

3.41 Uden notes that the phrase *certa fides* ("faith . . . certain") appears to recall both professions of faith in Christian literature and the *fides* of elegiac lovers, particularly Ovidian ones. See Uden (2009) at 214; see also Schneider (2003) at 218. Webster at 98 notes that the phrase occurs at Horace *Carmina* 3.16.30, Propertius 3.8.19, and Ovid *Tristia* 4.3.14. Franzoi and Spinazzè at 174 note that *modo certa . . . voluntas* ("just . . . certain . . . will") echoes Ovid *Ars amatoria* 3.617 (*modo certa voluntas*).

The adjective *inconcussa* ("unbroken") is somewhat rare, but Seneca uses it at least nineteen times.

3.42 Schneider (2003) at 87 argues that the false quantity of *passio* ("passion") reflects the satirical tone of the passage. See also Webster at 98. Uden argues that the word evokes martyrdom. Uden (2009) at 214; see also Roberts (1993) at 39–43. Spaltenstein (1983) at 208 and Goldlust (2013) at 154 mistranslate it as "*douleur.*"

By using "ruined" for *imminuit* I try to capture both the primary sense of "diminish" and the sexual sense of "deflowered" described in Uden (2009) at 214.

3.43 The term *stimulis* ("goads"), a reference to cattle goads or spurs, is common in elegiac poetry. See Anderson (1997) at 243. Cf. Claudian *De quarto consolatu Honorii Augusti panegyris* 252 (*stimulis nunc flagrat amorum*).

3.44 While the term *salutis* ("rescue") seems to suggest the Christian meaning of "salvation," Maximianus' use of the term is secular and the line probably echoes Ovid *Tristia* 1.2.33 (*nec spes est ulla salutis*).

3.45 Spaltenstein (1983) at 209 and Goldlust (2013) at 154 incorrectly assert that *carpebar* ("I was bothered" in the sense of "harried") "est rare dans ce contexte." The use of the passive form of *carpo* in association with the injuries of love goes back at least to Virgil's Dido. *Aeneid* 4.1–2 (*At regina gravi iamdudum saucia cura / vulnus alit venis et caeco carpitur igni*).

3.46 The phrase *vocis habet opus* ("took the place of words") literally means something closer to "had a word's function." But see Spaltenstein (1983) at 209.

3.47 Barnish argues that Boethius' role in assisting this love affair "recalls *Variae*, I.10, I.45, and II.40, in all of which he is called in by the government as a technical assistant and adviser." Barnish (1990) at 20. He also argues at 28 that Maximianus' familiarity with the written text of the *Consolatio*, which was probably not published before the death of Theodahad in 536, suggests that Maximianus "was likely to have enjoyed the confidence of Boethius' family," a conclusion that discounts many other possible ways that he could have obtained access to the manuscript before publication.

Uden argues, rightly I believe, that with this portrayal of the Ovidian *praeceptor amoris* ("teacher of love") Maximianus presents "a brutally deromanticizing reading of the elegiac tradition." See Uden (2009) at 217.

Some commentators see dark echoes in Maximianus' choice of the word *scrutator* ("searcher"). Shanzer cites Lactantius *De mortibus persecutorum* 10.1 and notes that Lactantius used the term in mockery "of Diocletian anxiously poking at viscera to discover the future." See Shanzer (1983) at 189–190. For Jerome's use of the term in *Vulgata proverbia* 25–27, see Uden (2009) at 216. Given Boethius' role in this elegy as a procurer, one has to wonder whether Maximianus was punning on *scortator* ("one who associates with prostitutes"), perhaps primarily for the amusement of a select number of insiders at a recitation. *Scrutator* was a rare term but a favorite of Ennodius. See, e.g., *Carmina* 2.16.7 (*Scrutator fulvum concessit pallidus aurum*). Cf. Boethius *Consolatio philosophiae* 1.6.2.6 (*rerum altius perscrutemur*). Shanzer (1983) at 189, probably inadvertently, lays the foundation for viewing this term as a pun by noting that *scrutator* "is normally used of poking, delving or grubbing around for things." See also Wasyl at 141.

Barnish speculates that *scrutator* had "been designed to put a harmless interpretation on those scientific studies which (citation omitted) had probably generated the charge of sorcery against Boethius" (27). One has to question whether Maximianus was as sympathetic to Boethius as that argument suggests. Zurli argues, based in part on his reading of the verb *scrutatur* in line 166 of the anonymous poem (probably from fifth-century North Africa) *Aegritudo Perdicae* (*sic fatus fessae scrutatur conscia venae*), that the term has a medical flavor. See Zurli (1991) at 313–314; see also Franzoi (2009) at 404.

Vitiello (2006) at 185 makes an interesting observation that suggests that the mockery of Boethius was even more nuanced than generally appreciated. Ennodius had a low opinion of Boethius for many reasons, including disputes over real estate. He also notes that in *Epistulae* 8.1.26 (miscited) Ennodius refers to Boethius as *avidus maximum rerum possessor* ("a greedy owner of things"). The verbal similarity to Maximianus' *magnarum scrutator maxime rerum* suggests that Maximianus is reminding his contemporaries of Ennodius' view of Boethius' greed and sexual procilivities. See Appendix C; see also Carini at 67–75; Anastasi (1948) at 81–84.

Shanzer notes that two critics (Alfonsi and Boano) comment on "an unusual feature of Maximianus' poetry: the almost total absence of myth and mythological baggage, aside from the most obviously metonymised deities." Shanzer (1983) at 192. Shanzer then suggests that the figure of Boethius in this elegy serves as a substitute for the traditional mythological characters. For an overview of scholarly comment on this scene, see Goldlust (2013) at 155–157. Fielding argues that this scene is based in part on an epigram of Maccius (*AP* 5.132=12 Sider). See Fielding (2016) at 11–12.

3.48 For a summary of varying critical reaction to Maximianus' portrayal of Boethius, see articles cited in Barnish (1990) at 21–22; see also Szövérffy (1968) at 360; Shanzer (1983) at 187–188; Bertini (1981) at 273–283; Fo (1986–1987) at 99–100. This portrayal of Boethius seems to have influenced Chaucer's description of Pandarus in *Troilus and Criseyde*. See Mitchell, "Chaucer's Portrayal of Pandarus in *Troilus and Criseyde*," 50, no. 4 *Notes and Queries* (2003) at 377–380. For metrical concern about *boeti* ("Boethius"), see Altamura (1981) at 822; Webster at 98.

The phrase *fers . . . opem* ("bring assistance") is common, particularly in Ovid. See, e.g., *Metamorphoses* 3.719 (*fer opem*), 5.618 (*fer opem*), 13.669 (*fer opem*), 13.671 (*ferre opem*). Webster at 98 and Shanzer (1983) at 190 see it as a pun; in Greek the verb "boethio" means "to bring help." Fielding suggests that it "seems to affirm his belonging to the Roman philhellenic movement in which Boethius had been a key figure." Fielding (2016) at 10–11.

The term *miseratus* ("showing pity") is a commonplace used by Virgil and analyzed by such grammarians as Priscian, Pompeius, and Servius. See, e.g., *Aeneid* 4.370 (*miseratus amantem*), *Georgica* 1.466 (*ille etiam extincto miseratus Caesare Romam*); see O'Sullivan (2004) at 107. Franzoi and Spinazzè at 176 note a surprising potential source of *fers miseratus opem* in Paulinus Petricordiae *De visitatione nepotuli sui* 19 (*fers miseratus*). Maximianus may have been searching for poems on old age; Franzoi's case is strengthened by the phrase *lamentae senectae* ("complaints of old age") in line 20. Cf. Franzoi (2011) at 164.

3.51 Webster at 98 notes that *peste teneri* ("gripped by . . . sickness") also closes Virgil *Aeneid* 4.90. A person who treats those sick with love by enabling them to obtain the affections of a beloved was a stock figure of the stage and poetry. See Barnish (1990) at 23; Wilhelm (1907) at 608–609.

Guardalben (1993) at 121 offers *prospiciens e tali* for Webster's *prospiciens tali me* ("Sensing . . . I . . . violent") and Baehrens' speculative *prospiciens e tacita*.

3.52 The phrase *mitibus alloquiis* ("softly"—more literally "with soft words") may echo Ausonius. See Shanzer (1988) at 260. Commentators tend to miss the humor of this phrase; Boethius' words that follow this description are brusque commands.

Spaltenstein at 211–212 mistranslates *pandere* ("opening") as a poeticism that means "to speak."

Shanzer argues that this line and the following lines "almost certainly parody Philosophia's help tendered to Boethius." Shanzer (1983) at 190.

3.53 For a thorough review of the variants of *dicito* ("Speak!"), see Schneider (2003) at 218. The command *dicito* appears rarely in classical poetry, although it appears six times in Cicero's *Orationes*. It does, however, appear thirty-four times in the comedies of Plautus, and one has to wonder whether Maximianus was cuing his reader to the comic content of his exchange with Boethius with a familiar comedic term. The role played by Boethius here—a man asked for advice by a lovesick young man—was a stock character in Roman comedy. The anaphora of *dicito* reinforces the theatricality of this distich. Guardalben (1993) at 121 argues for the variant *dic ait* over Webster's *dicito*.

The term *unde* ("from whom") is elevated with legal connotations. See Vidén (1984) at 127–131. Baehrens speculatively emends it to *quando*.

I have rejected Ellis' argument that Webster's *et* should be deleted in line 53 based on the Bodleian manuscript and metrical issues, see Ellis (1894) at 235, as well as his emendation of *dic ais* in line 53 and *dicas* in line 54 for *dicito*. See Ellis (1884b) at 159.

3.54 The term *edicti* ("claimed") has a bit of the legal/administrative flavor that comes from *edictum* and *edictio*, words closer to our "edict." Cassiodorus uses the term often in the *Variae*. The *Edictum Theoderici*, an important legal directive, was issued around 500 AD. The term may have a sarcastic undercurrent in this context. Guardalben (1993) at 121 accepts Webster's *et edicti* ("And . . . claimed") over Baehrens' *en dicti*.

3.55 For *non intellecti* as "undiagnosed," see Spaltenstein (1983) at 212.

For a discussion of the medical trope *curatio morbi* ("treatment for...disease"), see Agozzino at 43–44.

3.56 The phrase *inclusis ignibus* ("smothered flames") is an Ovidian echo. See Ovid *Heroides* 8.58 (*pectoraque inclusis ignibus usta dolent*).

For *antra fremunt* ("caverns bellow"), cf. Virgil *Aeneid* 1.56 (*circum claustra fremunt*).

Schneider (2003) at 219 notes that Baehrens, Guardalben, and Agozzino prefer *ut* to Webster's *et* ("and").

3.57 I collapse *pudor est tam foeda* (literally "it is a vile shame") into "it was shameful" and adjust the tense of the verb to correspond with standard English narrative techniques.

3.58 Webster at 99 and Franzoi and Spinazzè at 177 note that *agnovit . . . conscia signa* ("he recognized clear signs") echoes Ovid *Amores* 2.1.8 (*agnoscat flammae conscia signa suae*). See also *Amores* 2.8.8 (*furtivae Veneris conscia signa dedi*).

3.59 Webster at 99–100 argues that *causae* ("cause") has a medical flavor—undoubtedly looking back to lines 51 and 53—but looking ahead to line 60 the phrase *res causae* ("The matter's cause") may have more of a legal flavor. See Heidegger (1971) at 173. Guardalben (1993) at 121 accepts Webster's line over Baehrens' *occultae sat pestis prodita causa est*. But see Goldlust (2013) at 159.

3.60 This line has received inadequate scholarly attention. The term *veniam* ("forgiveness") could be interpreted in different ways. It could be a reference to the rule of *venia aetatis* ("forgiveness for age"), which allowed people younger than the age of majority, which was twenty-five, to appeal for the rights of adulthood. Males could do so at twenty and females at eighteen. See Cooper at 111. If this interpretation is correct, then Boethius is simply commending Maximianus for the mature way he is proceeding and observing that his appeal should be granted.

It is more likely that Maximianus is satirizing the Christian rite of confession by portraying a craven Boethius as granting absolution *in advance* of a sin. Cf. Boethius *De interpretatione* 4.1.2 (*venia*); *Consolatio philosophiae* 3.m12.27 (*veniam*); *De musica* 2.1.1 (*veniam*); Cassiodorus *Expositio in psalterium* 1.37 (*peccatis sui veniam petit*).

Perhaps the most likely alternative is that Maximianus is satirizing Boethius' personal conduct in some way we do not fully understand. One can read this conversation in conjunction with Ennodius' *De Boetio spata cincto* (see Appendix C), which suggests that Boethius' personal life fell far short of a model of Christian purity.

One can also read it in light of Ovidian echoes; Franzoi and Spinazzè at 177 note the parallel with *Heroides* 17.106 (*veniam vir dabit*). Of course, none of these interpretations entirely excludes the others.

The phrase *pone metum* ("Don't fret"—literally "set aside fear") often occurs in Ovid. See *Ars amatoria* 1.556; *Fasti* 2.759; *Tristia* 5.83; *Heroides* 16.68, 20.3; *Metamorphoses* 3.634, 5.227. Goldlust (2013) at 159 is almost certainly wrong in finding likely inspiration in Tibullus 3.10.15.

Shanzer argues that this line "is a joke, and the allusion to Aesculapius is intentional, intended to evoke reminisces of the healing God in Boethius' behavior." Shanzer (1988) at 260. Cf. note to 3.47.

3.61 Falling prostrate at someone's feet is more of a medieval activity. Maximianus' *prostratus pedibus* ("prostrate at his feet") is the preferred way of expressing the concept. But see Gregorius Turonensis *Miracula* 1.87.1 (*prostratus ad pedes*). Among other affectations, later Roman emperors expected visitors to lie prostrate at their feet and kiss their robes.

For *silentia rupi* ("I broke my . . . silence"), cf. Ovid *Metamorphoses* 1.208 (*silentia rupit*), 11.598 (*silentia rumpunt*); Virgil *Aeneid* 10.63 (*silentia . . . rumpere*); Lucretius *De rerum natura* 4.583 (*silentia rumpi*); Lucan *Bellum civile* 5.121 (*silentia rupis*); Seneca *Apocolocyntosis* 41 (*silentia rumpet*).

Altamura sees a metrical issue with *verecunda* ("shamefaced"). See Altamura (1981) at 822. Cf. note to 3.23.

3.62 Webster at 100 notes use of the phrase *ordine cuncta suo* ("all in sequence") and its most likely inspiration, Virgil *Aeneid* 11.241, as well as the less likely inspirations of Valerius Flaccus and Sedulius. Fo and Goldlust see inspiration by Orientius in this line, which I find highly unlikely. See Goldlust (2011) at 162.

3.63 For *munere formae* ("'gift' . . . beauty"), cf. Statius *Silvae* 3.51; Orientius *Commonitorium* 267. For *placitae . . . formae* ("beauty please you"), cf. Ovid *Ars amatoria* 3.353 (*nos facimus placitae late praeconia formae*); *Fasti* 2.777 (*sic quamvis aberat placitae praesentia formae*).

Textual uncertainty makes the meaning and tone of this line ambiguous. Webster has the first word as *Fare*, which is generally been translated along the lines of "Talk." This command would be very strange because the young Maximianus has just told *ordine cuncta* ("everything in sequence") in the previous line. Several manuscripts, see Webster at 41, have *Fac*, *Face*, and *Face ut* as alternatives. See Spaltenstein (1983) at 215 and Schetter at 79–81 for *Fac* and *Fac ut* as an imperative.The verb *facire* frequently served as a substitute for an obscene verb. See Adams (1982) at 3, 143, 204, 215, 221. While the best choice here is highly debatable, it seems the better choice is to view this command as an outburst that tells the young Maximianus exactly what he is supposed to act. The suggestiveness of *Fac* ("Do it!") might explain why a less suggestive alternative emerged in a text used in later centuries with schoolchildren. Accordingly, I emend Webster's text in favor of the *fac* of several manuscripts. Cf. Cato *Disticha* 2.5 (*Fac sumptum propere*), 3.11 (*Fac vivas contentus eo*), 4.12 (*Fac sapias*).

The rest of the line is also tricky, and translators have tended to overlook *an*, which makes the phrase an edgy question. The word *placitae* ("please you"—literally "be pleasing") may have associations with the noun *placitum*, which has the legal meaning "a condition of a deal."

3.64 The phrase *talia velle fugit* ("avoids such wishing") also appears at 3.92.

3.65 The phrase *in risum* ("laughing"—literally "into laughter") was an unusual one in classical times, but it does appear in Horace *Epistulae* 1.13.9 and Seneca *De tranquilitate anima* 15.5. Surprisingly, perhaps, it is a favorite of Augustine.

3.66 For issues with the prosody of this line, see note to 2.65; see also Altamura (1981) at 822.

3.67 This line echoes Ovid *Heroides* 19.205 (*non parcis dilectae parce puellae*).

3.68 A literal translation of this line would be something like: "If you want to be proper, here you will be improper (with her)." In other words, if you want to marry her, you must "consummate" the deal. The adjective *pius* ("proper") is common in Augustan poetry; it has primarily secular connotations. The paradox of being unfaithful in order to be faithful is nuanced here because *impius* seems to have a sense of rejected religious or moral values, whereas *pius* seems to be used in its standard elegiac sense. Depending on interpretation, the combination of these opposing adjectives may be an example of the rhetorical device of antithesis.

3.69 The phrase *unguibus et* . . . *morsu* ("by scratches and a bite") aptly describes aggressive elegiac lovemaking, but the combination of these two nouns is rare. But see Ovid *Metamorphoses* 3.69 (*unguibus et morsu*); cf. Cicero *Tusculanae disputationes* 5.77 (*unguibus morsu*); Jerome *Commentarii in Osee* 2.7.31(*morsu et unguibus*).

Erasmus, who wrote an elegy on old age that strongly suggests that he had read Maximianus (probably thinking he was reading Gallus), see note to 1.16, may have been echoing *teneri amores* ("Tender affairs") in *Elegia Erasmi de praepotenti virtute Cupidinis pharetrati* 3 (*Nutibus et signis teneri pascuntur amores*). See also Muretus *Epigrammata* 22.1 (*Sic age, pugnando teneri pascuntur amores*); Johannes Secundus *Basia* 67.85–86 (*pasci pugnando teneri volunt amores*).

3.70 Uden argues that the advice which closes with this line "is not merely cruel, but redundant, given Aquilina's preexistent *vulnera*; and not merely redundant, but illogical, since the major obstacle in their love-affair is not Maximianus' lack of assertion but the lovers' parental objection." See Uden (2009) at 216. I disagree—Boethius' advice may be venal, but it is neither cruel nor redundant. The joke here is premised on the major obstacle *not* being "the lovers' parental objection" but "Maximianus' lack of assertion." In the subsequent lines, once Boethius removes the parental objection by greasing palms, the affair fails because of Maximianus' lack of will to consummate the relationship. As in elegies 2, 4, and 5, the object of Maximianus' satire is not the *docta puella* but himself. This perspective takes these poems out of the category of elegy and into what I would call "antielegy"—use of the forms and themes of the genre to satirize its assumptions.

Translation of this line turns on interpretation of the supple word *res* ("business"), which here seems to demand a deromanticized verison of "affair."

Goldlust (2013) at 159–160 notes that *plagae* ("blows") is a metrical problem, an issue first raised by Wernsdorf. See Walsh, "Varia Latina" 27 *Classical Review* (1913) at 260; cf. Spaltenstein (1983) at 217; Altamura (1981) at 822. Walsh overreads by seeing a "recondite pun" on *plagae.*

3.71 The verb *permulcet* ("he pacifies") is rare but goes back at least as far as Lucretius. Lucretius *De rerum natura* 5.21 (*dulcia permulcet animos solacia vitae*). It is occasionally used by Augustan poets. See, e.g., Ovid *Metamorphoses* 4.599, 7.221, *Fasti* 4.551; Virgil *Aeneid* 5.816. It appears four times in Cicero *Philosophia*, including once in *De senectute* and once in a discussion of Epicurus. See Cicero *De finibus bonarum et malorum* 2.32, *De natura deorum* 2.114, *De oratore* 2.315, *De senectute* 4. The verb appears frequently in Cassiodorus. See *De anima* 12.21; *Expositio in psalterium* 0.0.7, 1.44.26, 3.106.50, 3.140.7, 3.145.2; *Institutiones* 2.5.39; *Variae* 9.35.2, 10.4.4 . Franzoi and Spinazzè at 179 note an arguable parallel to this line at Silius *Punica* 13.344.

3.72 I have translated the adjective *faciles* as a noun ("soft touches").

3.73 Webster at 100 argues for *nativum* as "inborn." Given the etymological root of *nascor* that is highlighted by the presence of *natae* ("daughter's") in the next line and advice from James Uden, I use "parental."

Heege at 14 notes that the phrase *auri caecus amor* ("Blind love of money") echoes Virgil *Aeneid* 1.349 (*auri caecus amore*).

Spaltenstein (1983) at 218 cites *amor . . . amorem* ("love . . . love") as an example of polyptoton.

3.74 Here the noun *crimen* ("guilt") has more of a secular/legal flavor than a religious sense. See Athanassiadi and Frede (1999) at 4; Webster at 100.

3.75 The phrase *iungere dextras* ("holding hands") is Virgilian. See *Aeneid* 1.408, 1.514, 6.697, 8.164. It implies the parents consented to an engagement.

3.76 The verb *concelebrare* ("filling") is uncommon although used frequently by Cassiodorus. See, e.g., *Complexiones in epistulis* 1.34, 1.36; *Expositio in psalterium* 0.4.1, 0.18.12, 1.8.4, 1.28.8, 1.48.9, 2.65.6, 2.69.6, 2.70.35, 2.73.25, 2.92.6, 3.102.27, 3.112.6, 3.113.17, 3.143.6; *Institutiones* 1.A.10, 1.11.3, 2.A.11; *Variae* 1.4.9, 2.40.7, 8.9.8.

Spaltenstein (1983) at 219 and Goldlust (2013) at 160 suggest *ludo* ("with play") is sexual when the point is almost certainly exactly the opposite. Maximianus' sexual aspirations are frustrated here because he isn't willing to cross the line into more physical activity. The phrase *totum ludo concelebrare diem* ("filling days with play") may be Plautan. See *Pseudolus* 1.2.33 (*dies . . . concelebrare*); but see Webster at 100. Franzoi and Spinazzè at 179 note that this line may also echo Plautus *Asinaria* 311 (*omnes . . . concelebrabuntur diem*).

3.77 The phrase *permissum . . . nefas* ("A sanctioned sin") is an oxymoron. Cf. note to 2.22. Citing Ovid *Amores* 2.19.3 and 3.4.9, Fielding (forthcoming) at 15 argues persuasively that the concept is Ovidian.

3.78 Schneider (2003) at 219 notes that Baehrens, Fels, and Agozzino have *tabida* for *languida* ("Exhausted"). But see Guardalben (1993) at 121; Goldlust (2013) at 160. There is no manuscript support for this emendation, although I find it attractive. Cf. Öberg at 171. I retain *languida* because of Maximianus' fondness for anaphora and because I cannot find a persuasive precedent for *tabida corda*.

Uden argues that this line reflects "a familiar Ovidian sentiment." See Uden (2009) at 217; cf. Ovid *Amores* 2.19.25–26, 3.4.45–46.

Webster at 101 seems oddly unclear as to whether *corda* ("hearts") is a classical usage.While *cor* may have been more common, Virgil often used *corda.* Juvenal, Lucan, Lucretius, Martial, Ovid, Seneca, Silius, and Statius also use the term.

3.79 Schetter (1970) at 10 notes that at least five manuscripts have *quaesitam* for *quaesita* ("pursuit"), an unclear word that probably refers to Maximianus' clumsy attempt at romance.

3.80 The phrase *illaeso corpore* ("with an unspoiled body") probably echoes Ovid *Heroides* 15.168 (*illaeso corpora pressit aquas*).

3.83–84 Some of the surprising popularity of Maximianus in the medieval period stems from a misreading of these lines, which in isolation seem to be praising virginity in a Christian way. In actuality, of course, the young Maximianus relinquishes Aquilina out of stifled lust, not devotion to chastity. For an overview of the changes in perceptions of virginity from the classical era through Late Antiquity, see Kelly (2000) at 1–16.

Schneider (2003) at 219 notes that the phrase *salve sancta* ("Hail holy") appears at Sedulius *Carmen Paschale* 2.63, but Webster at 101 is correct that *sancta* has classical roots and is not exclusively a Christian term. Cf. Virgil *Aeneid* 5.80 (*Salve sancte*).

The vocative *maneto* ("stay") is associated with Roman comedy. See, e.g., Plautus *Mercator* 2.4.30; Terence *Hecyra* 3.4.29. Franzoi at 181 argues that this line echoes Catullus 62.45 (*virgo dum intacta manet*).

The term *plena pudoris* ("most modest"—literally "full of modesty") appears in a line of debated authenticity, Ovid *Heroides* 7.98. See Fisher, "Two Notes on the *Heroides*," 74 *Harvard Studies in Classical Philology* (1970) at 193–198; see also *Heroides* 21.242 (*plena pudoris*); cf. Claudian *Panegyricus dictus Manlio Theodoro consul* at 247; Ausonius *Ordo urbium nobilium* 3.8, *Praefatiunculae* 5.3.8.

3.86 The noun *fluctus* ("moods") is often used metaphorically. See OLD 1c. It is a quintessentially Lucretian term used instead of the more common *unda* of Augustan poetry and is sexually loaded with hints of "wave of passion." For instance, Lucretius used *fluctus* to describe the movement of a woman's breast during sex. See *De rerum natura* 4.1271; see also Dyson, "Fluctus Irarum, Fluctus Curarum: Lucretian Religion in the *Aeneid*," 118, no. 3 *American Journal of Philology* (1997) at 449–457; Harrison, "Apuleius and the Epic Metaphor: Waves of Passion" in Harrison, Paschalis and Frangoulidid, *Metaphor and the Ancient Novel* (Groningen: Barkhuis Publishing and Groningen University Library, 2005).

3.87 For *Macte* ("Well done!"), see Allen, "Etymological Notes" 1 *American Journal of Philology* (1880) at 135–140. Uden suggests this word may recall use of the same word as a greeting in Horace *Sermones* 1.2.31, which then continues into a famous scene in which Cato congratulates a man exiting a brothel for satisfying his lust with whores rather than committing adultery with highborn wives. See Uden (2009) at 218. Franzoi notes many uses of the term in Virgil and Silius. See Franzoi (2011) at 164. Cf. Ennodius *Dictio* 9.26, *Carminum librum* 6.51.

Though the phrase *proprii dominator amoris* ("the lord of your own love") has the feel of an elegiac phrase, its roots are elsewhere; Franzoi notes arguable models in Avienus and Claudian. See Franzoi (2011) at 165. The term *dominator* is rare in the Augustan era, and Seneca was the first writer to embrace it fully. See Seneca *Phaedra* 7.49, 8.4; *Epistulae* 107.11; *Medea* 1.0.4. While it may seem like a short trip from the *domina* of Augustan elegy to *dominator*, *dominator* moved from the mistress/slave context to a male lover in control. Moreover, that control is more potent since Christian writers of Late Antiquity regularly use *dominator* to refer to God in a way analogous to our "The Lord." That point is punctuated by Maximianus' use of *proprii*, which makes the independence of the male lover even clearer. An elegiac lover might be a *magister amoris,* but that label means being an expert of an elaborate ritual in which objects of desire, obstructers of desire, and the gods all played important roles. The notion that a lover could control his own desires is a radical revision of elegiac teachings.

3.88 The noun *trophaea* ("some trophies") is the Late Antique version of the classical *tropaea*. The earliest literary user of *trophaea* I can identify is Seneca, who uses it frequently. Uden notes the possible association of *trophaea* in this line with commemorative structures erected to the martyrs. See Uden (2009) at 218; see also Roberts (1993) at 171; Mohrman, "À propos de deux mots controversies de la latinité chrétienne *tropaeum-nomen*," 8 *Vigiliae Christianae* (1954) at 158–167.

3.89 Franzoi notes parallels between this line and Ovid *Metamorphoses* 2.603 (*arma . . . arcum*) and Statius *Silvae* 5.2.49 (*arma arcus*). See Franzoi (2011) at 165.

3.89–90 Schneider at 220 notes that Baehrens, Fels, and Agozzino substitute *ceduntque . . . cedit* for Webster's *cedantque . . . cedat* ("yield . . . yield"). Four manuscripts support this emendation. See Öberg at 171; see also Goldlust (2013) at 161.

The adjective *armipotens* ("bold") often describes deities. See, e.g., Lucretius *De rerum natura* 1.33; Ovid *Fasti* 2.481, 5.559; Virgil *Aeneid* 2.425 (*armipotentis*), 6.839 (*armipotentis*). Spaltenstein (1983) at 222 notes that Minerva is often similarly described. See, e.g., Ovid *Amores* 2.6.35 (*armifera*), *Metamorphoses* 8.264 (*bellatrix*); Petronius *Satiricon* 5.9 (*armigera*).

Following my point about misreading in my note to 3.83–84, these final two distichs of elegy 3 summarize the import of this distich and the next one in a somewhat awkward fashion, perhaps to try to avoid future misreadings (that have, nonetheless, occurred).

3.91 Webster at 102 notes that the verse-close of *permissa potestas* ("a sanctioned license") originates in Virgil *Aeneid* 9.97 and is then used by Lucan, Avitus, and Paulinus of Nola. Cf. Claudian *In Rufinus* 2.1.74 (*permissa potestate*). It is a phrase redolent of law and government. See, e.g., *Codex Theodosianus* 4.8.6 (*potestas permissa est*); cf. Augustine *De civitate Dei* 10.21.1 (*potestas permissa*); Cassiodorus *Expositio in psalterium* 1.9.38. It also echoes 3.77.

3.92 See note to 3.64.

3.93 Although the text is not clear, Shanzer (1983) at 191 is almost certainly correct in arguing that *discedimus ambo* ("we split up, equally") refers to Boethius and Maximianus, not Boethius and Aquilina. But see Anastasi (1951) at 76; Barnish (1990) at 25; Fielding (2011) at 127–128. Cf. note to 3.21.

Spaltenstein (1983) at 223 and Goldlust (2013) at 161 wrongly suggest that *ingrati* ("resentful") is used here in a rare sense.

3.94 Webster at 102 notes that *discidii* ("the split") has legal connotations. Goldlust (2013) at 161–162 summarizes scholarly disagreements about the meaning of this distich.

Shanzer (1983) at 191–192 correctly notes the theatricality of this ending and suggests it invokes or parodies Horace *Sermones* 1.2.31–32 and Ovid *Amores* 1.15.33–34.

The weight of the manuscripts supports Baehrens' *vita* ("life") over Webster's *tota* in this line, and I prefer *vita*, primarily on literary instinct. See Öberg at 172.

Elegy 4

4.1 Webster at 103 notes that *restat adhuc* ("It still remains") appears at Ovid *Epistulae ex Ponto* 2.3.60 and that *turpesque revolvere* ("to tell of . . . shameful") appears in the same line location at 3.37 in the previous elegy.

Consolino notes that *revolvere casus* ("to tell of . . . falls") echoes Virgil *Aeneid* 10.61 (*revolvere casus*). See Consolino (1997) at 382. It also may echo the opening of elegy 3. Cf. note to 3.1–2.

4.3 The adjective *delirae* ("deranged") frequently described old age and old people. See, e.g., Cicero *De oratore* 2.75 (*deliros senes*); Jerome *Epistulae* 3.53.7 (*delirus senex*).

4.4 The vague noun *operi* ("work") would support a wide range of meanings here. Guardalben at 121 came to a similar conclusion.

4.5 I see the appeal of the manuscripts with *fallimus* but retain Webster's *fallimur* ('I am beguiled"). See Webster at 42.

4.6 For a discussion of the rhyme and wordplay of this line, see Fielding (2011) at 129. Franzoi and Spinazzè at 184 note that *tempora grata mihi* ("I am . . . grateful . . . seasons") echoes the same phrase in Ausonius *Ad patrem de suscepto filio* 32.

4.7 For a discussion of variants in this line, see Schneider (2003) at 220.

Guardalben (1993) at 122 defends Webster's *species* (collapsed with *candida* into "incandescence" in order to capture the pun) over the conjectured and more pedestrian *facies* of Baehrens. See also Goldlust (2013) at 163.

4.8 Butrica is harshly critical of Schneider's association of Candida with the *candida scrofa* of Juvenal 12.72. See Butrica (2005) at 562–564; but see Goldlust at 163. Fielding connects *candida diversis* ("Candida . . . fresh") with Ovid *Amores* 1.5.20 (*candida dividua*) and Catullus 68.70 (*candida diva*). See Fielding (forthcoming) at 51–52.

Welsh thoughtfully discusses issues in this line, but I do not endorse his emendations, including *composita* or *dispositis* for *diversis* ("fresh") and *stat* or *sat* for *nam* ("because of"). See Welsh (2011) at 219–220.

I substituted *modis* ("styles") of the Leidensis Lipsii and Britannicus Reg. 15, A.7 manuscripts for Webster's *comis*, primarily on the debatable assumption that it was more likely that she was constantly changing clothing and jewelry than hairdos. Guardalben (1993) at 122, Spaltenstein (1983) at 227, and Goldlust (2013) at 163 come to similar conclusions. But see Franzoi and Spinazzè at 185.

Webster and Baehrens agree on *nam* ("because of"), but nonetheless Goldlust (2013) at 163 prefers the variant *stat* after entertaining Mauger's (1996) *sat*.

4.9–10 Altamura sees *vidi pendentia* ("I saw . . . hanging") as echoing Ovid *Metamorphoses* 8.722 (*pendentia vidi*). See Altamura (1981) at 821.

Enk at 74 notes that *pulsa sonos* ("sounds when they are struck") echoes Propertius 4.2.8 (*pulsa sonos*).

4.11–15 Barnish suggests lines 4.11–12 echo Cassiodorus *Variae* 2.40.14 (*Musarum tela loquax, stamina verbosa, fila canentia, in quibus arguto plectro texitur quod dulcius audiatur*) and that other parts of this section echo other sections of *Variae* 2.40. Barnish (1990) at 19. I doubt that the similarities suffice to justify Barnish's arguments.

4.11 Schetter (1970) at 89, Guardalben (1993) at 122, and Spaltenstein (1983) at 228 argue for *pulsas* over *pulsans* ("struck") of Baehrens and Webster. The word is problematic, but given the number of variants and the absence of a compelling rationale for a change, I follow the Webster text. Many of the more important texts have *pulsat*, which may add a little weight to Welsh's clever argument for the speculative *pulsato* here. See Welsh (2011) at 220–221. Altamura notes that this line echoes Virgil *Aeneid* 6.647 (*digitis . . . pectine pulsat*). See Altamura (1981) at 821.

The noun *cordas* ("strings") is the Late Antique version of *chordas*.

4.12 For *loqui* ("warbled") as a musical term see OLD 1c.

For *murmure dulce* ("in a sweet . . . whisper"), cf. Statius *Silvae* 2.37 (*murmure dulce*).

Guardalben (1993) at 122 rejects Baehrens' *quiddam* for *quicquam* ("something"). Three of the manuscripts have *quidquid*. See Öberg at 172.

4.13 The phrase *diversis . . . partibus* ("with shifting parts") is probably wordplay referring back to both the changing songs of the previous distich and the moving body parts of the previous distich, as well as the Greek girl's *diversis . . . modis* in 4.8.

4.14 The precise sense here of *carpebat* ("was plucking") is unclear, and it possible that "was seducing" or something similar would be more appropriate. However, it seems to me that Maximianus is using wordplay by combining the senses of plucking the physical strings, plucking the metaphorical heartstrings, and maybe even metaphorically plucking a ripe fruit. Cf. OLD 1, 2, 7. Goldlust's (2013) translation of *carpebat* at 163 as "dechirait" is detached from the sense of the line; the verb does not retain the sense of "wounded" when not followed by *vulnere*.

4.15 Goldlust (2013) at 164 overstates his case that *subito correptus* ("being quickly smitten") "sans doute" echoes Ovid *Fasti* 3.681 (*correptus amore*).

4.17 Fielding argues that *singula visa* ("Each glance") seems to echo the *singula quaesita* of 1.101. See Fielding (2011) at 129–130.

Michael Roberts notes that there is a strong antithesis between *semel* ("each") and *semper* ("each time"); though each thing was only seen once, it was always pleasant to recall it.

4.18 Webster at 104 characterizes the phrase *nocte dieque* ("through night and day") as "an erotic commonplace," when, in fact, it is a cliché used by Christian authors too. See, e.g., Orientius *Commonitorium* 1.402. Franzoi and Spinazzè at 187 put too much weight on this phrase while using it to suggest an echo of Ovid *Heroides* 7.25–26.

4.19 For *velut visae . . . imagine formae* ("her figure's lifelike image"—literally "an image of a figure as if seen"), cf. note to B.1.19; Franzoi and Spinazzè at 188. It is arguable that *formae* here should be translated as "beauty."

4.19–22 Maximianus returns to the rhetorical device of anaphora with the repetition of *saepe* ("often") and *velut* ("as if" in line 21—in line 19 collapsed into "vision") in these two distichs.

4.20 The phrase *voce et manuque* ("from voice and touch") is a common one. See, e.g., Martial 8.65.6; Dracontius *Satisfactio ad Guntharium* 118; Ovid *Metamorphoses* 1.205; Silius *Punica* 6.458, 12.510; Statius *Thebaid* 9.161.

4.22 Webster at 55 and 104 concedes that the manuscript that has *cantabam* ("I kept on singing") instead of *captabam* may be correct. I share his doubt in a stronger form and accept Baehrens' *cantabam*.

4.23 The similarity of *demens* ("demented") and *sine mente* ("mindless") seems oddly redundant, though it may be rhyming wordplay reinforcing the anaphora of *quotiens*. Ellis' argument for the Britannicus Add. 21, 213 *sine arte* has some merit. See Ellis (1884b) at 160.

For elegiac love as sickness, see Fielding (2011) at 20.

4.24 Baehrens emends *fallebar* ("was I . . . tricked") to *fallebat*, and Wernsdorf emends it to *fallebam*. Spaltenstein (1983) at 232 expresses concern that *fallebar* "n'est pas attesté." But see Goldlust (2013) at 164 (criticizing Spaltenstein's analysis and acrobatic interpretation). The verb in this form is not common, but it is a "low" term of comedy. See, e.g., Plautus *Epidicus* 2.2.59 (*nec sermonis fallebar tamen*). See also Webster at 55. Guardalben (1993) at 122 supports Webster's *fallebar*, which I retain with reservations.

4.25–26 As a teenager, humanist scholar Pomponius Gauricus deleted this distich from the text in 1501 when he fraudulently passed off Maximianus' elegies as the work of Cornelius Gallus, whose elegies have been lost except for a handful of lines. See generally Schneider (2001) at 445–461; Altamura (1981) at 818–820. Impressive recent scholarship indicates that scattered false attributions to Gallus preceded the Gauricus fraud. See Franzoi and Spinazzè at 50–62. For Pulmann's 1569 response to the fraud and later efforts to set the record straight, see Arcaz Pozo (2011) at 20–21.

Despite this line's mention of Maximianus, some commentators declare that "Maximianus" is a fiction, including Webster (an unidentified author between 524 and 650), Ratkowitsch (an unidentified author of the ninth century), Öberg (an unidentified author of the sixth century), and Tyson (a classroom exercise of the sixth century). For a brief yet brilliant skewering of Ratkowitsch's poorly conceived and poorly supported theory, see Shanzer (1988) at 259–261. Webster at 16 skates perilously close to academic dishonesty in order to defend his theory of authorship when he asserts the existence of a French grammarian named Maximianus solely based, or so it appears, on an unsupported statement in the Manutius introduction to the fraudulent Gauricus edition of 1501. For more information on the Manutius introduction, see Navarro López (2002) at 147–156.

For *cantat cantantem* ("She sings . . . singer"), cf. Augustine's *De vera religione* 17.90 ("*Qui ergo invidet bene cantati, non amat bene cantantem, sed rursus qui eo indiget non cantat bene*"). Webster at 104 notes the "double entendre in *cantat cantantem*; each word has the idea of witchery in it, and song has a special place in the arts of love." Although a number of manuscripts have *canta*, *cantat* is almost surely correct. But see Ellis (1884b) at 159–160. Schneider (2003) at 221 notes that Baehrens and Agozzino have *cantans* for *cantat*, a position Guardalben rejects at 122. Cf. note to 2.60. For support of *cantantem* as "the singer," see Spaltenstein at 165.

4.28 Welsh is troubled by the repetition of *clauso* (incorporated into "closed-lipped") in this line and *clausae* ("cloistered") two lines later, and proposes the plausible *clarae* for *clausae*. See Welsh (2011) at 221. The repetition could be wordplay or a scribal error: Franzoi at 189 calls it polyptoton even though the two words are in different distichs and his version, unlike mine, translates the distichs as separate sentences.

4.29 Webster at 104 notes parallels for *pallorque ruborque* ("blush and paleness") in Statius, Dracontius, and Corippus, along with some significantly less compelling parallels with other authors.

4.30 Despite Guardalben (1993) at 122, Schetter (1970) at 51, Goldlust (2013) at 165, Franzoi and Spinazzè at 189–190, and Tandoi at 143, I reject Baehrens' *interdum*; some manuscripts have *interius* instead of Webster's *internum* ("private"). See Webster at 43; see also Spaltenstein (1983) at 234, Schneider at (2003) 221, Öberg at 173.

The idiom *habebat opus* ("performed the . . . task") is Ovidian. See *Epistulae ex Ponto* 4.7.26 (*habebat opes*); *Fasti* 1.348 (*habebat opus*), 3.50 (*habebat opes*), 4.400 (*habebat opes*), 6.420 (*habebat opus*).

For *clausae*, see note to 4.28.

4.31–34 Spaltenstein (1983) at 235 notes Lucretius *De rerum natura* 5.1158–1160 and Tibullus 1.9.26–27 as precedents for involuntary speech during dreams. See generally Bouquet, "La nuit, le sommeil et le songe chez les elegiaques latins" 74 *Revue des études latines* (1996) at 182–211.

4.33 For *oblivia* ("amnesia") and *sopitos* ("drowsy"), cf. Lucretius *De rerum natura* 3.1067 (*aut abit in somnum gravis atque oblivia quaerit*), 4.822 (*quod ne miremur sopor atque oblivia curant*); Claudian *De raptu Proserpinae* 2.1.274 (*aegra soporatis spumant oblivia linguis*). Webster at 104 notes that *oblivia* occurs in the same location in 1.123.

For precedents for *premerent* ("had submerged"), cf. Ovid *Metamorphoses* 14.779 (*ore premunt voces et corpora victa sopore*), 15.21 (*pressum gravitate soporis*); Claudian *In Eutropium* 1.70 (*Eutropium tantasque premunt oblivia noctes*); Pliny *Naturalis historia* 8.127 (*tam gravi somno premuntur*).

4.34 For *confessa est facinus* ("confessed . . . crime"), Franzoi and Spinazzè at 190 see an echo of Dracontius 159 (*confessus facinus*), which is line 135 in the version edited by Eugene of Toledo.

4.35 Fielding argues that the dreaming Maximianus who blurts "*propera cur Candida tardas*" ("hurry! Why delay, Candida?") is paraphrasing Ovid *Amores* 1.13.33 (*invida quo properas*). Fielding (2011) at 131–132. Franzoi and Spinazzè at 190 suggest that *propera* in this context is Plautan.

4.36 Webster at 105 notes *nox abit* ("Night flees") echoes Ovid's *nox abiit* in *Fasti* 4.721. A more likely inspiration is *Amores* 1.5.6 (*nox abiit*).

Webster at 105 also notes that the phrase *lux inimica* ("light, unkind to") occurs at Virgil *Aeneid* 9.355 in the same location. See also Macrobius *Saturnalia* 5.13.39.

For *furtis* as "trysts," see OLD 2b.

4.37 Guardalben (1993) at 122 and Franzoi and Spinazzè at 191 accept Webster's *mecum* over *me tum* of Baehrens and Withof. I have taken some poetic liberties in rendering *proximus ut genitor mecum comitatus amatae virginis* as "just as my girlfriend's father . . . while nestled close to me."

4.38 Goldlust (2013) notes that *forte iacebat* ("by chance . . . sprawled upon" in line 37 of the translation) echoes Virgil *Aeneid* 12.897 (*forte iacebat*).

4.38–39 Eavesdropping was a common device in Roman comedy. Terence used eavesdropping in his extant plays an average of fourteen times; Plautus used it an average of nine times in his extant plays. See Duckworth (1994) at 109.

4.39 This line may echo Statius *Thebaid* 11.545 (*turbatus colligit artus*). Guardalben (1993) at 122 defends the *turbatos* ("restless") of Webster, Schetter, and Spaltenstein over Baehrens' *turbatus*, which is also accepted by Öberg and Schneider (2003). Hunt defends *turbatus* in part on metrical grounds. See Hunt (1978) at 59–60; see also Franzoi (2009) at 404–405 and (2011) at 166.

Some manuscripts have *exitat* or *excitat* for *excutit* ("shakes"). Franzoi argues that an almost surely coincidental parallel with Tertullian *De anima* 25.3 (*ad novum sonum excutitur*) tends to support *ad . . . excutit*. Franzoi (2009) at 405, (2011) at 167.

The phrase *illius ad nomen* ("at that name") may echo romantic advice in Lucretius *De rerum natura* 4.1065 (*illius et nomen dulce observatur ad auris*). Franzoi suggests, wrongly I believe, that this phrase echoes Juvencus *Evangelia* 2.221 (*illius ad nomen . . . turbine*). Cf. Franzoi (2009) at 405.

4.41–42 Webster at 105 notes this distich parallels the *omnia conlustrans . . . prospexi* of Virgil *Aeneid* 3.651–652. Cf. Cicero *De natura deorum* 2.92. See also Franzoi and Spinazzè at 192.

The phrase *somnum . . . afflantem* ("slumbering"—literally "breathing sleep") is a bit unclear. It may mean the heavy breathing of sleep, but it may also mean something funnier and closer to yawning or snoring. Surreptitious observation of a sleeping person does suggest a Roman comedy. I emend Webster's *afflantem* to *efflantem*; the latter is rare but the former is nonexistent in the key databases. Franzoi makes the same choice and sees a parallel to Statius *Thebaid* 209 (*efflantem somno*). See Franzoi (2011) at 167–168. For *somnum* paired with *pectore* ("my . . . chest"), cf. Plautus *Pseudolus* 1.2.12 (*nisi somnum socordiamque ex pectore oculis exmovetis*). Goldlust (2013) at 167 also points out the parallel to the less humorous Virgil *Aeneid* 9.326 (*pectore somnum*).

Franzoi calls *toto . . . pectore* ("with my whole chest") an elegiac phrase and cites as support Tibullus 3.1.20 and Ovid *Heroides* 12.142, *Ars amatoria* 2.536, 3.56. Franzoi (2011) at 167.

For *nec meminisse* as "being inattentive," see OLD 3.

4.43 This line may echo Livy *Ab urbe condita* 6.14.11 (*omisso discrimine vera* *an vana iaceret*). Ellis (1884b) at 160 argues unpersuasively for *lactans* over *iactat*.

The words *vana . . . ludibria* ("false illusions") may echo Martial 10.4.7 (*vana . . . ludibria*). For an argument that this line parallels Macrobius on dreams, see Consolino (1997) at 385; Wasyl at 147–148.

I concur with Guardalben (1993) at 122, Franzoi and Spinazzè at 192, and Goldlust at 167, all of whom accept Webster's *putas* ("Do you believe") over Baehrens' *putabo*.

James Uden privately makes a strong case for the speculative emendation of *en* for *an* ("or").

4.44 Spaltenstein notes that *pectoris ardor* ("the heart's . . . passion") also appears at Ovid *Ars amatoria* 3.714 (*quis adtoniti pectoris ardor erat*).

In light of the problematic nature of Webster's *hoc et* to start this line, I have followed the *an te* of Britannicus Reg. 15, A.7.

Guardalben (1993) at 122, Franzoi and Spinazzè at 192, and Goldlust (2013) at 167 accept Webster's *verus* ("true") over Baehrens' *serus*.

4.47 Schneider (2003) at 222 notes that Baehrens and Schadd have *tamquam* for *tamen* ("still").

Franzoi and Spinazzè at 193 claim *perplexaque murmura* echoes "non improbabile" Paulinus Petricordiae *Vita Sancta Martini* 5.349 (*murmura perplexis*), a claim with which I disagree even with the double negative phrasing.

4.48 Ellis (1884b) at 161 argues unpersuasively for *discere* over *dicere*. Guardalben (1993) at 122 and Goldlust (20130 at 167 accept Webster's *tacitis precibus dicere* ("with hushed questions . . . disclosure") over Baehrens' *tacitus strepitu discere*.

4.49 For *habebar* ("I . . . considered"), see OLD 25.

For *sic ego* ("So I"), cf. Ovid *Metamorphoses* 5.604.

For an overview of scholarly debate about the proper translation of this line and the following two, see Wasyl (2011) at 148.

4.50 Webster at 105 comments on *vitio . . . meo* ("my . . . vice") as follows: "Notice that in all these elegies there is this refinement on the motifs of the classical period. the [*sic*] fault is always the lover's." This assessment is Victorian revisionism. Tibullus, for instance, blames all three of his lovers, and part of what we find unsatisfying in Tibullus is his inability to come to terms with his own failure to advance beyond transient, self-centered relationships. In contrast, Maximianus fails in *all* of his relationships and to varying degrees accepts responsibility for those failures, even if he never adopts an explicit explanation for the pattern.

This acceptance of guilt by Maximianus also undercuts Szövérffy's argument that the object of this satire "is not Maximian, who utterly fails in his manly functions, but the young *Graia*, whose sensuous nature is perfectly characterized by this phallic hymn. This turns the whole poem into a cleverly formulated invective against women, who are always bent on their own pleasure and sexual satisfaction as the center of not only their own life but also of the universe." Szövérffy (1968) at 364. Szövérffy is simply wrong. It is clear in the hilarious elegy 5 that Maximianus is not denying the fairness of what the Greek girl claims is due—he just can't "deliver." Szövérffy sees satiric elements in these elegies, but he misses the technique and target. In each of these elegies Maximianus is engaging in the self-deprecatory satire of many of Horace's *Sermones*. Particularly in dangerous times, self-mockery is generally safe, and self-deprecatory humor is effective because of its inherent humility and authority.

Schetter (1970) at 52–53 follows Baehrens' preference for the Florentinus manuscript and substitutes *indicio* for *et vitio* and *ipse* for *ille*. Without comment Goldlust (2013) at 167–168 embraces the Baehrens emendation and sees Horatian and Ovidian echoes in *indicio*.

4.51 Webster's argument that the term *crimine* "is used in the technical sense of the erotic poetry" and that the line should be paraphrased as "And now the luck's against me—I'm so good I never have love adventures any more" is truly awful. The phrase *sine crimine* ("without reproach") had strong connotations in both a secular and religious sense. See, e.g., Jerome *Vulgate Titus* 1:6, 1:7 (*si quis sine crimine*) (*sine crimine esse*); Cato *Disticha* 5 (*nemo sine crimine vivit*). Schneider (2003) at 222 and Franzoi and Spinazzè at 194 also note Virgil *Aeneid* 4.550 (*sine crimine vitam*). Goldlust (2013) at 168 rejects Baehrens' ill-considered emendation of *in* for *sine*.

Schneider at 185 omits *tota* ("all") from this line.

Schetter at 159 runs counter to the scholarly consensus and argues unsuccessfully for including this line and the following lines through line 58 to the following elegy. See Guardalben (1993) at 122.

Boano argues this line is echoed in Corippus *Iohannis* 6.139. See Boano (1949) at 201.

4.52 For a helpful discussion of the comments by Fo, Consolino, and Webster on the tense of *non potuisse* ("unfit"), see Wasyl (2011) at 148.

For a sound argument against the argument of Spaltenstein (1983) at 240 that elegy 4 should end at line 52, see Consolino (1997) at 385.

4.54 For a weak argument for *voluisse* ("I haven't wanted") in the present tense, see Spaltenstein (1983) at 242. Cf. Wasyl (2011) at 148.

The syntax of this line is tricky; with reluctance I translate it as a double negative rather than a triple negative and followed the *et* ("and") of the Leidensis Gronovii 87 and Palatinus 1573 manuscripts rather than the *nec* of the Webster text. Franzoi and Spinazzè at 194–195 hear echoes of Ovid and Paulinus of Nola I do not hear.

For *non . . . meum est* ("I . . . not"), cf. Terence *Heauton Timorumenos* 3.2.28 (*non est mentiri meum*).

4.55–56 This distich is so difficult it has sparked almost as much discussion with my colleagues as the entire rest of the text.

The phrase *serior aetas* ("older age") is Ovidian, perhaps indirectly by way of Tibullus 1.4.33. See, e.g., *Amores* 2.4.45, *Ars amatoria* 2.667, *Tristia* 5.9.7. For Ovid older age was not necessarily a bad thing—older women are presented as an amorous opportunity in the *Ars amatoria.*

Welsh reminds us that the division of this text into six elegies is a creation of an ethically troubled teenager almost a thousand years after the likely completion of the text. Welsh also argues, along with Franzoi at 196 and other scholars, that this line more naturally demarcates the beginning of elegy 5 with its focus on age disrupting sexual escapades. See Welsh (2011) at 222; Fo (1986–1987) at 104–105. For a summary of scholarly disagreement on this issue, see Goldlust (2013) at 168. A problem with Welsh's reading is *hoc* ("this") in line 54, which would make the line an abrupt start, particularly with *etiam* ("too") suggesting a connection to the previous distich. I read *hoc* as referring to the rest of the distich.

Welsh also makes the speculative but seductive suggestion of emending the problematic *laeta* ("numerous") with *vena,* which would make the line far more clever and its translation less acrobatic than the alternatives supported by manuscripts or the less satisfactory speculative emendations of Wernsdorf's *lena* or Baehrens' *lingua* (which Guardalben (1993) at 123 rightly calls "*fantasiosa*"). Goldlust (2013) at 168–169 defends Spaltenstein's (1983) emendation of *lenta* for *laeta,* which doesn't resolve the awkwardness of the distich. For *laeta* as "numerous" see OLD 1d. Cf. Welsh (2011) at 222; Webster at 107.

The phrase *licet meminisse* ("One may remember") appears at Ovid *Epistulae ex Ponto* 1.7.1. Cf. Appendix Virgiliana *Dirae* 1.103 (*meminisse licebit*). The parallel to Ovid makes it reasonably clear that *licet* is being used as a verb instead of an adverb, although it is not clear whether Ovid is using *licet* in the sense of capability or in the sense of permission.

Schetter (1970) at 159 would end elegy 5 at line 55.

4.57–58 There is disagreement in the manuscripts about the first words of these lines. See Webster at 45; Schneider (2003) at 222. With hesitation I embraced *quis ad has* ("who . . . these") of the Leidensis Gronovii 87 and Palatinus 1573 manuscripts to make this distich and the previous one more coherent.

Webster at 106, Goldlust (2013) at 169, and Franzoi and Spinazzè at 197 note that line 57 seems to echo Virgil *Georgica* 2.483 (*naturae . . . partes*). The phrase *naturae partes* ("parts of nature") often referred to genitals, see Adams (1982) at 59–60, so there may be some high/low wordplay.

There is an oddness in these lines that has escaped scholarly attention. First, they feel like a *non sequitur.* Second, who is Maximianus referring to in line 58 when he is criticizing an unmentioned person who is *clarus et . . . sapiens* ("famed and wise")? There is no reason, other than proximity in the text, to believe that he is referring to Candida's father. Indeed, Candida's father does not come off as particularly bright and there is no reason to think he is famous. "Famed and wise" might seem to refer to Boethius, as would the wishing for "what is wrong" if you believe his critics, but there is no foundation for that observation in this elegy. Another possibility is that Maximianus didn't write *clarus.* Five of the manuscript have *gnarus* ("known" or "having knowledge"), a reading embraced by Spaltenstein at 243, but that emendation would just leave us with a muddier version of the same problems.

Guardalben (1993) at 123 and Franzoi and Spinazzè at 197 reject Baehrens' conjecture of *cur* for *et ut* ("when . . . and").

For *adtingere* as "detect," see OLD 3.

4.59 Guardalben (1993) at 123 and Goldlust (20130 at 169 accept Webster's *volentes* ("willingly"—the adjective is used as an adverb) over Baehrens' speculative and almost surely wrong *videntes*. Franzoi and Spinazzè at 197 note the paradox of *rapimur . . . volentes* ("We're . . . ravaged willingly").

4.60 For an argument that Webster's *capiunt* ("get") is better translated as "to be capable of," see Spaltenstein (1983) at 244. I almost followed Baehrens and Guardelben (1993) in substituting *cupiunt* for *capiunt*, the version in Britannicus Add. 21, 213. See Goldlust (2013) at 169.

Elegy 5

5.1–3 There is considerable interest in the diplomatic mission alluded to in these lines. Barnish places the mission later than some scholars; he argues that the two poems praising Theodahad in the *Appendix Maximiani* were written by Maximianus and that they must have been written about the time of Maximianus' diplomatic work. See Barnish (1990) at 37; cf. Merone (1948) at 345–350. Procopius describes negotiations between Theodahad and Justinian in 533–534. Procopius *Historia arcana* 4.13.2, 6–29; 5.3.3–9.There was also a mission sent by Amalasuntha and Theodahad from 534 to 535. See Romano (1968–1969) at 317.

Another mission was the very large one sent led by Pope Agapetus I that arrived in Constantinople in early 536 to petition Justinian to withdraw from Sicily. Mastandrea also makes a strong case for a diplomatic mission of 535 described by Procopius as including two named senators, Petrus Marcellinus Felix Liberius and Opilio, and one unnamed senator. See Mastandrea (2005) at 162–162; see also O'Donnell, "Liberius the Patrician" 37 *Traditio* (1981) at 31–72. Vitiello (2014) at 261–262 notes certain parallels between Cassiodorus *Variae* and elegy 5 that support a 535 or 536 date.

There was also a mission sent by Totila in 546 or 549, see Bertini (1981) at 313, but those dates are far too late based on Maximianus' description of his mission and the text's influence on Corippus. Another possibility would be the various desperate diplomatic missions of Witigis in 538 and 539, but Maxiananus' likely ties to Theodahad make that hypothesis less likely.

I use the contemporary phrase "for diplomatic service" instead of the literal "in the duty of a legate" for *legati munere*. See generally Gillett (2003). Barnish (1990) at 21 notes that Maximianus' impotence during his diplomatic mission may echo Horace's impotence (albeit of a more temporary nature) during his diplomatic mission of *Sermones* 1.5.

Vitiello (2014) at 93 has recently claimed "we know that Maximianus would eventually abandon Theodahad and cross over to the Byzantine cause." In fact, "we know" nothing of the sort.

5.1 For *eoas . . . partes* ("the East"—literally "the eastern regions"), cf. Ovid *Fasti* 1.140 (*eoas partes hesperiaque simul*); Horace *Carmina* 3.35.31–32 (*Eois . . . partibus*). The phrase is a favorite of Ammianus. See *Res gestae* 18.4.2 (*ad tuendas partes eoas denuo missus*); see also *Res gestae* 16.10.1, 26.5.2, 31.10.11. Barnish asserts that these "lines have no direct verbal parallel to those numerous *Variae* which deal with the diplomacy of the Gothic wars, but they do show a strong resemblance." Barnish (1990) at 20; cf. Cassiodorus *Variae* 10. Mastandrea (2005) at 159 sees this line as a fusion of Ovid *Fasti* 1.140 and Ovid *Epistulae ex Ponto* 4.7.1 (*Missus es Euxinas quoniam Vestalis ad undas*).

5.2 The verb *nectere* ("close"—literally closer to "bind") is a cognate of *nexum*, originally the tethers on a hostage or slave. It came to mean the debt a hostage owed his captor, and eventually the Senate abolished this type of obligation for Roman citizens. See Berger, "From Hostage to Contract" 35 *Illinois Law Review* (1940–1941) at 281–285; cf. Varro *Lingua* 7.4 (*Liber qui suas operas in servitutem pro pecunia quam debebat nectebat*); Cicero *De re publica* 2.59 (*Sunt propter unius libidinem omnia nexa civium liberate nectierque postea desitum*). Use of the infinitive to denote purpose is a construction that became more common in Late Antiquity.

Spaltenstein (1983) at 246 overreads *cunctis* ("worldwide") by suggesting it is paradoxical and that for Maximianus it has some connection to "la guerre pour moi seul." The term here is a fairly straightforward one that means the peace being negotiated was universal (as Romans understood their world).

5.3 The phrase *gemini . . . regni* ("twin realms") describes the split between Ravenna and Constantinople; silence on the fall of Ravenna suggests that this episode and its composition occurred before its fall in May of 540. See Boano (1949) at 202; cf. Cassiodorus *Variae* 1.1.4 (*res utrasque publicas*); 10.32.4 (*utrasque res publicae*). Mastandrea sees possible echoes of Claudian and Sidonius in this line. Mastandrea (2005) at 159. Vitiello (2014) at 282 sees political and sexual metaphors in this line and notes the parallel between *gemini . . . foedera* in 5.3 and *geminas . . . foedere* in 5.115.

5.5 By identifying himself as an Etruscan, Maximianus may be revealing himself as "an original Roman" as opposed to simply a native of what we would now call Tuscany. Cf. Propertius 2.29 (*gentis Etruscae*). While this self-identification could be either fact or pretension, his inclusion of it here, as with his preference for dark-haired women over blondes at 1.93–97, hints at a strain of suppressed Roman pride beneath his allegiance to the Ostrogothic rulers of his time. But see Webster at 106–107 (arguing that "Etruscan" at this time simply meant "Italian"). See also Franzoi (2009) at 405–406. Barnish, relying on a parallel to Ovid *Amores* 3.15.3, criticizes Spaltenstein (1983) and Ratkowitsch (1986) for suggesting that *Etruscae* is "no more than a poetic periphrasis for 'Italian.'" Barnish (1990) at 17. While his logic is thin on this point, he does make the worthwhile observation that Tuscany was the power base of Theodahad. Barnish (1990) at 17, 30. See also Vitiello (2014) at 32–33.

It is likely that this elegy had strong political overtones for the poet and his audience. In the late 530s the image of a crumbling old Italian succumbing to, and failing to satisfy, a vibrant younger Greek would almost inevitably evoke the shift of power from the West to the East.

Ellis and Spaltenstein misread *suscipiens* ("sizing me up") by assuming it is occupational rather than personal. See Spaltenstein at 247; Ellis (1884a) at 3.

5.6 The phrase *Graia puella* ("a girl from Greece") probably echoes Ovid's description of Helen of Troy as the *Graia puella* in *Ars amatoria* 1.54. But see Butrica (2005) at 563 ("How can the *Graia puella*, who laments that the penis was her 'wealth' (608), be a symbol of the 'heroic' age of Greece—evoking the Trojan War, no less—rather than a simple whore?"). Butrica misses the point. By tapping into this resonant image, Maximianus is not only describing the *Graia puella* as intensely beautiful, he is setting up the epic expectations that he thoroughly deflates in the self-deprecatory comedown of "the Greek girl's lament." For possible allusions to Juvenal and Martial, see Mastandrea (2005) at 160.

Fielding has thoughtfully identified another likely inspiration for "the Greek girl," a Philodemus epigram (*AP* 5.132=12 Sider). See Fielding (2016) at 3–10.

5.7–8 Franzoi, citing Propertius 2.24.47 (*simulatum*), 4.5.49 (*simulare*), and Ovid *Amores* 1.8.71 (*simulatus*), suggests *simularet* ("she faked") has elegiac connotations. See Franzoi (2009) at 406–407. He also sees *vero . . . amore* ("truly . . . love") as echoing *Amores* 1.617 (*amor verus*). *Id.* at 407.

The repetition in these lines falls a bit short of the classic serpentine verse discussed in my note to 3.5–6. Goldlust at 171 describes these lines as examples of polyptoton and chiasmus.

5.9 Goldlust at 171 and Franzoi and Spinazzè at 199 see *nocte fenstras* ("windows . . . night") as an echo of Propertius 3.20.29 (*nocte fenstras*).

In an unpublished 2012 lecture at Brown University James Uden noted echoes of 5.9–10, 5.17–18, and 5.109–110 in Kenneth Rexroth's 1949 poem "Maximian, Elegy V."

5.10 If this line's *murmure dulce* ("in soft tones") echoes the *murmure dulce* of Statius *Silvae* 2.37, it should evoke a babyish voice.

The use of *nescio quid Graeco* ("something Greek") is another example of Maximianus' often overlooked use of humor, which is Horatian in its dry and self-deprecatory wit. Maximianus is gently poking fun at the foolishness of his own rapture because he doesn't even care what it was that the Greek girl was singing. Commentators tend to overlook the humor of the gender-based role reversal here; classical Roman poetry does not even imagine a love-struck female on watch and wooing a male beneath his window. The gender reversal for comic effect continues; Wasyl (2011) at 152 notes parallels for the Greek girl's lament at Ovid *Amores* 3.7 and Petronius *Satyrica* 130, but notes that in those cases it is the male who laments impotency, not the female.

5.11 This litany of noises and physical reactions is also part of the gender role reversal of this scene.

5.13–14 Spaltenstein (1983) at 249 notes an echo of Virgil *Aeneid* 4.370 (*aut* *miseratus amantem est*). Note the wordplay *miseratus* ("pitying") paired with *miserandus* ("pitiful").

5.15 Franzoi and Spinazzè at 200 note an echo of *egregiae formae* ("special beauty") in Corippus *In laudem Iustini minoris* 2.77.

5.16 I concur with Spaltenstein's (1983) rejection at 250 of Webster's argument at 107 that *grata* ("pleasing") is adverbial.

The noun *arte* ("art") probably also has multiple meanings in this line.

5.17 For *loqui* as "strum," see OLD 1d. The implicit trope of "fingers speaking" would have been understood by Maximianus' audience.

Webster at 107 notes the "elaborate chiasmus" of this line.

For influence on Rexroth, see note to 5.9.

5.18 My choice of "to stimulate" for *sollicitare* reflects my attempt to capture the sexual association of the term. See Adams (1982) at 184 citing Maximianus 5.58 as an example of *sollicito* for "masturbation" along with Ovid *Amores* 3.7.74, Petronius *Satyrica* 20.2, and Martial 11.22.4.

5.19 For *sirenis* ("the Sirens"), cf. Cassiodorus *Variae* 2.40.10 (in looking for a lute player for Theoderic, Cassiodorus unfavorably compares the toxic sweetness of the Sirens to the Psalms of David); Boethius *Consolatio philosophiae* 1.1.8–11 (calling the Muses a sweet method for destruction and comparing them to theatre whores). Schneider (2003) at 223 notes that Guardalben and Schetter follow Webster's *sirenis*, Petschenig and Schadd substitute *sireniis*, and Baehrens substitutes the improbable *sereni*. The angst of these emenders is driven by the metrical issue noted by Altamura (1981) at 822. Pliny, Priscian, Solinus, and Martianus Capella used *sirenis*; I have been unable to identify an author who used *sireniis*.

5.20 Despite note to 3.11, the phrase *alter Ulixes* ("the new Ulysses") may echo Propertius 3.12.23 (*alter . . . Ulixes*). Ellis argues that *Ulixis* would be the proper form of the nominative for this name. See Ellis (1884b) at 161. There is also a possible metrical issue. See Altamura (1981) at 822.

5.21 Schneider (2003) at 223, along with Guardalben and Baehrens, would substitute *et quia non poteram* for the *et qui non poteram* ("and I, who was unable") of Webster, Petschenig, and Schadd.

Franzoi and Spinazzè at 200 list many translations of the vague noun *moles* ("reefs").

5.22–23 Heege at 14 and Spaltenstein (1983) at 252 note that *vada caeca feror* ("I . . . was borne . . . to unseen shoals") echoes Virgil *Aeneid* 1.536 (*in vada caeca tulit*).

5.24 My "beat/feet" echos the end rhyme of *moventes/pedes*. The use of end rhyme, still rare in this period, may reflect Maximianus' aspirations for lyrical intensity and surprise. The exact meaning of *suspensos pedes* ("arching feet") is open to debate, but it probably means something along the lines of "on tiptoes." See Seneca *Controversiae* 1.0.22 (*suspensos pedes*); cf. Ovid *Fasti* 6.338 (*suspensos plantis*), Propertius 1.20.27 (*suspensis . . . plantis*), Quintilianus *Declamationes maiores* 2.16 (*suspensis gradibus*), Ammianus *Res gestae* 24.4.23 (*suspensis gradi-*

bus); see generally Mozley, "The Uses of *Pendeo* and *Suspendo* in Latin Poetry" 713 *Classical Weekly* (1933) at 177–180. Franzoi and Spinazzè at 201 see *plausibus . . . pedes* ("feet . . . applause") as an echo of Virgil *Aeneid* 6.644 (*pedibus plaudunt*). Guardalben (1993) at 123 and Goldlust (2013) at 172 reject Baehrens' *suis* in favor of Webster's *novis*. See also Agozzino at 286.

5.25–26 Maximianus uses the intensifying effect of anaphora here in a way that parallels the intensity of the passage. But see Franzoi and Spinazzè at 201.

5.27 The verb *urebant* ("were . . . burning up") is common in love elegies. Uden and Fielding note that this line and the following three echo Ovid's description of the naked Corinna in *Amores* 1.5. See Uden and Fielding (2010) at 452–453.

5.29 Schneider (2003) at 224 supports the *fultura* of Webster and Ellis over the *iunctura* ("joined") of Baehrens, Agozzino, Petschenig, Schadd, and Guardalben, which I have followed. Knox thoughtfully criticizes both these alternatives by looking to Ovid *Amores* 1.5.19–22 for guidance, but I am not persuaded by his proposed *factura*, the version in Leidensis Gronovii 87 and Palatinus 1573. See Knox (2011) at 411–412.

5.30 The phrase *exhausto pectore* ("exhausted chest") puzzles my advisors and me, but the key may be Martial 13.63.1 (*exhausto inguine*), which reflects the Roman belief that "sexual overexertion could cause males of all species, including humans, to become unappealingly skinny." Williams (2011) at 134; cf. Knox (2011) at 411–412. The Greek girl is, of course, female, but this elegy is rife with reversals of gender roles, so one more reversal is not necessarily problematic. Knox sees some merit in the comparison to Martial but would nonetheless emend *exhausto . . . pectore* to *exusto pectine* and make the phrase describe the Greek girl's pubic hair rather than her chest. Knox (2011) at 412.

5.31 Schneider (2003) at 224 reviews the variants for Webster's *terrebar* ("I was scared"); Ellis' speculative suggestion of *torrebar* has some merit. See Ellis (1884b) at 162. But see Webster at 108. Welsh is unduly perturbed by *terrebar*, and prefers Baehrens' *pellebar*, the *urebar* of several manuscripts, Ellis' *torrebar*, or the unsupported *pergebam*. See Welsh (2011) at 222–223. The previous two distichs establish a significant difference in weight between Maximianus and the Greek girl that makes his fear of squeezing her, and hence the retention of *terrebar*, eminently reasonable. Cf. Guardalben (1993) at 123; Goldlust (2013) at 172; Ovid *Epistulae ex Ponto* 3.6.50, *Heroides* 5.41.

5.33 Schneider (2003) at 224 notes that Baehrens uses *sic* for Webster's *nunc* ("now") and that Petschenig uses *summe*.

5.33–34 Maximianus is extending his self-deprecatory humor here by painting himself in a grotesque fashion. Franzoi and Spinazzè at 203 see unlikely echoes of Rutilius, Paulinus Petricordiae, and Reposianus in this distich.

5.35 Translating *dirigui* ("I froze") is a challenge. The primary meaning would be closer to "I stiffened" but the sexual connotations of that choice run counter to the gist of the line. Franzoi and Spinazzè at 203 note that *dirigui . . . calor* echoes Virgil *Aeneid* 3.308 (*deriguit . . . calor*).

5.36 For *venae* ("pecker") as the male sexual organ, see OLD 1e; Adams (1982) at 35. Schneider (2003) notes its use in Martial 4.66.12, 6.49.2, 11.16.5, and Persius 6.72.

The adjective *nata* as "old" relies on the Lewis and Short (1879) entry.

5.37–38 Spaltenstein notes parallels between this distich and Prudentius *Cathemerinon* 3.66–70 (*Spumea mulctra gerunt niveos / ubere de gemino latices, / perque coagula densa liquor / in solidum coit et fragili / lac tenerum premitur calatho*) and suggests that Maximianus is satirizing Prudentius' description of a Christian diet by using the same terms for sexual functions. See Spaltenstein (1983) at 258. Spaltenstein's point strikes me as more persuasive if one considers the first sixteen lines of Prudentius *Prefatio* to the *Cathemerinon*, which deal with old age and offer an autobiography of the poet eerily similar to what appear to be the facts of Maximianus' life. For conspiracy theorists such as Tyson and Ratkowitsch, this comparison might reinforce their views that the protagonist of these elegies is a totally fictional character. Others will note that most of the best poets of Late Antiquity had similar biographies; they had training in rhetoric, used that training early in adulthood in the courts, advanced into public administration (often by using their poetic talents to write sycophantic panegyrics), and wrote poetry in a community that highly valued poetry. See generally, Barnish, "Liberty and Advocacy in Ennodius of Pavia: The Significance of Rhetorical Education in Late Antique Italy," in *Hommages à Carl Deroux V–Christianisme et Moyen Âge: Néo-latin et survivance de la latinité* (Brussels: P. Defosse, 2003) at 20–28.

5.37–44 Schetter (1970) at 149–154 proposes deleting these lines. Franzoi provides a helpful but overly sympathetic overview of scholarly reaction to Schetter's misguided proposal. See Franzoi (2009) at 407–408.

5.38 The phrase *liquidi . . . liquoris* is another example of wordplay close to polyptoton, which I try to mimic with "on flowing fluid." Guardalben (1997) at 123 supports Webster's *liquidi* over Baehrens' *calidi*. Cf. Spaltenstein (1983) at 257–258.

5.39 Barnish suggests this line "may echo" Cassiodorus *Variae* 5.40.5. Barnish (1990) at 20.That letter praises a Cyprian—perhaps the Cyprian who accused Boethius—for not falling prey to Greek treachery. Greek treachery, as Barnish himself reminds us, was a cliché of the time, so without more evidence I am dubious of a true connection here. Webster at 108 suggests this line may echo Juvenal 11.100 (*tunc . . . Graias mirari nescius artes*). Mastandrea (2005) at 160–161 notes that *nescius artis* ("unschooled about . . . tricks") appears at Lucan *Bellum civile* 4.744 and Corippus *Iohannis* 3.412.

5.40 For *Tusca* ("Tuscan") see note to 5.5.

5.41–42 Guardalben at 123 supports Webster's *qua* ("which") over Baehrens' conjectured *cum*.

Franzoi and Spinazzè at 204 note that *superata . . . troia* ("Troy / was beaten") echoes Ovid *Metamorphoses* 11.215 (*superatae Troiae*). The *superata/superare* pairing is an example of polyptoton.

This distich is essentially a comment on the *Graiae . . . artis* ("Greek tricks") of the previous distich. With another gender role reversal, Maximianus paints himself as the helpless victim and compares the Greek girl to the epic hero Odysseus.

5.43 I have tried to capture multiple connotations of the phrase *muneris iniuncti* ("for the ordered duties") by translating it in a way that captures the sense of both the bonds of contract and the bonds of sexual commitment. Cf. Augustine *Sermo* 3.309.5 (*muneris iniuncti*); Justinian *Codex Iustinianus* 11.38 (*iniuncti muneris*). Spaltenstein at 253 overstates a valid observation by declaring that the expression is "de la langue administrative." In fact, the phrase is probably Ovidian here. Cf. note to 5.48.

For *curam* as "concern," see OLD 5a.

5.44 The phrase *saeve Cupido* ("cruel Cupid") was common in the Augustan era. See, e.g., Juvenal 14.175 (*saeva cupido*); Horace *Carmina* 1.19.1, 4.1.5 (*saeva cupidinum*); Ovid *Metamorphoses* 1.453 (*saeva cupidinis*).

5.47–48 For *sua munera solvit* ("paid its . . . debt"), cf. Ovid *Metamorphoses* 11.104, 11.153 (*munera solvit*). It is perhaps not coincidental that Maximianus took this phrase from a passage on the evils of wanting something too much. There are many defensible translations of this phrase; one scholar has suggested that Ovid used it twice in the same poem with opposite meanings. See Griffin, "A Commentary on Ovid *Metamorphoses* Book XI" 162–163; *Hermathena* (1997) at 98. Cf. note to 5.52.

The phrase *munere subeunda* ("pending debt") has a legal flavor. Cf. Justinian *Digesta Iustiniani* 650.6.6.3 (*munera . . . subeunda*).

5.49–50 I translate *recedit* as "shrank" to mimic the sexual innuendo of the original text. Franzoi (using different line numbers) notes a strong echo of Ovid *Amores* 3.7.14–15 (*segnia . . . destituere . . . ut ante fui*). Some texts use the Baehrens *recessit* for *recedit*. See, e.g., Franzoi at 204–205.

Goldlust at 175 ties this line to Ennodius *De Boethio spata cincto* (see Appendix C), but the theme of impotency and the presence of the common phrase *In Venerem* ("in love") seems rather slight to suggest a connection "sans doute."

5.52 Spaltenstein at 260 argues that *debita* ("what's owed") has a sense of conjugal obligation common among Christian authors of Late Antiquity.

Relying on Franzoi (2011) at 168, Goldlust (2013) at 175 sees an echo of Silius Italicus *Punica* 2.250 (*instat atrox terga increpitans fugienta victor*) in *instat et increpitat* ("pursues and snarls"). Franzoi notes the alliteration and internal rhyme of this phrase and argues, unpersuasively, that these techniques create a sense of urgency. Franzoi (2011) at 168.

5.53 Franzoi and Spinazzè at 205 refer to *nil . . . nihil* ("no . . . no") as anaphora.

5.54 The phrase *natura negat* ("nature cancels") may have been proverbial. See Webster at 109. Schneider (2003) at 225 notes parallels with Cato *Disticha* 2.9 (*cui vim natura negat*); Sedulius *Carmen Paschale* 4.8 (*et quidquid natura negat*); and Claudian *De raptu Proserpinae praefatio* 4 (*quas natura negat*). Cf. *Historia Augusta* 11.2.4 (*natura negat*).

5.55 For *verecundia* ("shame"), see note to 3.23. Ennodius includes a six-line poem with this title near the beginning of *Ambrosio et Beato*. Ennodius at 403. For the metrical issue, cf. notes to 3.23, 3.61.

Schetter (1970) at 53–55 argues unpersuasively for substituting Baehrens' *simul verecundia motus* for *quia tunc verecundia mentem* ("Since shame then . . . my mind"). Cf. Seneca *Hercules Oetaeus* 4.8.2 (*mentem abstulit*). See also Guardalben (1993) at 123. This line varies widely in the manuscripts.

Franzoi (using a text with different words and lineation) notes that *erebui stupui* ("I blushed, I froze") appears to be echoed in Corippus *Iohannis* 8.151 (*erubuit stupefacta*). Franzoi (2011) at 168.

5.56 The verb *ademit* ("cut off") has a wide range of meanings, including an association with castration. See OLD 1a.

Goldlust (2013) at 175 hears *blandum opus* ("alluring task") as an echo of Virgil *Georgica* 3.127 (*blando . . . labori*).

5.57 For this sexual sense of *contrectare* ("fondling"), see Adams (1982) at 186.

Without comment (there seems to have been a bit of a rivalry here), Webster at 56 follows Ellis' critique of Petschenig's inclusion of *virilia* over the much more common *flagrantia* ("burning") in the manuscripts. See Ellis (1894) at 235. Spaltenstein (1983) at 261 seriously considers the proposed Baehrens emendation of *flaccentia* for *flagrantia* ("burning"), which would radically change the meaning of the line, an emendation supported by Guardalben (1993) at 123. Welsh tends to side with Baehrens, but prefers his unsupported *languentia*. I agree that *flagrantia* read just within the distich seems odd, but it makes some sense when conjoined with the metaphorical *tactus . . . ignis* ("strokes of passion") of the following distich. Goldlust (2013) at 175 thoughtfully defends *flagrantia*. Franzoi and Spinazzè at 205–206 express sympathy for the *frigentia* of Wernsdorf, Puget (in Nisard), and Agozzino.

5.59 Barnish suggests this line echoes Cassiodorus *Variae* 1.35.4 (*forte natae praedictarum navium tactu torpedinis segnissime torpuerunt.*). See Barnish (1990) at 19. This suggestion, based on the parallel of *tactu/tactus* and *torpenti/torpedinis*, strikes me as tenuous. For the sexual sense of *tactus* ("strokes"), see Adams (1982) at 186.

Goldlust (2013) at 175 thoughtfully supports Spaltenstein (1983) at 261 in rejecting Baehrens' emendation of *illis* for *ignis* ("passion").

5.60 The phrase *in medio . . . foco* ("within the hearth") may be a playful echo of Plautus. See *Aulularia* 0.4.7 (*in medio foco*); cf. 2.8.16 (*in foco nostro Lari*).

5.62 For *arma* ("my arms") as sexual wordplay as "weapons," see note to 5.77.

5.63 Although the most likely source for *curis . . . mordacibus* ("gnawing cares") is Lucan *Bellum civile* 2.681 (*curis . . . mordacibus*), it is intriguing to note *mordacibus curis* at Augustine *Confessiones* 9.1.1. See also *Confessiones* 7.5.7 (*curis mordacissimis*).

For *animum . . . uri* ("my spirit was inflamed"), cf. note to 1.96.

5.65 Although Spaltenstein (1983) at 263 and Goldlust (2013) at 176 overstate their case, there is a possible echo in this line of Virgil *Aeneid* 4.296 (*dolos . . . amantem*).

5.66 Schneider (2003) at 226 notes that he joins Baehrens and Petschenig in supporting *certus* ("Constant"), whereas Agozzino, Schadd, and Guardalben support *caecus*.

5.67 See OLD 3c for *quin potius* as "What's more."

I follow Spaltenstein (1983) at 263 and substitute *placito* ("pleasing") for *placido*.

Schneider at 226 notes that Schadd supports Webster's *inquit* ("She says"), but that he joins Baehrens, Spaltenstein, and Guardalben in prefering *unquam*, which is in four of the manuscripts.

5.68 I render *renovare* ("be restored") in the passive to capture a bit of the sense of "renovate," which I think is part of its flavor and another example of the imagery of ruin in the text.

5.69–70 To show that *curarum pondera* ("loads of burdens") was a poetic commonplace, Spaltenstein (1983) at 263 cites Lucan *Bellum civile* 9.951 (*cetera curarum projecit pondera soli / intentus genero*) as well as Statius *Thebaid* 4.38 (*aeger / pondere curarum*) and 9.575 (*per attonitas curarum pondere noctes*).

The term *sarcina* ("weight") is a favorite of Augustine, who used it at least sixty-nine times. Ovid used it eleven times. None of their uses closely parallel this line, which has a proverbial feel. Cf. Augustine *Enarrationes in Psalmos* 59.8 (*sarcina pondus habet*). I see sexual innuendo here, but I have not persuaded some of my advisors.

5.71 Spaltenstein (1983) at 264 supports the variant reading in four manuscripts, originally used by Baehrens, of *versatus* over *nudatus* ("naked"). See Webster at 48; cf. Catullus 50.11–12. Spaltenstein's argument, which is unclear, ignores the randy context of the line and unpersuasively argues that *nudatus* "ne propose pas une vision efficace." Goldlust (1983) at 176 also supports *nudatus*. Enk at 74 supports *versatus* and argues that *versatus corpore lecto* may echo Propertius 2.1.45 (*versantes proelia lecto*).

5.73 Schneider (2003) at 226 notes that Petschenig and Schadd concur with Webster's *heuque senes* ("Alas, old men"), while Baehrens has *ecce senes*. Spaltenstein (1983) at 264 believes that the *que* after the *heu* is highly unlikely, and leans toward *ecce senes* over *hercle senes*, whereas Guardalben (1993) at 124 supports the *hercle senes* rejected by Spaltenstein. The Leidensis Gronovii 87 manuscript has *heus senes* and the Palatinus and Britannicus Reg. 15, A.7 manuscripts have *heu segnes*. Franzoi and Spinazzè at 207 adopt *heu segnes* despite the metrical issue and note the parallel of Prudentius *Psychomachia* 511 (*heu segnes*). Goldlust (2013) at 176 also embraces *segnes*, though he translates it as a characteristic rather than a term of invective. Welsh would replace *segnes/senes* with *nostrum*, a solution unsupported by the manuscripts that would produce redundancy and odd blandness in the line. Welsh (2011) at 224. Cf. Öberg at 178.

5.75 Spaltenstein (1983) at 265 misdescribes the manuscripts while arguing that *voluntas* should replace *voluptas* ("appetite") and relies on Wernsdorf's speculative emendation to support his position. See Webster at 48, 57. This emendation may have made the text "plus satisfaisant" for Spaltenstein, but it only extends the squeamishness of his equally strained reading of 5.71. But see Franzoi and Spinazzè at 208.

5.76 Spaltenstein (1983) at 265 continues his misreading of this passage by arguing that the verb in this line should mean the opposite of what it means. The verb *vindicor* ("I'm excused") is a legal term, see OLD 3, 4, and may have a hint of the mistress/slave trope common in love elegy. While the exact meaning may be open to debate, there is no basis for Spaltenstein's assertion that Maximianus "ait confondu *vincor* et *vindicor*." Wernsdorf offers the plausible but speculative emendation *judicor* for *vindicor*. Cf. Giles at 51.

For *infelix* as "Jinxed," see OLD 2, 3.

5.77 For *arma* ("the arms") as a metaphor for sexual organs, see Adams (1982) at 224 citing Ovid *Amores* 1.8.47, 1.9.26 as well as Adams at 19–22. For *tradimus arma* ("I give . . . arms"), cf. Statius *Achilleid* 1.532 (*tradimus arma*).

Spaltenstein (1983) at 265 sees a pun with *situ* ("disuse"). His second alleged meaning of "pour dire la vieillesse" does not work, but the word does have an engineering flavor consistent with the recurring ruin theme.

For possible influences of Petronius *Satyrica* on this and the following lines, see Merone (1950) at 329; see also Wasyl (2011) at 151–159.

5.79–80 There is a split in the manuscripts about the last word in this line, and I retain the Webster *ipso* over the Baehrens *ipsa*. Cf. Öberg at 179. This distich is murky with regard to both meaning and syntax, but it seems that *ipso* has to share the ablative with *hoc*. The gist here, I believe, is that his acknowledgement of inability to perform sexually makes him even less able to perform. Accordingly, I view *hostis* ("the foe") here as impotency or the broader physical decay that has rendered him impotent.

Guardalben (1993) at 124 defends Webster's *nos cessimus* ("I've yielded") and rejects Baehrens' *successibus*. See also Goldlust (2013) at 177. In the same line Guardalben also follows Schetter (1970) at 55 in accepting Webster's *hoc* ("this . . . fact") and rejecting the *haec* of three manuscripts.

5.81 Spaltenstein (1983) at 266 correctly rejects Baehrens' *argivas*, which is present in two manuscripts, for *argutas* ("cunning"). See Webster at 48; Schneider (2003) at 226; Guardalben (1993) at 124. But see Franzoi (2014) at 208.

5.82 Prior to this probably sacrilegious use, the verb *vivificare* ("revive") seems to have been a term of Christian writers, perhaps beginning with Zeno of Verona. Ratkowitsch (1986) at 118 cites this verb in support of her discredited theory that Maximianus was a Christian addressing a late ninth-century monastic audience.

5.84 Adams (1982) at 57 correctly points out that many editors, including Baehrens, uncritically accept Ommeren's speculative eighteenth-century emendation of *onus* for *opus* ("the job"). Spaltenstein's (1983) vain effort at 84 to find other examples where "burden" would make sense makes Adams' argument for retaining the term in the texts exceptionally persuasive. Given the colloquial nature of the term as used here and its engineering/architectural heritage, as well as my agreement with Green that the word has a sexual connotation, I render it as "tool" (which has sexual connotations in American and British slang). See also Green (2000) at 449; Adams (1982) at 156–157.

The particple *expositum* ("laid out") plays off imagery of the previous line and has a strong connotation of a corpse laid out for a funeral.

5.85 The phrase *viduoque toro* ("on her widowed bed") is a favorite of Ovid. See *Amores* 3.5.42, *Heroides* 5.108, 10.16, 16.318, *Tristia* 5.314; see also Propertius 2.9.16; Seneca *Phaedra* 3.18.

The term *laniata* ("torn") is Ovidian and it implies torn hair (*capillos* or *comas*) associated with grieving. See, e.g., Ovid *Fasti* 6.493, *Heroides* 12.159, 14.52, *Metamorphoses* 4.139, 6.532. It might also suggest a lacerated *sinus* ("breast"), see, e.g., Ovid *Heroides* 14.52, *Metamorphoses* 2.335, or images from early martyrologies. Goldlust at 177 rejects Baehrens' speculative *flammata* for *laniata*.

Guardalben (1997) at 124 rejects Baehrens' *resurgens* for *recumbens* ("prone").

5.86 The noun *damna* ("damage") has economic and legal associations, and its use sets the stage for the Greek girl's almost contractual demand for sexual services. Despite Spaltenstein's (1983) assertion at 267 that *damna* is synonymous with *luctus* ("grief"), *luctus* is a very different word loaded with strong emotion. In other words, Maximianus is describing head and heart. Spaltenstein is correct, however, in criticizing Webster at 86 for using one parallel with Statius to suggest that Maximianus was using "the language of the consolatory poems."

5.87 The noun *cultrix* ("celebrator") originally meant "cultivator" and later came to mean "worshipper" or "celebrator." It is rare in the classical era, and even rarer in Late Antiquity because of its strong connotation of pagan worship. See, e.g., Augustine *Sermones* 10.121.3 (*idolorum cultrix*).

For a discussion of this parody of classical laments, see Ramírez de Verger (1984) at 149–156. Barnish makes a thoughtful comparison between the Greek girl's lament and Philosophy's efforts to assist Boethius. Barnish (1990) at 26. Schneider at 93–96 argues that her lament is Lucretian. Thematically, if not linguistically, there are parallels between these lines and Ovid's account of his own unexpected impotence at *Amores* 3.7.1–24. See also Fo (1987) at 350–352.

Spaltenstein at 268 notes that Maximianus is echoing Ovid's declarations that holidays are for sex. Cf. Ovid *Amores* 3.10.47; *Fasti* 1.101. Goldlust at 179 calls the phrase *operosa dierum* ("holidays") Ovidian. See *Fasti* 1.101 (*operose dierum*), 3.177 (*operose dierum*); see also Pasco-Pranger, "*Vates Operosus*: Vatic Poetics and Antiquarianism in Ovid's *Fasti*," 93, no. 3 *The Classical World* (2000) at 275–291. Pasco-Pranger at 275 suggests that the phrase may be inspired by Hesiod—a pun on *Opera et dies* ("*Works and Days*").

5.88 For *deliciae*, see note to 1.154.

5.90 Spaltenstein at 268 notes that *digna de* ("worth") is a phrase of Late Antiquity. See Herman (2000) at 60. Both this phrase and *meritis* have a contractual flavor—a sense of what is "owed" in a sexual relationship.

5.92 Maximianus may have found the rare verb *ludificare* ("tease") in Plautus. See, e.g., Plautus *Cistellaria* 2.1.12–13 (*ita me Amor lassum animi ludificat*); *Mostellaria* 3.3.52 (*ubi ludificat cornix una uolturios duos*), 4.5.51 (*quid med exem-*

plis hodie ludificatus est), 5.3.3 (*quoque modo hominem advientem servos ludificatus sit*); *Amphitruo* 4.3.13 (*ludificant ut iubet*); *Menaechmi* 3.2.58 (*ita me ludificant*); *Miles Gloriosus* (*ita me ludificant*); *Bacchides* 3.4.28 (*quod eum ludificatus est*); *Casina* 3.2.20 (*iam hic est ludificatus lepide*).

5.93 The post-Augustan phrase *per totam noctem* ("all through the night") became suddenly popular among Christian writers of the late fourth and early fifth centuries. See Ambrose *Expositio evangellii secundum Lucam* 4.76a; Augustine *Sermones* 30.311.5; Cassianus *Collationes* 2.17.1.1; Jerome *Epistulae* 4.120a.4, *Samuelis I* 28.25, *Iudith* 6.21, *Lucas* 5.5; Orosius *Historiae* 4.10.6; cf. Cassiodorus *Historia ecclesiastica* 8.1.42.

5.96 The wordplay in my translation is present in the original text; *astans* captures the erect penis/guard "standing tall" at attention. Cf. Wasyl (2001) at 153–154.

5.97 Shanzer notes that this line echoes Lucan *Bellum civile* 7.75 (*quo tibi feruor abit aut quo fiducia fati?*). See Shanzer (1988) at 260; see also Goldlust (2013) at 179.

Spaltenstein (1983) at 270 notes a metrical issue with the second syllable of *feritura* ("foreplay"—literally "being about to strike"). See Adams (1982) at 148–149. See also Altamura (1981) at 822; cf. Hall (2004) at 240 (noting prosodical issue with *feritura* in Claudian).

5.98 Spaltenstein (1983) at 270 notes the parallel to *Priapea* 83.4 (*nec viriliter / iners senile penis extulit caput*), another lament for a limp penis.

For *cristatum . . . caput* ("crested . . . head"), cf. Claudian *In Rufinum* 2.1.355 (*cristato vertice*); Adams (1982) at 72. Spaltenstein (1983) at 270 and Wasyl (2011) at 153–154 note that with the adjective *cristatum* ("crested") Maximianus appears to be mixing erotic and military imagery the way he does with *astans* in 5.97 and *feritura* in 5.98. *Cristatus* is often used to describe military helmets. See, e.g., Claudian *De tertio consolatio honorii Augusti* 7.133; Sidonius *Carmina* 5.13–14.

5.99 For issues with the prosody of this line, see note to 2.65.

The most likely inspiration for the phrase *suffusa rubore* ("engorged with red") would be Ovid *Amores* 3.3.5 (*suffusa rubore*); cf. Petronius *Satirica* 128 (*perfusus rubore*), 132 (*rubore perfundi*); Pliny *Epistulae* 1.14.8 (*rubore suffusa*); Apuleius *Metamorphoses* 2.2 (*rubore suffusus*); Horace *Sermones* 1.8.5 (*ruber porrectus*). Schneider notes that Baehrens and Guardalben (1993) supports *perfusa* for the *suffusa*, as do Webster, Petschenig, and Schadd.

5.99–100 This distich is another example of serpentine verse.

5.100 This line may echo Ovid *Amores* 2.6.20 (*infelix auium gloria nempe iaces*). For a thoughtful discussion of this line and its relation to lines from Propertius and other poets, see Heyworth (2007) at 29–30.

5.101 The noun *blandities* ("flattery") is somewhat rare. But cf. Ovid *Amores* 3.7.11 (*blanditias*).

The anaphora of *nil . . . nil* ("no . . . no") is enhanced by the negatives of *nullo* ("no") in the previous distich and *non* (collapsed into "nothing") in the next line.

5.102 Schneider (2003) at 227 notes that the possibly tongue-in-cheek *sollici-*

tare solet ("tends to stimulate") parallels Claudian *Panegyricus de sexto consulatu honorii Augusti, Praefatio* 12 (*sollicitare solet*).

5.103 This line is a rare instance where I (along with Uden and Spaltenstein) side with Ellis against Webster. See Webster at 49; Ellis (1884b) at 162. Webster's *meritam te fungere* does not allow a coherent reading of the line in context. With some reluctance, I concur with Ellis' support for *funere* ("corpse") from the Regius manuscript. Cf. Augustine *Sermones* 21.158.2 (*quo funus tegebatur exposito*). Once we make this emendation, the case of *meritam* becomes problematic and the *merito* ("as befits") of the Florentinus, Leidensis (Gronovii), and Palatinus manuscripts becomes irresistible. But see Spaltenstein (1983) at 271 (conjecturing *emeritam* for *meritam*); Goldlust (2013) at 179–180 (harshly criticizing Spaltenstein's views on this line). If *merito te funere* is correct, it offers a parallel between its *exposito . . . funere* ("laid-out corpse") and the *expositum . . . opus* ("tool . . . laid out") in 5.84.

5.104 The adjective *assueto* ("customary") is rare, and rarer yet in Late Antiquity, but Propertius uses it three times to modify words for amorous attachment. See 1.1.36 (*assueto . . . amore*), 1.4.4 (*assueto . . . servitio*), 2.348 (*assueto . . . iugo*).

5.105 Enk at 74 notes that *deducta voce* ("her voice subdued") echoes Propertius 2.33b.38 (*deducta . . . voce*). Cf. Macrobius *Saturnalia* 6.4.12 (twice: *voce deducta*; *deducta mihi voce*); Lucilius ap.Non.289.16 (*deducta tunc voce leo*).

Works familiar to Maximianus also start lines with *hanc ego* (this . . . I). See, e.g., Virgil *Aeneid* 9.286; Horace *Sermones* 2.4.73.

5.107 I emend the Webster text to *languorem* ("slackness") consistent with note to 1.6. For manuscript support for *languorem*, see Schetter (1970) at 11.

5.108 Although in my opinion Maximianus takes a charitable view of his women compared to many of his predecessors and contemporaries, Spaltenstein (1983) may be correct in pointing out at 272 that with *morbo . . . graviore* ("a worse disease") Maximianus is making the standard charge of female lasciviousness against the Greek girl. One has to wonder, though, whether he is also being somewhat satirical at his own expense here—there seem to have been two quite willing participants until nature intervened. Uden and Fielding connect the *morbo* of this line with Philosophy's banishment of the Muses in Boethius *Consolatio philosophiae* 1.p.1.9 (*hominum mentes assuefaciunt morbo non liberant*). See Uden and Fielding (2010) at 455.

5.109 The phrase *perfide nescis* ("You're clueless, traitor!") echoes the *perfide nescis* that closes Ovid *Epistulae ex Ponto* 4.3.17, including the use of the adjective *perfide* as the noun "traitor." Cf. Prudentius *Peristephanon* 10.818 (*appello ab ista, perfide, ad Christum meum crudelitate*); Lewis and Short (1879) at 599.

For echoes in Rexroth, see note to 5.9.

For the parenthetical phrase *ut cerno* ("as I see it"), see Quintilian *Institutio oratoria* 7.9.3.1 (*ut cerno*).

5.110 The noun *chaos* ("hell") does not mean "chaos" as we use it today. Originally a description of the primeval nothingness, it had evolved to some extent by Late Antiquity into a term for the Christian hell. Here the *generale chaos* may recall the *sponsus generalis* of 1.72 so that we contrast the earlier vision of order and optimism with the later vision of decay and despair. Spaltenstein (1983) at 273 underestimates the power of this image when he argues that *chaos* here means confusion, not hell. Uden correctly notes that *generale chaos* is a cue that these lines are commenting on the broader political situation as well as the personal situation of the two lovers. See Uden (2009) at 209; cf. note to 1.72.

5.111–122 Wasyl (2011) at 155–156 notes that in this section the satirical fun eases and the Greek girl appears to making a challenge to the prevailing Christian view on the relation between *eros* and the soul. Wasyl makes a fair criticism of a somewhat similar argument made by Schneider (2003) at 463–464 when she reminds us that criticism of asceticism is not inherently a criticism of Christianity. She further notes that Maximianus may have had an unexpected ally in this view in Ennodius, who criticized excessive asceticism in an epithalamium. On the other hand, Uden argues that lines 5.113–116 parody Lucretius' hymn to Venus (*De rerum natura* 1.1–49). See Gold (2012) at 472. Fielding argues for a more serious Lucretian echo from *De rerum natura* 4.1198–1199. See Fielding (2016) at 18.

For a prose translation of this line and the next three lines, see Shanzer, "Latin Literature, Christianity and Obscenity in the Later Roman West" in McDonald (2006) at 184.

5.112 Boano correctly sees *quicquid toto spirat in orbe* ("everything that breathes throughout the world") as playing off of Boethius *Consolatio philosophiae* 4.6.2.30 *(quicquid vitam spirat in orbe)*. See Boano (1949) at 199.

5.113–114 The repeated phrase *hac sine* ("Without it . . . without it") creates another example of serpentine verse.

5.114 The phrase *gratia summa* ("the highest grace") may be a twist on a phrase Maximianus learned during studies in rhetoric. See Cerutti (1996) at 24–28. Although the meaning here of *gratia* is unclear, I think it is best understood (remembering "the Greek girl," not Maximianus, is speaking) in its postclassical sense of "grace."

5.115 For *geminas . . . foedere* ("coupled . . . bond"), see note to 5.3.

5.116 While the sentiment of love creating "one flesh" seems familiarly Christian (in the Vulgate *et erunt duo in carne una* appears at Genesis 2:24, Matthew 19:5, and Mark 10:8), it is also Ovidian. See *Tristia* 4.4.72 (*qui duo corporibus, mentibus unus erant*).

For *faciat* as "combine," see OLD 8.

For a metrical issue with *unius* ("one"), see Altamura (1981) at 822.

5.117–118 Spaltenstein (1983) at 274 mistranslates *perdit* ("loses") with "user en vain." The sense of this line is that a woman who is not having sex cannot stay beautiful because sex is essential to the spiritual bond that sustains her physical beauty. The following line adds that this phenomenon is the same for men. After misunderstanding this distich Spaltenstein characterizes it as "banal."

Guardalben (1993) at 124 rejects Baehrens' *defit . . . deficiet* for Webster's *desit . . . defuerit* ("it goes . . . it's gone"). See also Schneider (2003) at 227.

5.119 For *gemma micans* ("bright gem"), see Prudentius *Psychomachia* 1.334 (*gemmarum luce micantem*); Dracontius *Romulea* 5.88 (*non gemma micans*); cf. Virgil *Aeneid* 10.134 (*qualis gemma micat . . . aurum*).

The exact meaning of this line has been debated for over a century and has caused heated debate about emendation. Webster at 57 refers to the proposed emendation by Petschenig and Huemer of *conferat aurum* ("embellish . . . gold") to *conserat arvum* as "intolerable." Polara thoughtfully makes the case that *conserat arvum* has roots in Lucretius and other writers. See Polara (1989) at 198–201. In particular, he relies on Lucretius *De rerum natura* 4.1107 (*conserat arva*). Cf. Boano (1949) at 216. With *fallax* in line 120, Polara also points to Ovid *Ars amatoria* 1.399 (*fallacibus arvis*) and Manilius *Astronomica* 4.401 (*fallacia rura*). I have reluctantly retained *conferat*, which may be playing off of Virgil *Aeneid* 10.134 (*qualis gemma micat fulvum quae dividit aurum*).

Goldlust (2013) at 182 rejects Baehrens' emendation of *ut* for *haec* ("this").

5.120 The verb here is inferred and the distich unclear, but the gist seems to be that it is natural for gold and a jewel to combine in a marriage ring, just as it is natural for a man and woman to unite in marriage. Christian leaders of Late Antiquity discouraged most personal ornamentation but generally made an exception for marriage rings.

Guardalben (1997) at 124 amusingly rejects Baehrens' emendation of Webster's *externum* ("strange"—with the sense that anything outside the borders of Rome was strange) for *est arvum* (cf. note to 5.119) by understandably calling it "*la congettura piuttosto fantasiosa*." Goldlust (2013) at 182–183 argues for substituting the *aeternum* of the Leidensis Lipsii 36 manuscript for Webster's *externum*, a case supported by Spaltenstein, Polara, Öberg, and Schneider. On Michael Roberts' urging I reversed myself and accepted *aeternum* ("forever").

5.121 Webster at 121 notes that *pura fides* ("pure vows") occurs in the same location at Dracontius *De laudibus Dei* 3.248. More significantly, see Ovid *Amores* 1.3.6 (*qui pura novit arnare fide*), *Epistulae Ex Ponto* 4.10.82 (*puram non temerasse fidem*); cf. Lucan *Bellum civile* 8.572 (*fides si pura foret*). For *fides* as "vows," see OLD 2.

Guardalben (1993) at 124 and Goldlust (2013) at 183 rightly reject Baehrens' speculative *colentur* for Webster's *loquuntur* ("are declared").

5.122 Guardalben (1993) at 124 and Goldlust (2013) at 183 rightly reject Baehrens' *faustum* for Webster's *nostrum* ("of mine").

5.123 On Michael Roberts' urging I have accepted the Leidensis Lipsii 36 *vale* for Webster's *valde* ("quite"). The subsequent wordplay, including the best translation of the polyptoton *felix . . . felicis* ("happily . . . happy"), is not clear.

5.124 I have emended the Webster *en tibi* in favor of the Palatinus 1573 *et mihi* ("and . . . for me") based on the sense of the surrounding text.

Webster notes a parallel in Thetis' lament in Statius *Achilleid* 1.92 (*cognatis utere fretis*).

The adjective *cognatis* ("those kinds of") is ambiguous here. Imagination starts to run amok, which perhaps is the point, as to the exact nature of the recommended *deliciis* ("pleasures").

5.126 There may be some phallic wordplay here with the use of *sceptra* as a metonym for a "ruler."

5.127 Schneider (2003) at 228 notes that Baehrens, Spaltenstein, Schadd, and Guardalben use the conjectured *substrata* for the *subdita* ("obeying") of Webster and Petschenig. Various manuscripts have *subtracta, subiuncta, substracta,* and *subiecta*. See Öberg at 181; Webster at 50.

5.128 Goldlust (2013) at 183 notes disagreement as to whether this distich should trade places with the following distich; Baehrens placed it much earlier in the text. I see no compelling reason to undo Webster's editorial decision.

5.129–130 For most Late Antique poets, a personification of wisdom would have evoked the Old Testament. See, e.g., Wisdom 6:17. Personification of an abstract concept such as a goddess or goddess-like figure is also a common technique in classical poetry. Maximianus may be satirizing Boethius' Lady Philosophy. Cf. note to B.3.17; Corippus *Iohannis* 1.56 (*sapientia mundi*); Franzoi and Spinazzè at 9–10.

5.130 Heege at 25 notes that *porrigit invictas ad tua iussa manus* ("extends unvanquished hands at your command") echoes Ovid *Amores* 1.2.20 (*porrigimus victas ad tua iura manus*).

5.131–134 The "virgin" here is probably Aquilina (or an imagined young virgin), not the personification of wisdom in the previous distich. Although I cannot identify a specific martyrology that Maximianus might be satirizing, it seems that he is satirizing the popular tales of young Christian virgins who suffered death for their faith and comparing them to young girls who sacrifice their virginity. The welcoming of the wounds, the mocking of lost body parts, and the treatment of the torturer as a tool of salvation are common themes of Christian martyrology.

5.131 Spaltenstein (1983) at 277 notes a use similar to *votivo* ("prayed-for") at Apuleius *Metamorphoses* 7.13.1 (*tota civitas ad votivum conspectum effunditur*). But see Webster at 112 (restricting it to "of the marriage vow"). Both times Ovid uses *votivo* it is associated with blood. Cf. *Heroides* 20.238 (*votivo sanguine*); 21.95 (*votivo sanguine*).

5.132 Altamura notes that *perfusa . . . cruore* ("immersed in . . . blood") may echo the *perfusos sanguine* of Virgil *Aeneid* 11.88. See Altamura (1981) at 821.

5.133–134 This distich seems to display sympathy for the deflowered virgin/martyr, sympathy that it is overlooked by critics who wrongly accuse Maximianus of misogyny, such as Szövérffy. The modifier *laniata* is nuanced and captures much of the emotional and physical violence of deflowering; my use of "bloodied" tries to mimic both the sense of emotional tearing and the tearing of the hymen. The term is Ovidian and often associated with torn *capillos* ("hair"), a symbol of extreme grief. Cf. Ovid *Fasti* 6.493; *Heroides* 12.159, 14.52; *Metamorphoses* 6.532; cf. *Metamorphoses* 4.139 (*laniata comas*). The Greek girl also uses *laniata* to describe Maximianus' beleaguered penis at 5.85.

The term *percussori* ("her abuser") suggests the sense of repetitive striking present in both violence and sexual intercourse. Even the choice of *plaudit* ("claps for") is more physical than the more obvious, but less visceral, verb *laudat*.

5.137 Heege at 25 notes that *magnis nunc viribus usa* ("then with the use of heavy force") echoes Ovid *Metamorphoses* 7.440 (*magnis male viribus usus*). Maximianus uses anaphora in this line and the following two with *nam* ("yes" . . . "Yes") and *nunc* ("first" . . . "then").

5.138 Green (2000) at 449 harshly, but fairly, criticizes Öberg's proposed emendation of *nec his* for *nunc his* ("then . . . these"). In general, the manuscripts have widely divergent versions of this distich. See Webster at 162. Schetter (1970) at 91–95 discusses these variations in detail, but comes to the same conclusion as Webster, although Schetter's conjecture of *vincis quae Veneri* has merit.

Schetter (1970) at 95 and Guardalben (1993) at 124–125 rightly reject Baehrens' wholesale emendation of this line as *has pugnas quod poenis non es amica malis*. Guardalben also reluctantly follows Schetter's argument for *magis* over *malis* ("schemes"). Cf. OLD 7a. If Webster's version is correct, *sunt inimica malis* ("schemes are . . . adverse") might unexpectedly echo Augustine *Confessiones* 2.6.13 (*quandoquidem opera sua malis inimica sunt?*). Goldlust at 184 defends the speculative *vincis quae veneri sunt inimica magis* of Schetter and Schneider; I find their reasoning too thin to justify abandoning Webster's version.

5.139–140 Schetter (1970) at 50 compares these lines to Tibullus 1.2.25–28, and Spaltenstein (1983) at 278 compares them to Ovid *Ars amatoria* 2.231–232. Goldlust (2013) at 184 overconfidently asserts that the model for these lines is "sans doute" Tibullus 1.2.31–34.

Spaltenstein (1983) argues for *inpendunt* over *intendunt* ("target") on the basis of one manuscript, Leidensis Lipsii 38, but the proposed emendation makes little sense. Moreover, *inpendere* is very rare and had almost disappeared by Maximianus' era in favor of *impendere*. See, e.g., Cassiodorus *De anima* 11.3 (*et illis impendunt*).

I accept Spaltenstein's (2013) argument at 278 for *nives* ("snow") instead of Webster's *rates* ("ships"), but it is a close call. Cf. Schetter at 49–51.

5.141 Based on the number of parallels, Maximianus appears to have enjoyed Plautus. This line suggests he may have enjoyed drama as well because *feri . . . cordi tyranni* ("fierce tyrants' hearts") may echo a play often attributed to Seneca. See Pseudo-Seneca *Octavia* 88 (*fera quam saevi corda tyranni*). The noun *corda* ("hearts") is used at least as far back as Lucretius and is immensely popular with Christian writers as a trope for the soul.

5.142 Mars is often characterized as covered with blood. See, e.g., Virgil *Aeneid* 12.332 (*sanguineus Mauors*); Ovid *Remedia amoris* (*sanguinei . . . Martis*); Silius *Punica* 17.488 (*ferventi sanguine Mauors*).

5.143 Spaltenstein (1983) at 279 notes that although the amorous frolics of Jupiter and the War of the Giants are familiar stories, this combined account "semble unique." See, e.g., Ovid *Metamorphoses* 2.847–850.

5.144 Spaltenstein (1983) at 279 notes the strong echo of Ovid *Amores* 2.5.51–52 (*qualia possent / executere irato tela triscula Iovi*).

5.145–146 Spaltenstein (1983) at 279 rightly criticizes Baehrens' proposed reordering of these lines. Webster at 113 sees these lines echoed at Corippus *Iohannis* 7.253.

Spaltenstein (1983) at 164 provides multiple examples of the lion/tiger pairing in Roman poetry.

5.147 For a prose translation of this line and the next three lines, see Shanzer, "Latin Literature, Christianity and Obscenity in the Later Roman West" in McDonald (2006) at 184.

5.147–150 For the use of polyptota and chiasmic arrangements in these lines, see Uden and Fielding (2010) at 456; Fielding (forthcoming) at 29–30.

5.149 The phrase *vires animosque* ("strength and spirits") is common. See, e.g., Martial 8.73.3–4 (*si dare vis nostrae vires animosque Thaliae / et victura petis carmina*); Ovid *Metamorphoses* 6.690 (*saevitam, et vires, iramque, animosque minaces*).

5.151 Spaltenstein at 280 argues unconvincingly for *voluntas*, which appears in the Palatinus manuscript, over Webster's *voluptas* ("joy"). Guardalben (1993) at 125 also defends *voluptas*.

5.153–154 Though there are no linguistic parallels, in both this passage and 6.5–12 the "living dead" theme in this distich reflects the Lucretian view of life summarized in 6.5–8. However, instead of accepting the disintegration of the body with the cheery resignation of a happy guest leaving a party, cf. Lucretius *De rerum natura* 3.938–939; Horace *Sermones* 1.1.117–119, Maximianus alters the image of the party to one of a funeral both in this distich and at 6.11. In short, he rejects both Christianity and traditional Roman religion for a dreary form of materialism. Boethius also follows this Lucretian line of thought at *Consolatio philosophiae* 3.10.5–6, but in an ontological argument concludes instead that disintegration into imperfect parts demands a perfect ultimate source, and the consolation of a benevolent ultimate order.

Wasyl (2011) at 157 aptly compares this distich to a stage direction.

Elegy 6

6.1 There is a theatrical "coming full circle" in the direct address of *aetas verbosa* ("Chatty old age") in the first line of the closing elegy that echoes the direct address of *aemula senectus* ("jealous old age") in the opening line of the first elegy. Elegy 6 very much has the feel of a play's epilogue. Cf. Fo (1986–1987) at 111.

6.2 The noun *vitium* ("failure") is a moral and religious term, but it is also rich with connotations from Maximianus' likely professional activities. *Vitium operis* ("structural failure") and *vitium soli* ("ground failure") were engineering terms probably familiar to him if he is the Maximianus directed by Theoderic to undertake historic preservation in Rome. See Appendix A; Berger (1953) volume 43 at 769–770. *Vitium rei* ("a general defect in title") and *vitium possessionis* ("a limited defect in title that involves only a previous owner") would also have been familiar terms to an experienced advocate. *Id.*

6.3 I cannot identify a previous or subsequent use of the phrase *indignum . . . pudorem* (compressed to "scandal"), and probably for good reason. The most straightforward definition would be something like the redundant "shameful shame." Manuscript variants do not provide an easy rescue, although the *laborem* of the Bodleian manuscript is tempting. Cf. Öberg at 183. Franzoi and Spinazzè at 217 are unpersuasive in connecting the phrase with Catullus 101.6.

6.4 The idiom *crimen habent* ("is wrong") was Ovidian. See, e.g., *Amores* 2.5.6 (*crimen habent*); *Ars amatoria* 1.586 (*crimen habet*), 2.634 (*crimen habet*), 2.72 (*crimen habent*); *Heroides* 18.144 (*crimen habet*); *Fasti* 2.162 (*crimen habet*), 3.782 (*crimen habere*); *Tristia* 4.285 (*crimen habebo*). Goldlust (2013) at 186 notes the polyptoton of *crimina crimen* ("wrongs . . . wrong").

The word *contractata* ("massaging") is sexually loaded and striking in this context.

6.5 The phrase *leti via* ("Death's journey") had a long and honorable pedigree long before it appeared in this line. See, e.g., Virgil *Aeneid* 3.685 (*viam leti*); Tibullus 1.3.50 (*via leti*); Horace *Carmina* 1.28.16 (*via leti*). The journey metaphor also suggests a resonance with the Ovidian theme of exile—old age being an exile from the joys of youth. See Bellanova (2004) at 101 ("La condizione del vecchio Massimiano viene ad essere strodinariamente simile a quella del'Ovidio in esilio").

6.9 Webster at 113 sees a verbal echo of *vitabile nulli* ("unavoidable" in line 10 of the translation) in Corippus *In laudem Iustini* 1.265 (*nulli evitabilis*). See also Boano (1949) at 201.

For metrical issues with *ergo* ("thus"), cf. notes to 1.263, 2.43.

6.12 See notes to 5.153–154. The paradoxical conclusion, which has the feel of a closing couplet in light of its end rhyme, is typical of Maximianus' rhetorical approach. Goldlust (2013) at 187 makes a cautious case for Öberg's theory that this distich should close elegy 5.

While many readings are possible, Uden and Fielding (2010) at 457 stretch to find a sexual meaning in this use of *parte*. Cf. 1.5, 1.16, 1.117; but see 1.258 (*hac . . . parte*); see also Fielding (2011) at 140–141; Bellanova (2004) at 114; Fo (1986–1987) at 112–113; cf. Goldlust (2013) at 187–188; Gärtner (2004) at 153. The phrase *hac parte* is a usage of rhetoricians and lawyers and is almost always preceded by a preposition. See, e.g., Justinian *Digesta* 3.6.7.2.2, 12.2.28.10.2, 37.10.1.9.3; Quintilian *Institutio oratoria* 1.1.17.5, 5.4.2.1; Cicero *De officiis* 3.9.11. Without a preposition, I render *hac* as the adverb "here" instead of the pronoun.

For me Maximianus' sadly qualified *vivere* ("living") in this final line is a striking contrast to Ovid's confidently predictive *vivam*, the literal last word of his *Metamorphoses*. Aside from manuscript evidence, this parallel is perhaps the most compelling argument for rejecting the Öberg and Goldlust suggestion of moving this distich to the end of elegy 5.

My reading is darker than that of most other translators, who translate this line as an affirmation of immortality through poetry. I understand the desire to translate this line in that fashion, but in my opinion that interpretation is inconsistent with the bleak Lucretian view of the universe offered throughout the elegies.

Appendices

A. This marvelously nuanced piece of lyrically coercive bureaucratese nearly defeated my Latin. I want to acknowledge assistance from Michael Roberts, Shane

Bjorlie, and James O'Donnell, who generously provided me with their skillful, though quite different, versions. The successes of my translation are largely theirs and the failures are entirely mine.

For an overview of conflicting views on Theoderic's building and *renovatio* program, see Arnold (2008) at 172–174.

Paragraph 2, line 6: The phrase *indaginem veritatis* ("hunter of the truth") brings to mind Maximianus' self-description as a hunter in 1.21–24.

B. Title: Four of the six poems of the evolving "Appendix Maximiani," many of them with evident textual issues, were first collected in Garrod (1910) at 263–266 from the thirteenth-century Bodleianus 38 folios 13–16, which follow a copy of Maximianus' elegies. A half-century later Schetter corrected and expanded Garrod's work using a fifteenth-century manuscript from the Royal Library of Copenhagen, Hafniensis Thott 1064. See Schetter (1960) at 116–120; Fo (1984–1985) at 153–161. See also Spinazzè (2011) at 36–38. Later in the decade Romano made further emendations, and most editions since that time have followed most of his textual conclusions, as I have. See Romano (1968–1969) at 307–335; D'Angelo (2005) at 471–473.

On far from conclusive analysis, commentators argue for and against an attribution of these poems to Maximianus. Schetter became more dismissive of attribution to Maximianus as time passed. Cf. Schetter (1970) at 163–180; Schetter (1960) at 116–120; but see Romano (1968–1969) at 308–315; see also Tandoi (1973) at 148. Perhaps the most dismissive commentator is Butrica, who said, "[The] poems of the *Appendix Maximiana* . . . really have nothing to do with Maximianus apart from an association in a fifteenth-century MS and the fact that some of them are at least contemporary." See Butrica (2005) at 562–564.

The most thorough consideration of these poems has been that of Alessandro Fo, see Fo (1984–1985) at 151–230, but there is still ample opportunity for insight into these poems. See also Schneider (2003) at 133–145; Salanitro (1987) at 138–143; Salemme (1988) at 98–101; Stiene (1986) at 184–192; Vitiello (2006) at 135–151.

My text is not taken from one particular manuscript or edition but draws on all the best scholarly thinking to date. I created titles for four of the translations; titles are not part of the original texts except arguably for B.4 and B.6. For the best critical apparatus, which covers the two primary manuscripts and subsequent manuscripts, see Fo (1984–1985) at 165–170; see also Franzoi and Spinazzè at 67. Franzoi and Spinazzè have provided a very useful electronic version listing textual variants at Musisque Deoque: A Digital Archive of Latin Poetry (www.mqdq.it); see also Schetter (1970) at 168–174.

B.1.1 I substitute the variant *facunda* ("rich") for the Bodleian manuscript's *fecunda* and the *secunda* of Garrod. See Garrod (1910) at 264; Fo (1984–1985) at 171. Franzoi and Spinazzè at 239 note that the case for *facunda* is strengthened by Ovid *Fasti* 4.245 (*facunda voce*).

Franzoi and Spinazzè at 239 argue that *praemia formae* ("your points of beauty") echoes Ovid *Ars amatoria* 1.683 (*praemia formae*) and notes Luxorius *Anthologia latina* 354.7 (*praemia formae*).

B.1.2 Franzoi and Spinazzè at 239 note *dicere musa* ("Muse . . . to express") also appears in Rufinus *De numeris oratorum* 6.1.

B.1.3 Garrod read the second word of this line in the manuscripts as *normalis*. In classical Latin, the adjective *normalis* means "forming a right angle"; it is highly technical and rare. See, e.g., Quintilian *Institutio oratione* 11.3.141 (*normalem*); Solinus *Mirabilia* 38.3 (*normalis*); Manilius *Astronomica* 2.289 (*normalis*). It is unclear when the term lost its technical meaning and evolved into the "normal" we know today, but the technical meaning does not come close to working in this line. The only harbinger of a broader meaning I can identify may be Martianus Capella *De nuptis Philologiae et Mercuri* 4.327 (*nil normale putans*). The rarity of *normalis* does support the view of most scholars that Garrod simply misread difficult script and that *normalis* should be read as *votivas* ("promised"), which I use reluctantly. See Fo (1984–1985) at 171. The phrase *votivas . . . voces* ("in promised speech"), if correct, perhaps echoes Tibullus 1.3.29 (*votivas . . . voces*), but several scholars have emended *voces* in 1.3.29.

B.1.4 The phrase *verba deficiunt* ("words fall short") appears to be restricted to Christian authors. See, e.g., Augustine *Sermones* 10.120.2 (*verba deficiunt*); Jerome *Ecclesiasticus* 0.3 (*deficiunt verba hebraica*).

Franzoi and Spinazzè at 239 note that *pectus anhelat* ("as my . . . chest is heaving") parallels Virgil *Aeneid* 6.48 (*pectus anhelum*).

B.1.5 A less contorted version of line 5 is in *Carmina Burana* 142.11 (*si tu esses Helena, vellem esse Paris*). There are at least three reasonable translations of this line depending on how one punctuates it.

On Michael Roberts' advice, I have followed the emendation of Schetter (1970) at 173 and used *Helenae* over Garrod's *Helena*.

For *nuda Venus* ("nude Venus"), cf. Ovid *Ars amatoria* 3.224 (*nuda Venus*).

Schetter (1970) at 170 emended Garrod's *quid* to *quia*; another manuscript has *qua*. See also Schneider (2003) at 229.

For fluency, I have rendered *quid fama teneris in pretio* (literally, "What fame you hold for worth!") more colloquially.

B.1.6 The phrase *in pretio* ("in worth" in line 5 of the translation) is fairly common; it appears in Ovid *Fasti* but not in his other work. See *Fasti* 1.217, 5.316, 6.33, 6.349. As with much of Maximianus' vocabulary in the elegies, the phrase *in pretio* is common in legal writing of his era. See, e.g., Justinian *Digesta Iustiniani* 4.4.16.4 (*Pomponius ait in pretio emptionis*).

Goldlust (2013) at 189–190 defends the Schetter, Schneider, and Fo emendation of *te dare* for *cedere*, although he and others believe that the distich is corrupt. I think this line as amended originally by Schetter becomes more defensible once you accept *dare* as referring to bearing a child (i.e., "given birth to you"). See OLD 23, 24.

B.1.7 I follow Fo and Schetter (1970) in rejecting Garrod's *caro crines* for *auro crines* ("locks . . . gold"). See Fo (1984–1985) at 172–173; Schetter at 174. Franzoi and Spinazzè at 239 bolster this choice by citing Virgil *Aeneid* 4.138 (*crines . . . in aurum*) and, to a far lesser extent, Luxorius *Anthologia latina* 18.38 (*auro . . . crines*).

B.1.9 Schetter (1970) emends Garrod's *lilia* to *cilia* ("lashes"), as I do, with support from Fo (despite metrical reservations), Romano, and Salemme. Tandoi proposes the attractive alternative *lumina* for reasons of meter, style, and vocabulary. See Tandoi (1973) at 148. Salinitro, who supports the Tandoi alternative, provides a helpful summary of this issue. See Salinitro (1988) at 138; see also Fo (1984–1985) at 173,189. For a harsh critique of Tandoi's *lumina*, see Salemme (1988) at 98–101; cf. B.1.13 (*lilia*).

For *blanda* ("coy"), cf. 1.129.

B.1.10 I follow the scholarly consensus in emending the Bodleianus 38 manuscript's *ante Venus . . . nitet* for *ebenus . . . nitent* ("ebony shines"). See Fo (1984–1985) at 173. Fo (1984–1985) at 189 notes a metrical issue with *ebenus*. Two apparent aficionados of the *Appendix Maximiani*, Paul McCartney and Stevie Wonder, topped the charts in 1982 with their much-parodied "Ebony and Ivory."

B.1.11 Fo notes a metrical issue with *rubor* ("blush"). Ibid.

Franzoi and Spinazzè at 239 note that the phrase *in ore decus* ("Grace . . . upon a face") also appears in Paulinus of Nola *Carmina* 25.210.

B.1.13 For *lilia multa* ("abundant lilies"), cf. Virgil *Aeneid* 11.68–69 (*aut mixta rubent ubi lilia multa / alba rosa*).

For *lactea colla* ("milky neck"), cf. Virgil *Aeneid* 8.660, Statius *Silvae* 2.1.50, Martial 1.31.6. For the neuter plural used for the singular, see Gummere "The Neuter Plural in Vergil," 10, no. 17 Issue 1 *Language Dissertation* (March (1934) at 5–55.

B.1.14 I reluctantly follow Schetter's endorsement of Garrod's emendment of the rare *vernant* for its even rarer use in the passive voice, *vernantur* ("are budded"). See Schetter (1970) at 175; cf. Salemme (1974) at 316.

Franzoi and Spinazzè at 239 note that the phrase *membra decora* ("your gorgeous limbs") exactly echoes Virgil *Aeneid* 4.559.

B.1.15 Romano and Stiene would overenthusiastically emend Garrod's *delecto* ("plucked" in line 16) for *detecto*. See Romano (1968–1969) at 329; Stiene (1986) at 186. I retain Garrod's version in part due to the fruit trope in the following line.

For the phrase *tumidas . . . papillas* ("perky breasts"), see Prudentius *Contra Symmachum* 2.1.38 (*tumidas . . . papillas*). This description of the young woman's breasts has some similarity to the description of the Greek girl's breasts in Elegy 5.27–28.

B.1.16 For the phrase *manibus tractet* ("stroke"), cf. Horace *Sermones* 2.4.79 (*tractavit calicem manibus*). Franzoi and Spinazzè at 240 see a parallel with Avitus *Carmina* 2.214 (*manibus pomum . . . retractat*), which I believe is coincidental.

The term *poma* ("fruit") is somewhat uncommon but favored by Martial, Ovid, and Pliny. It is a favorite of Christian authors.

Fo notes a metrical issue with *fecunda* ("ripened"). See Fo (1984–1985) at 189.

B.1.17 Schneider (2003) at 229 notes that this entire line is lifted from Ovid *Amores* 1.5.21. See also Goldlust at 190; Stiene (1986) at 186–187. In part for that reason I reject Garrod's *castigatus plano* for the more precisely Ovidian *castigato planus* ("flat . . . shapely").

B.1.18 For the phrase *iuvenile femur* ("young a thigh"), cf. Ovid *Ars amatoria* 3.781 (*cui femur est iuvenale*). Stiene would emend the Garrod text to make it exactly correspond to Ovid's language; since there is no compelling reason based on meaning or the manuscripts for the change, I accept the Garrod text. See Stiene (1986) at 186–187.

B.1.19 The phrase *imagine formae* ("beauty glimpsed"—literally "a glimpse of beauty") also closes the line at 4.19. Both classical and Christian writers often use this phrase. See, e.g., Virgil *Aeneid* 6.293 (*sub imagine formae*); Ovid *Metamorphoses* 3.416 and 4.676 (*visae correptus imagine formae*); Claudian *De raptu Proserpine* (*tardatur imagine formae*); Prudentius *Contra Symmachum* 1.1.446 (*sub imagine formae*); Venantius Fortunatus *Vita Sancta Martini* 1.91 (*sub imagine formae*), 4.690 (*sub imagine formam*).

I follow the Bodleianus 38 *latet* ("lurks") over the Garrod *latent.*

Both *inguina* ("groin") and *his* ("it") are plural in the Latin.

B.2.1 For Romans the light from a woman's eyes was not primarily a picturesque trope; they believed, based on Greek scientific theories, that eyes emitted rays that permitted vision. See, e.g., Virgil *Aeneid* 9.110 (*nova lux oculis offulsit*), 9.731 (*nova lux oculis effulsit*); Ovid *Heroides* 9.169 (*tu lux oculis hodierna novissima nostris*); Silius *Punica* 11.282 (*luxus oculis mirantibus*); Prudentius *Cathemerinon* 5.153 (*tu lux vera oculis*). Cf. Lucretius *De rerum natura* 3.1026 (*lumina sis oculis*).

B.2.2 The phrase *clarum . . . diem* ("bright day") is Senecan. See *Medea* 1.0.5 (*clarumque . . . diem*), 2.2.120 (*clarum . . . diem*); *Hercules Furens* 821 (*clarum diem*); cf. Sedulius *Carmen Paschale* 3.146 (*clarum largire diem*). Schneider (2003) at 195, 230 (and some of my advisors) would emend *clarum* ("bright") to *claram*, which would make the adjective modify *te* ("you").

The reference to *lucifer* is the planet/goddess Venus.

On Michael Roberts' advice, I have emended Garrod's *te* for *se* collapsed into *fert* as "brings." See OLD 11; but see Franzoi and Spinazzè at 240. Virgil, Circero, and Quintilian used *se fert*; I was unable to find antecedents for *te fert* and it is at best an awkward fit within the line.

I have received conflicting advice regarding *sic* ("like") in this line. I believe *sic* is not being used to connect a conlusion to a premise, but is introducing a comparison with the implied verb *esse.* Cf. OLD 10, 11.

B.2.3 Roman elegy often uses the image of fetters and chains of slaves—either *catenis* ("chains") as in this line or *vinclis*—as a trope for a man's love. It is frequently used in association with *colla* ("neck"). See, e.g., Ovid *Ars amatoria* 1.215 (*onerati colla catenis*); Propertius 2.133 (*circumdata colla catenis*), 3.12.12 (*collo dulcia vincla meo*). Cf. Boethius *Consolatio philosophiae* 1.2.1.25 (*et pressus gravibus colla catenis*); note to 1.55.

Franzoi and Spinazzè at 240 see, though I do not, *constrictum blanda catenis* ("fettered by sweet chains") as an echo of Catullus 64.296 (*restrictus membra catena*).

B.2.4 There is disagreement in the manuscripts between *sub perdideris*, *per* *subdideris*, and other variants. I uneasily follow Schetter's conjectured *dum me subdideris* ("when you subdue me") over the Garrod *dum sub perdideris* and the improbable Franzoi hapax *persubdideris*. See Schetter (1970) at 176–177; Franzoi and Spinazzè at 240–241; see also Stiene (1986) at 187–188; Goldlust (2013) at 190.

B.2.5 The most likely source for the reference to Leander is Ovid *Heroides* 18.

For a discussion of why *remeabat* ("swam . . . back") is "problematisch," see Schetter (1970) at 177–178. Cf. Stiene (1986) at 187–189; Salemme (1974) at 177; but see Fo (1984–1985) at 174–175. Garrod at 264 notes the parallel between *remeabat in undis* ("swam . . . back through . . . waves") and Manilius *Astronomica* 5.610 (*remeavit in undis*), but a more likely inspiration is Lucan *Bellum civile* 3.701 (*remeavit ad undas*).The phrase *gelidis . . . undis* ("cold waves") is a familiar one. See, e.g., Ovid *Tristia* 4.10.3 (*gelidis . . . undis*); Silius *Punica* 10.363 (*gelidis . . . undis*); Valerius Flaccus *Argonautica* 5.350 (*gelidis . . . undis*); cf. Ovid *Metamorphoses* 15.310 (*unda . . . gelida*); Silius *Punica* 17.314 (*gelidas undas*); Tibullus 3.760 (*gelida unda*).

B.2.6 Goldlust (2013) at 190 comments on the corruption of this line and reluctantly embraces Schetter's *inter quas dubium* ("between which . . . risk") over Fo's *inter quem dubio*, which tracks Bodleianus 38. See Fo (1984–1985) at 175. Schetter's (1960) version is the least unhappy of the unhappy options. Cf. Ovid *Epistulae ex Ponto* 1.3.72 (*inter quas dubium*). For *dubium*, cf. B.3.5 (*dubiam*).

B.2.7 The most likely source for the reference to Achilles and Briseis is Ovid *Heroides* 3. Fo notes a metrical issue with *Achilles*. See Fo (1984–1985) at 189.

B.2.8 Goldlust (2013) at 190–191 has a helpful note on *cognitor* ("champion"). Cf. Fo (1984–1985) at 175. Franzoi and Spinazzè at 241 note an echo of Horace *Saturae* 2.5.38 (*cognitor ipse*).

B.2.9 The most likely source for the reference to Daphne is Ovid *Metamorphoses* 1.452 ff. (*Primus amor Phoebi Daphne*); cf. Martial 11.43.7 (*torquebat Phoebum Daphne fugitiva*); Cassiodorus *Historia ecclesiastica* 33.4 (*in Daphne festa celebrari*).

Shanzer (1983) at 192 (citing Alfonsi at 344 and Boano at 211) notes the almost total absence of mythological references in Maximianus' elegies. Given that fact, this sequence of mythological references does make one question the attribution of this poem to Maximianus. However, one has to hold open the possibility that his earlier verse was more formulaic.

I follow Fo over Garrod in choosing *Phoebum . . . pectore* ("Phoebus in his heart") over *Phoebi . . . pectori*. See Fo (1984–1985) at 175.

B.2.11 The verb *cremat* ("consumes") is unusual, but it probably echoes Ovid. Cf. Ovid *Fasti* 4.639 (*igne cremat vitulos*), *Metamorphoses* 8.823 (*innumerasque trabes cremat*), 14.444 (*QUO DEBUIT IGNE CREMAVIT*), *Tristia* (*et cremat insontes hostica flamma casas*). Cf. also Virgil *Aeneid* 7.295 (*num incensa cremavit*), 11.208 (*nec numero nec honore cremant*).

I follow Fo's *nos* ("us") over the *hos* of Garrod and Romano.

B.2.13 Fo notes a metrical issue with *anulus* ("ring"). Fo (1984–1985) at 189.

B.2.14 This line may echo Lucretius *De rerum natura* 4.1103 (*nec manibus quicquam teneris abradere membris*).

The phrase *manibus teneris* ("with tender hands") is less common in Roman literature than one might expect; it may have some Lucretian inspiration. See *De rerum natura* 4.1103 (*nec manibus quicquam teneris abradere membris*), 6.797 (*et manibus nitidum teneris opus effluit ei*); cf. Lactantius *Divinae institutiones* 6.6.3 (*quod teneri manu potest*).

Franzoi and Spinazzè at 241–242 note that the phrase *tu mea membra* ("you . . . my parts") appears in Eugene of Toledo *Carmina* 18.2.

B.2.17 The noun *ceris* means "wax," but it became a metonym for wax sculptures and writings on wax tablets.

B.2.18 I follow Fo in using *labiis* ("lips") of Hafniensis Thott 1064 over the *labris* of Bodleianus 38, although *labris* could be construed to mean "lips" as well. See Fo (1984–1985) at 176. Fo also notes the parallel between *oscula blanda dabis* ("you'll give sweet kisses") and *oscula blanda dedi* in 2.14. Fo (1984–1985) at 183–184; cf. note to 2.14.

My solution of "pressed" for *applicitum* seemed the best of the unsatisfactory alternatives.

B.3.0 Barnish sees strong thematic, but no linguistic, parallels between this poem and Cassiodorus *Variae* 1.17 and 3.48. See Barnish (1990) at 18.

This poem and the following poem are probably set at the fortress on the Isola Martana at Lake Bolsena in Tuscany. Tuscany was Theodahad's stronghold (Gregory of Tours referred to Theodahad as *rex Tuscia*) and Maximianus' familial home. In this fortress Theodahad jailed his co-regent, Queen Amalasuntha, in 534. Amalasuntha was assassinated there shortly after her arrival, almost surely by agents of Theodahad. The date of this poem is probably 534–535, a time period when one could still have been optimistic about a reign that was brief and disastrous.

B.3.1 Schneider (2003) at 133 has *quis* rather than *quisquis* ("who") to begin this line. Cf. Mastandrea (2005) at 173; Franzoi and Spinazzè at 242 (citing Ovid *Epistulae ex Ponto* 1.59).

The phrase *fastigia . . . montis* ("mountain peaks") is unremarkable, but Franzoi and Spinazzè at 242 note its use at Silius *Punica* 5.488 and Juvencus *Evangeliorum libri* 1.731.

B.3.1–2 Mastandrea (2005) rightly sees *excelsi . . . varium . . . opus* ("lofty . . . varied building features") as echoed in Corippus *Iohannis* 2.274–277 (*varium . . . opus . . . excelsis*). Cf. note to B.3.17. His argument is somewhat strengthened by the fact that *varium . . . opus* appears in the same locations in both lines.

B.3.3 With reluctance I follow the scholarly consensus and embrace the Bodleianus 38 gloss *gentes* ("tribes").

In this line and the following two lines, the poet (like any good political propagandist) is trying to paint his leader's failings as a virtue. Theodahad was not adverse to assassinating rivals, but he was notoriously uninterested and inept in military matters. His education focused on Platonic philosophy rather than traditional Gothic military arts. See Vitiello (2014) at 21–24.

Weyman (1926) at 163 notes that *sine funere* ("with no . . . death") mirrors Ovid *Tristia* 1.3.89; Manilius *Astronomica* 5.548, and Silius *Punica* 1.154. Cf. Cicero *Pro Milone* 86.10.

B.3.4 Weyman at 163 notes that *non opus est* ("There is no use") also appears at Lucan *Bellum civile* 2.319.

The phrase *caecoque furore* ("by dark rage" in line 5 of translation) may echo Virgil *Aeneid* 2.244 (*caecique furore*). See also Catullus 64.197 (*caeca furore*); Livy *Ab urbe condita* 28.22 (*cum caeci furore*).

B.3.5 For *dubiam* ("at stake" in line 4 of translation), cf. B.2.6 (*dubium*). Weyman at 163 notes that *casibus incertis* ("at risky odds") precisely echoes Lucan *Bellum civile* 5.66.

B.3.6 Goldlust (2013) at 192 sees *cedant arma* ("let arms yield") as an echo of Cicero *De officiis* 1.77 (*cedant arma togae concedat laurea laudi*), an argument first made almost a century ago. See Weyman at 164. I doubt that there is any conscious echoing here. Moreover, Mastandrea and Fo undercut the Weyman-Goldlust point by using the *cedunt* of Bodleianus 38 rather than the *cedant* ("yield") of Hafniensis Thott 1064. See Mastandrea (2005) at 173; Fo (1984–1985) at 176.

B.3.7 For information on the fort, see note to B.4.0.

The phrase *turriti scopuli* ("Stone towers") also appears in the same location at Virgil *Aeneid* 3.536.

B.3.8 I have followed Mastandrea's *praeruptaeque* ("steep") for the Fo *praerupta quae*. Mastandrea (2005) at 173. Based on context and line location, Franzoi and Spinazzè at 243 make a good case for an echo of Ovid *Remedia amoris* 179 (*praeruptaeque*).

Weyman at 164 notes that *undarumque minae* ("the waves' threats") precisely echoes Lucan *Bellum civile* 5.454.

B.3.9–13 These lines repeat the elegies' theme of a deteriorating world that is thoughtfully tracked in Uden and Fielding (2010) at 439–460. The closing line returns to this image as well.

Mastandrea in Franzoi and Spinazzè at 11 make an unsuccessful argument that these lines begin a section echoed in Corippus *Iohannis* 1.402–410.

B.3.9 Weyman at 164 notes that *pendente . . . ruina* ("looming . . . ruin") echoes Juvenal 3.196 (*pendente . . . ruina*).

B.3.10 Weyman at 164 and Franzoi and Spinazzè at 243 note that *per tot discrimina* ("for . . . many hazards") echoes Virgil *Aeneid* 1.204.

B.3.12 Garrod emended the *tutam* of Bodleianus 38 for its gloss *cuncta* (combined with *de culmine* as "skyward" in line 13), a change that has satisfied subsequent scholars. See Fo (1984–1985) at 176–177.

B.3.13 For *prospicit et placido* ("gazes and . . . peaceful"), Franzoi and Spinazzè argue at 244 argues for debatable echoes of Catullus 64.62 and Ovid *Metamorphoses* 7.226. He also notes that *et placido fruitur* ("and lazes . . . peaceful") is lifted exactly from Martial 12.9.2. *Id.*

B.3.14 Weyman at 163 notes that this line parallels Virgil *Aeneid* 6.487 (*nec vidisse satis est iuvat usque morari*).

B.3.15 For a helpful note about scholarly speculation about the location of this fort, see Goldlust (2013) at 192. Cf. note to B.40.

B.3.17 Mastandrea (2005) at 153 argues that the reference to *Theodade* ("Theodahad") in the present tense suggests a composition date between 534 and 536 AD, cf. note to B.3.0, and that this suggestion is strengthened by two echoes in Corippus of *cuius sapientia mundo* ("whose wisdom . . . world") later in this line. See Franzoi and Spinazzè at 8–9. They also note Maximianus' use of these words in the *Elegies*. See 5.129 (*sapientia mundum*); cf. Corippus *Iohannis* 3.81 (*cuius sapientia*); *In laudem Iustini* 1.56 (*sapientia mundi*). Ibid. at 154–155. Mastandrea (2005) dates *Iohannis* at 548–549 AD and *In laudem Iustini* at 565–566 AD. Cf. note to B.3.1–2. Fo notes a metrical issue with *Theodade*. See Fo (1984–1985) at 189.

B.3.18 Amid many manuscript variations and proposed emendations, Schetter (1970) at 178–180, supported by Tandoi, argues for *ne quid minus esset* ("so nothing's lacking") over the *nec prominus esset* of Bodleianus 38 and the *neque minus esset* of Hafniensis Thott 1064. See Tandoi (1973) at 149. Fo has a useful summary. See Fo (1984–1985) at 177; see also Weyman at 163–165; Salemme (1974) at 317. I have followed Schetter.

B.3.19 Franzoi and Spinazzè at 244 argue that *permiscuit utile* ("united . . . with . . . craft") echoes Horace *Ars poetica* 343 (*miscuit utile*).

B.3.20 Franzoi and Spinazzè at 244 note that *magna quidem virtus* ("What power") exactly parallels *Laus Pisonis* 97.

Franzoi notes that *prosternere gentes* ("to slaughter tribes") also ends the lines of Lucan *Bellum civile* 7.659 and Cyprianus Gallus *Deuteronomium* 163. Ibid.

B.3.22–23 These lines are baffling with regard to syntax and content, and probably corrupt; the variants only compound the issues. Fo properly rejects Weyman's emendation of *redemptos* for *demptos* ("saved"). See Fo (1984–1985) at 177; Weyman at 163. I follow Garrod and most subsequent scholars in using *titulo* instead of the *titulum* of Bodleianus 38. The phrase *titulo pietatis* (collapsed as "legacy") mirrors Lucan *Bellum civile* 10.363.

Fo notes a possible parallel between this line and 3.23 based on the familiar *ruina/ruinam*. Fo (1984–1985) at 183.

Goldlust (2014) at 193 makes the important observation that *instante ruina* (collapsed as "crisis") strongly echoes 1.171 (*non secus instantem cupiens fulcire ruinam*). See generally, Uden and Fielding (2010) at 439–460.

B.4.0 The fortress portrayed in this poem "may be the island stronghold at Bolsena guarding Theodahad's Tuscan domains, where Amalsuintha was imprisoned and put to death." Barnish (1990) at 30. Cf. note to B.3.15. It is probably the same fort mentioned in the previous poem. See also Fo (1984–1985) at 207–219.

For four of the six poems in the *Appendix Maximiani*, I invented a title. For this one I have used the *De saxo vario decore ornato* title included in Bodleianus 38, but not in other texts. See Goldlust (2013) at 193; Franzoi and Spinazzè at 245;

but see Schetter (1960) at 120. Eva Oledzka of the Bodleian Library confirmed for me that the titles for this poem and B.6 are both in a different handwriting from the body of the text, an observation which increases the likelihood that these titles were tacked on by a scribe.

B.4.3 Schneider (2003) at 231 and Goldlust (2013) at 193 note that *pelagi volucres* (collapsed as "seabirds") is an echo of Virgil *Georgica* 1.383 (*pelagi volucres*). See also Virgil *Aeneid* 3.241 (*pelagi . . . volucres*).

B.4.4 Fo notes a metrical issue in *aestuarentur* ("were churned"). Fo (1984–1985) at 189.

B.4.5–6 The phrase *horrida bella* ("cruel wars") is Virgilian. See *Aeneid* 6.86, 7.41 (*horrida bella*). Cf. Corippus *Iohannis* 8.289; Franzoi and Spinazzè at 9.

Franzoi and Spinazzè at 245 note that *nova castra* ("New forts") parallels Ovid *Fasti* 3.174 and *tutus eris* ("you will be safe") parallels Ovid *Ars amatoria* 2.58.

B.4.10 Fo notes metrical issues with *aridi* ("dry") and *theodadus* ("Theodahad"). Fo (1984–1985) at 189.

B.4.11 Franzoi and Spinazzè at 246 argue that this line may echo Priscian *Periegesis* 521 (*potens . . . aspera tellus*).

B.4.15 The phrase *diversaque pignora* ("assorted treasures") may be a veiled reference to Queen Amalasuntha if *pignora* has the sense of "hostages," or it may be redundant and mean "produce of the earth." For the straddling "treasures" I have relied on Lewis and Short II.B.2. Cf. Lucan *Bellum civile* 7.376 (*pignora tanta*). Franzoi at 246 notes that *pignora servat* ("it guards . . . treasures") echoes Ovid *Ars amatoria* 3.489.

B.4.17 I follow Romano in emending *viles* of Bodleianus 38 to *vilis* ("cheap"). See Romano (1968–1969) at 329. Fo does note a metrical issue with this emendation. Fo (1984–1985) at 189.

For *pretii tanti* ("worth as great"), see Knapp, "Studies in the Syntax of Early Latin," 35 *American Journal of Philology* (1914) at 292–293.

B.4.19 For *tranquilla tempora vitae* ("calm times of life"), cf. 1.289 (*tranquillam vitam*).

B.4.20 Franzoi and Spinazzè at 246 see two Ovidian echoes in this line. *Fasti* 6.742 (*per scopulos dominum duraque saxa trahunt*); *Epistulae ex Ponto* 2.2.36 (*porrigit ad spinas duraque saxa manus*).

B.4.21 I concur with Schetter's view that *natura* ("Nature") is personified here. See Schetter (1970) at 119; but see Fo (1984–1985) at 178.

Goldlust (2013) at 194 argues, overconfidently, that "sans doute" *grates . . . referret* ("offer thanks") echoes Virgil *Aeneid* 11.508–509 (*grates referre*). For a thoughtful overview of *grates*, See Williams, "Some Uses of *Gratus* and *Gratia* in Plautus: Evidence for Indo-European?" new series 9, no. 2 *Classical Quarterly* (1959) at 155–163; see generally Moussy (1966).

B.4.22 Franzoi and Spinazzè at 246 argue that *ministrant opes* ("works . . . make") echoes Ovid *Epistulae ex Ponto* 3.1.104 (*ministrat opes*).

B.5.1 There is some chance that our punning poet provides a hint of the location of this poem's house with his choice of word *atria* ("palace") in the opening line. The once-coastal Tuscan port city (now twenty miles from the ocean) of Atria (now Adria, probably the source of "Adriatic Sea") was located a little more than fifty miles north of Ravenna. Theodahad owned many lavish residences, some of them confiscated simply because Theodahad wanted them, but there is nothing specific tying the house in this poem to any of his residences.

For an overview of this poem, see Goldlust (2013) at 217–242.

B.5.6 Franzoi and Spinazzè at 247 note that this distich echoes Virgil *Eclogae* 10.42–43 (*hic gelidi fontes hic . . . / hic*). The unusually concentrated anaphora creates a sense of immediacy.

The phrase *in orbe placet* ("pleases all the world") is Ovidian. See *Heroides* 21.148 (*in orbe placet*).

B.5.7 Fo notes a metrical issue with *platanus* ("plane tree"). Fo (1984–1985) at 189.

Franzoi and Spinazzè at 247 note that *vitreis . . . undis* ("clear streams") parallels Ovid *Metamorphoses* 5.49; Martial 1.45; Ausonius *Mosella* 195.

B.5.8 I do not follow Schetter (1970) at 180 in emending Garrod's *aspectoque* ("in sight"—literally "seen") to *aspectaque*.

B.5.9 Franzoi and Spinazzè at 247 argue that *arbore lucus* ("a . . . tree . . . the… grove") echoes Ovid *Amores* 3.13.7 (*arbore lucus*), and *niger patula* ("spreading . . . darkened") echoes Marius Victor *Alethia* 2.498 (*niger patula*).

B.5.11–12 Goldlust (2013) at 195 notes that *vernat avis* ("a . . . bird / exults") echoes Ovid *Tristia* 3.12.8 (*vernat avis*).

James Uden noted for me that *aestibus in mediis* ("In midday heat") probably echoes Virgil *Georgica* 3.331 (*aestibus . . . mediis*). See also Franzoi at 247.

Franzoi and Spinazzè at 247 note that *viridi sub fronde* ("beneath green leaves") exactly echoes Appendix Virgiliana *Culex* 3.331.

B.5.14 For concerns that this line might be a scribal notation, see Fo (1984–1985) at 158. The line expresses a standard principle of Late Antique esthetics. Cf. note to 1.32. Franzoi and Spinazzè at 247 undermine Fo's argument by noting that this line and the previous line seem to parallel 5.31–32. It also would be odd for a gloss to fit the metrical pattern. Goldlust (2013) at 194 notes similarities to the elegies.

B.6.0 In Bodleianus 38 this poem carries the title *De viridario*, which seems, perhaps, more appropriate for the previous poem. Cf. note to B.4.0 (title in different script). The term *viridario* was extremely rare and its connection with this poem is most likely the act of a medieval scribe, but it could have been familiar to Maximianus. See Petronius *Satyrica* 10.2 (*viridarius*); Cicero *Epistulae ad Atticum* 2.3.2.3 (*viridarium*); Seneca *Controversiae* 10.9.8 (*viridarium*). The title may also be a corruption of the more plausible *de rivi ductio* or *de rivi ductione*. See Fo (1984–1985) at 178. Fo also raises the possibility that it is a title borrowed from Merobaudes *Carmina* III. Fo (1984–1985) at 222. The key Merobaudes manuscript is mutilated and the title is less than clear, however. See Clover, "Flavius Merobaudes: A Translation and Historical Commentary" new series, 61, no. 1 *Transactions of the American Philosophical Society* (1971) at 28, 61. *Carmina* III has certain other parallels to this poem and that Merobaudes also wrote panegyrics similar in several regards to the fourth and fifth poems of the *Appendix Maximiani.*

It is possible, as with the previous poem, that its location is Atria. The river flowed into a broad delta sculpted for centuries to create lagoons around the city. The scene might have been one of Theodahad's spectacular properties. Cf. Vitiello (2014) at 31–37.

B.6.1 The phrase *devia cursu* ("a winding course") probably echoes Ovid *Epistulae ex Ponto* 3.1.27 (*devia cursu*). Franzoi and Spinazzè at 248 (2014) make a case for this line echoing Valerius Flaccus *Argonautica* 8.54 (*haec ait atque furens rapido per devia passu*).

B.6.2 I have translated the phrase *perdebat meritum* as "was diminishing" (literally "was losing its worth") in order to capture the senses both of diminished stature and diminished size. The phrase may reflect the commercial vocabulary of Maximianus. A similar phrase is *augebat meritum* ("It helped my stature") at 1.29. Cf. Cassiodorus *De anima* 9.2 (*perdiderat meritum*); Ovid *Heroides* 7.7–8 (*meriti . . . perdiderim*).

B.6.3 The Bodleianus 38 manuscript has *lumina* but I accept the Schetter (1970) emendation *culmina* ("lofty"). See Fo (1984–1985) at 170. Franzoi and Spinazzè at 248 note that *quae nunc tecta* ("where . . . buildings now") also starts the line at Statius *Silvae* 2.2.55.

B.6.5 Goldlust (2013) at 196 suggests that *varios . . . quaestus* ("different uses") may echo Manilius *Astronomica* 4.166 (*varios quaestus*).

B.6.6–10 Barnish argues that this section "strongly recalls" Cassiodorus *Variae* 12.15.4 and may echo *Variae* 5.38.2. See Barnish (1990) at 18.

B.6.8 The manuscripts vary as to the last word of this line. I rely on a thoughtful defense of Schetter's *lacus* ("lagoons") by Salanitro. See Salanitro (1987) at 142–143; but see Fo (1984–1985) at 178.

The adjective *perspicuos* ("clear") was rare, but Cassiodorus did use it to describe water. See Cassiodorus *Variae* 8.33.5 (*perspicuos liquores*).

B.6.9 For *carcere* ("in a . . . jail" in line 10 of translation), cf. Maximianus 1.3.

B.6.10 For *fovet sinu* ("warms . . . in . . . the harbor" in line 9 of translation), cf. Ovid *Heroides* 19.62 (*fovere sinu*). This allusion is wryly funny if it associates the fish with Hero's recurring dream of embracing a wet Leander.

C. I rely on Hartel's edition of Ennodius for the text of this epigram. See Ennodius at 602. For a discussion of the manuscripts relied upon by Hartel, see Ennodius at I-LXXXVII.

C.1–5 Shanzer argues persuasively that *languescit* ("droops"), *rigidus* ("rigid"), *emollit* ("enfeebles"), and *improbe* ("falsely") are sexually loaded terms. See Shanzer (1983) at 184. She correctly notes that phallus/sword jokes are common and includes a literal translation of this epigram. Shanzer (1983) at 183.

One might extend Shanzer's argument about sexual language in this epigram by arguing that *dextra* ("right hand") is a masturbatory image, which admittedly seems odd when one recalls that this poem was written by one future saint about another future saint. There has been speculation about the source of Ennodius' spite toward Boethius, including speculation that it stemmed from a real estate dispute memorialized in a letter from Ennodius to Boethius, but we do not understand all the intrigue.

Shanzer makes a strong case that "the word *substantia*, an intrusion from philosophical terminology, reinforces the identification" of Boethius. Shanzer (1983) at 183.

C.4 The noun *colus* ("distaff") was a weaving implement, and weaving was viewed as women's work, so this line implies that Boethius was engaging in effeminate activity.

D. The *Imitatio Maximiani* is a plodding eighth- or ninth-century imitation of Maximianus' elegies; the author is unknown. The fifteenth-century manuscript containing this poem is in the Biblioteca Apostolica Vaticana (Pal. Lat. 487 IX e s). I have followed the version published in Baehrens (1883) at 313–314.

For background on the poem, see Schneider (2003) at 147–151; Leotta (1985) at 91–106.

E. For information about *Le regret de Maximian* I am indebted to correspondence with M. Leigh Harrison as well as his article "The Wisdom of Hindsight in *Layamon* and Some Contemporaries" in Allen, Roberts and Weinberg (2013). This poem is found in a late thirteenth-century manuscript, MS Digby 86 in Oxford's Bodleian Library, and in a manuscript from the first half of the fourteenth century, Harley 2253 in London's British Museum. For facsimiles, see Tschann and Parkes (1996) at 134v–136v; Ker (1965) at f. 82.

Bibliography

Translations, Editions, Concordances, and Commentaries

Agozzino, T. *Massimiano, Elegie, a cura di Tullio Agozzino*. Bologna: Silva, 1970.

Arcaz Pozo, J. *Maximiano Etrusco, Poemas de amor y vejez*. Madrid: Escolar y Mayo, 2011. (includes Spanish translation)

Ashton-Gwatkin, F. *Max: Poet of the Final Hour, Being the Elegies of Maximianus the Etruscan*. London: Paul Norbury Publications, 1975. (loose English translation)

Baehrens, E. *Poetae latini minores recensuit et emendavit Aemilius Baehrens. Vol. V*. Leipzig: Teubner, 1883.

Canali, L. *Massimiano: Elegia della vecchiaia: Testo latino a fronte*. Borgomanero: Guiliano Ladolfi Editore, 2011. (includes Italian translation)

Centre Traditio Litterarum Occidentalium. *Imitatio Maximiani*. Turnhout: Brepols, 2010.

Dapunt, A. *Der Eligiker Maximianus und sein Verhältnis zu seinen Vorgangern, besonders Ovid*. Ph.D. thesis, University of Innsbruck, 1949.

Fels, W. *Maximianus, Elegien, der alte Mann und die Liebe; Appendix Maximiani, Von Mädchen und Mauern*. Heidelberg: Books on Demand GmbH, 2000. (includes German translation)

Franzoi, A. and Spinazzè, L. *"Elegie" e "Appendix Maximiani": Testo, traduzione, commento*. Amsterdam: Adolf M. Hakkert, 2014. (includes Italian translation)

Galdi, M. *Cornelio Gallo e la critica virgiliana*. Padua: Prosperini, 1905.

Garrod, H. "Poeseos saeculi sexti fragmenta quattuor." 4 *Classical Quarterly* (1910), 263–266. (four of the six poems now called the *Appendix Maximiani*)

Giardelli, P. *Studio sulle Elegie di Massimiano*. Savona: Tipografia D. Bertoletto, 1899.

Goldlust, B. *Maximien Élégies*. Paris: Les Belles Lettres, 2013. (includes French translation)

Guardalben, D. *Massimiano: Elegie della vecchiaia; Traduzione e introduzione*. Florence: Ponte alle Grazie, 1993. (includes Italian translation)

Heege, F. *Der Elegiker Maximianus*. Blaubeuren: Druck der Fr. Mangoldschen Buchhandlung, 1893.

Lekusch, V. "Zur Verstechnik des Elegikers Maximianus." In S. Frankfurter (ed.) *Serta Harteliana*, 257–262. Vienna: F. Tempsky, 1896.

Lind, L. (trans.) *Gabriele Zerbi, Gerontocomia: On the Care of the Aged; Maximianus, Elegies on Old Age and Love*. Philadelphia: American Philosophical Society, 1988. (includes English translation)

Mastandrea, P., Tessarolo, L. and Sequi, C. *Concordantia in Maximianum: Concordanza ad "Elegiae" e "Appendix Maximiani."* Hildesheim: Olms-Weidmann, 1995.

Mauger, B. *Présentation, édition, traduction et commentaire des "Élégies" de Maximianus*. Ph.D. thesis, University of Lille, 1996.

Nisard, D. *Oeuvres complètes d'Horace, de Juvenal, de Perse, de Sulpicia, de Gallus et Maximien, de Tibulle, de Phèdre et de Syrus*. Paris: Imprimeurs de L'Institut de France, 1863. (includes French translation by L. Puget)

Öberg, C. *Versus Maximiani: Der Elegienzyklus textkritisch herausgegeben, übersetzt und neu interpretiert*. Stockholm: Almquist and Wiksell International, 1999.

Petschenig, M. *Maximiani Elegiae: Ad fidem codicis Etonensis recensuit et emendavit Michael Petschenig*. Berlin: Berliner Studien für Klassiche Philologie und Archaeologie, Volume 11, no. 2, 1890.

Prada, J. *De inter metri dactylici disciplinam et sermonem in Maximiano paeta exsistunt quaestiones*. Ticini: Mattei, 1914.

———. *Sul valore e la parentela dei codici dei Massimiano*. Abbiategrasso: De Angeli, 1918.

———. *Maximiani elegiae, codicibus denuo collatis cum apparatu critico locupletissimo codicum et editonum*. Abbiategrasso: De Angeli, 1919.

———. *Lamenti e guai di un vecchio. Versione metrica delle elegie di Massimiano*. Abbiategrasso: De Angeli, 1920.

Schadd, J. and Schröder, A. *Maximianus Elegieën: Tekst en vertaling*. Amsterdam: Straat, 1987. (includes Dutch translation)

Schetter, W. *Studien zur Überlieferung und Kritik des Elegiker Maximian*. Wiesbaden: Otto Harrassowitz, 1970.

Schneider, W. *Die elegischen Verse von Maximian: Eine letzte Widerrede gegen die neue christliche Zeit*. Stuttgart: Steiner Verlag, 2003. (includes German translation)

Spaltenstein, F. *Commentaire des élégies de Maximien*. Rome: Institut Suisse de Rome, 1983.

Strazzulla, V. *Massimiano etrusco elegiografo*. Catania: Galati, 1893.

Tyson, M. *The First Elegy of Maximianus: A Translation and Commentary Based on an Analysis of Possible Earlier Latin Influences Found by a Computer Search on the Phi CD-ROM Disk*. M.A. thesis, University of Ottawa, 1996. (Includes English translation of most of Elegy 1.)

Walker, H. *The Impotent Lover accurately described in six elegies upon Old Age, with the doting old lecher's resentments on the past pleasures and vigorous performances of youth*. London: Peacock and Bible, 1688. (loose English translation)

Webster, R. *The Elegies of Maximianus*. Princeton: Princeton Press, 1900.
Wernsdorf, J. *Poetae latini minores, tomi sexti qui carmina amatoria et ludibria complecitur pars prior*. Helmstedt: G. S. Fleckeisen, 1794.
Withof, J. *Encaenia critica sive Lucanus, Avianus et Maximianus, triga scriptorium veterum primaevae integritati restituti*. Vesaliae, 1741.

Other Sources

Adams, J. *The Latin Sexual Vocabulary*. Baltimore: Johns Hopkins University Press, 1982.
———. *Social Variation and the Latin Language*. Cambridge: Cambridge University Press, 2013.
Allen, R., Roberts, J. and Weinberg, C. (eds.) *Reading Laȝamon's Brut: Approaches and Explorations*. Amsterdam: Rodopi, 2013.
Amory, P. *People and Identity in Ostrogothic Italy, 489–554*. Cambridge: Cambridge University Press, 1997.
Anderson, W. (ed.) *Ovid's Metamorphoses: Books 1–5*. Norman: University of Oklahoma Press, 1997.
Athanassiadi, P. and Frede, M. *Pagan Monotheism in Late Antiquity*. Oxford: Oxford University Press, 1999.
Baehrens, E. *Miscellanea critica, Corollarium*. Groningen: In Aedibus J. B. Woltersii, 1878.
Balch, D. and Osiek, C. (eds.) *Early Christian Families in Context: An Interdisciplinary Dialogue*. Grand Rapids: Eerdmans, 2003.
Berger, A. *Encyclopedic Dictionary of Roman Law*. Philadelphia: American Philosophical Society, 1953.
Boethius. *The Theological Tractates; The Consolation of Philosophy*, trans. S. Tester. Cambridge: Harvard University Press, 1973.
———. *Consolation of Philosophy*, trans. J. Relihan. Indianapolis: Hackett, 2001.
Borgolte, M. and Spilling, H. *Litterae medii aevi: Festschrift für Johanne Autenrieth zu ihrem 65 Geburtstag*. Sigmaringen: J. Thorbecke, 1988.
Broering, J. *Quaestiones Maximianeae*. Ph.D. thesis, University of Münster, 1893.
Brown, R. *The Art of Suicide*. London: Reaktion Books, 2001.
Burton, R. *The Anatomy of Melancholy*, intro. W. Gass. New York: New York Review of Books, 2001.
Calboli, G., Degani, E., Ghiselli, A., Mariotti, I. and Traina, A. *Scritti in onore di Giuseppe Morelli*. Bologna: Pàtron Editore, 1997.
Cardini, R. and Coppini, D. *Il rinnovamento umanistico della poesia: L'epigramma e l'elegia*. Firenze: Edizioni Polistampa, 2009.
Cerutti, S. *Cicero's Accretive Style: Rhetorical Strategies in the Exordia of the Judicial Speeches*. Lanham: University Press of America, 1996.
Chin, C. *Grammar and Christianity in the Late Roman World*. Philadelphia: University of Pennsylvania Press, 2008.
Copeland, R. and Sluiter, I. *Medieval Grammar and Rhetoric: Language Arts and Literary Theory, AD 300–1475*. Oxford: Oxford University Press, 2009.

d'Andeli, H. *The Battle of the Seven Arts: A French Poem*, ed. and trans. L. J. Paetow. Berkeley: University of California Press, 1914.

Dickey, E. and Chahoud, A. *Colloquial and Literary Latin*. Cambridge: Cambridge University Press, 2010.

Duckworth, G. *The Nature of Roman Comedy: A Study of Popular Entertainment*. Norman: University of Oklahoma Press, 1994.

Enk, P. *Sex: Propertii Elegiarum Liber I (Monobiblos)*. Leiden: Brill, 1946.

Ennodius. *Magni Felicis Ennodius opera omnia*, ed. G. Hartel. Vienna: Academiae Litterarum Caesareae Vindobonensis, 1882.

Faral, E. *Recherches sur les sources latines des contes et romans courtois du moyen âge*. Paris: E. Champion, 1913.

Forni, K. *Chaucerian Apocrypha: A Counterfeit Canon*. Gainesville: University Press of Florida, 2001.

Gaertner, J. (ed.) *Ovid Epistulae ex Ponto, Book I*. Oxford: Oxford University Press, 2005.

Gaisser, J. (ed.) *Catullus*. Oxford: Oxford University Press, 2007.

Galán Vioque, G. *Martial, Book VII: A Commentary*, trans. J. Zoltowski. Leiden: Brill, 2002.

Gibson, R. (ed.) *Ars amatoria, Book 3*. Cambridge: Cambridge University Press, 2003.

Gillett, A. *Envoys and Political Communication in the Late Antique West, 411–533*. Cambridge: Cambridge University Press, 2003.

Gold, B. (ed.). *A Companion to Roman Love Elegy*. Oxford: Wiley Blackwell, 2012.

Gowers, E. *Horace: Satires, Book I*. Cambridge: Cambridge University Press 2012.

Guardalben, D. *Studi su Massimiano*. Ph.D. thesis, University of Rome, 1978.

Günther, H. *Quaestiones Propertianae*. Leiden: Brill, 1997.

Hall, J. (ed.) *Claudian: De raptu Proserpinae*. Cambridge: Cambridge University Press, 2004.

Harries, J. *Law and Empire in Late Antiquity*. Cambridge: Cambridge University Press, 1999.

Hass, P. *Der locus amoenus in der antiken Literatur: Zu Theorie und Geschichte eines literarischen Motivs*. Bamberg: Wissenschaftlicher Verlag, 1998.

Heidegger, M. *Poetry, Language, Thought*, trans. M. Hofstadter. New York: HarperCollins, 1971.

Herman, J. *Vulgar Latin*, trans. R. Wright. University Park: Pennsylvania State University Press, 2000.

Heyworth, J. *Cynthia: A Companion to the Text of Propertius*. Oxford: Oxford University Press, 2007.

Hodgkin, T. *Italy and Her Invaders: The Ostrogothic Invasion, 476–535*. Oxford: Clarendon Press, 1885.

James, S. *Learned Girls and Male Persuasion: Gender and Reading in Roman Love Elegy*. Berkeley: University of California Press, 2003.

Kaster, R. *Guardians of Language: The Grammarian and Society in Late Antiquity*. Berkeley: University of California Press, 1988.

Kelly, K. *Performing Virginity and Testing Chastity in the Middle Ages*. London: Routledge, 2000.

Kennedy, D. *The Arts of Love: Five Studies in the Discourse of Roman Love Elegy.* Cambridge: Cambridge University Press, 1993.

Kennell, S. *Magnus Felix Ennodius: A Gentleman of the Church*. Ann Arbor: University of Michigan Press, 2000.

Ker, N. R. *Facsimile of British Museum MS Harley 2253*. London: Published for the Early English Text Society by the Oxford University Press, 1965.

Kleywegt, A. *Valerius Flaccus, Argonautica, Book I: A Commentary*. Leiden: Brill, 2005.

Knox, P. *Heroides: Selected Epistles*. Cambridge: Cambridge University Press, 1995.

Lattimore, R. *Themes in Greek and Latin Epitaphs*. Urbana: University of Illinois Press, 1962.

Lavan, L., Ozengel, L. and Sarantis, A. *Housing in Late Antiquity: From Palaces to Shops*. Leiden: Brill, 2007.

Lawrence-Mathers, A. *Manuscripts in Northumbria in the Eleventh and Twelfth Centuries*. Woodbridge: Boydell Press, 2003.

Lewis, C. and Short, C. *A Latin Dictionary*. Oxford: Oxford University Press, 1879.

Maes, C. *Children in the Roman Empire*. Cambridge: Cambridge University Press, 2011.

Mann, J. *Chaucer and the Medieval Estates Satire: The Literature of Social Classes and the General Prologue of the Canterbury Tales*. Cambridge: Cambridge University Press, 1973.

Marenbon, J. (ed.) *Poetry and Philosophy in the Middle Ages: A Festschrift for Peter Dronke*. Leiden: Brill, 2001.

Masters, J. *Poetry and Civil War in Lucan's Bellum Civile*. Cambridge: University Press, 1992.

Maxwell, V. *The Military Decorations of the Roman Army*. Berkeley: University of California Press, 1981.

McBrine, P. *The English Inheritance of Biblical Verse*. Ph.D. thesis, University of Toronto, 2008. (forthcoming in revised form as a book from the University of Toronto Press)

McDonald, N. (ed.) *Medieval Obscenities*. Woodbridge: Boydell Press, 2006.

McGill, S. *Virgil Recomposed: The Mythological and Secular Centos in Antiquity.* Oxford: Oxford University Press, 2005.

McGinn, T. *The Economy of Prostitution in the Roman World*. Ann Arbor: University of Michigan Press, 2004.

Montaigne, M. de. *The Complete Essays*, trans. M. Screech. London: Penguin, 1987.

Moorhead, J. *Theoderic in Italy*. Oxford: Oxford University Press, 1992.

Moussy, C. *Gratia et sa famille*. Paris: Presses Universitaires de France, 1966.

Nathan, G. *The Family in Late Antiquity: The Rise of Christianity and the Endurance of Tradition*. London: Routledge, 2000.

Navarro Antolín, F. *Lygdamus: Corpus Tibullianum III.1–6: Lygdami elegiarum liber*. Leiden: Brill, 1996.

O'Connell, R. *Soundings in St. Augustine's Imagination*. New York: Fordham University Press, 1994.

O'Daly, G. *The Poetry of Boethius*. Chapel Hill: University of North Carolina Press, 1991.

O'Sullivan, S. *Early Medieval Glosses on Prudentius' Psychomachia: The Weitz Tradition*. Leiden: Brill, 2004.

Oxford Latin Dictionary (OLD). Oxford: Oxford University Press, 2006.

Parkin, T. *Old Age in the Roman World*. Baltimore: Johns Hopkins University Press, 2003.

Peachin, M. (ed.). *The Oxford Handbook of Social Relations in the Roman World*. Oxford: Oxford University Press, 2011.

Post, G. *Studies in Medieval Legal Thought: Public Law and the State, 1100–1322*. Princeton: Princeton University Press, 2015. (First published 1964.)

Prada, G. *Sul valore e la parentela dei codici di Massimiano*. Pavia, 1918.

Ratkowitsch, C. *Maximianus amat: Zu Datierung und Interpretation des Elegikers Maximian*. Vienna: Verlag der Österreichischen Akademie der Wissenschaften, 1986.

Relihan, J. *The Prisoner's Philosophy: Life and Death in Boethius' Consolation*. Notre Dame: University of Notre Dame Press, 2007. (includes English translation of Elegy 3)

Reynolds, P. *Marriage in the Western Church: The Christianization of Marriage During the Patristic and Early Medieval Periods*. Leiden: E. J. Brill, 1994.

Roberts, M. *Poetry and the Cult of Martyrs: The Liber Peristephanon of Prudentius*. Ann Arbor: University of Michigan Press, 1993.

Roller, M. *Constructing Autocracy: Aristocrats and Emperors in Julio-Claudian Rome*. Princeton: Princeton University Press, 2001.

Sandoz, L. (ed.) *Au-délà de l'élégie d'amour: Métamorphoses et renouvellements d'un genre latin dans l'Antiquité et à la Renaissance*. Volume 2. Paris: Garnier, 2011.

Sandys, J. *A History of Classical Scholarship*. Cambridge: Cambridge University Press, 1906.

Sessa, K. *The Formation of Papal Authority in Late Antique Italy: Roman Bishops and the Domestic Sphere*. Cambridge: Cambridge University Press, 2012.

Skei, A. *Jacob Handl's Moralia, Vol. 1*. Ann Arbor: University of Michigan Press, 1965.

Spinazzè, L. *Per un'edizione critica digitale: il aso di Massimiano elegiaco*. Ph.D. thesis, Università Ca'Foscari Venezia, 2011.

Stevenson, J. *Women Latin Poets*. Oxford: Oxford University Press, 2008.

Styka, J. (ed.) *From Antiquity to Modern Times: Classical Poetry and Its Modern Reception: Essays in Honor of Stanisław Stabryła*. Krakow: Ksiegamia Akademicka, 2007.

Sullivan, J. *Propertius: A Critical Introduction*. Cambridge: Cambridge University Press, 1976.

Thomas, H. *The English and the Normans: Ethnic Hostility, Assimilation, and Identity, 1066–c. 1220*. Oxford: Oxford University Press, 2003.

Thomson, R. *England and the 12th-Century Renaissance*. Aldershot: Ashgate, 1998.

Tschann, J. and Parkes, M. *Facsimile of Oxford, Bodleian Library, MS Digby 86*. Oxford: Published for the Early English Text Society by the Oxford University Press, 1996.

Vitello, M. *Il principe, il filosofo, il guerriero: Lineamenti di pensiero politico nell'Italia ostragota*. Stuttgart: Steiner, 2006.

———. *Theodahad: A Platonic King at the Collapse of Ostrogothic Italy*. Toronto: University of Toronto Press, 2014.

Walsh, P. *Love Lyrics from the Carmina Burana*. Chapel Hill: University of North Carolina Press, 1993.

Wasyl, A. *Genres Rediscovered: Studies in Latin Miniature Epic, Love Elegy and Epigram of the Romano-Barbaric Age*. Krakow: Jagiellonian University Press, 2011.

Weyman, C. *Beiträge zur Geschichte der christlichen-lateinischen Poesie*. Munich: Olms, 1926.

Williams, C. *A Martial Reader: Selections from the Epigrams*. Mundelein: Bolchazy-Carducci, 2011.

Zurli, L. and Mastandrea, P. (eds.) *Poesia latina, nuova e-filologia: Opportunità per l'editore e per l'interprete*. Volume 1. Rome: Herder, 2009.

Key Articles and Presentations

Alfonsi, L. "Sulle elegie di Massimiano." 101 *Atti del Reale Istituto Veneto di Scienze, Lettere ed Arti* (1941–1942), 333–349.

———. "De quibusdam locis quos ex antiquiis poetis Boethius et Maximianus repetisse videntur." 16 *Aevum* (1942), 86–92.

———. "De boethio elegiarum auctore." 102 *Atti del Reale Istituto Veneto di Scienze, Lettere ed Arti* (1942–1943), 723–727.

Altamura, D. "De Maximiani poetae sermone." 40 *Latomus* (1981), 818–827; reprinted in 30 *Latinitas* (1982), 90–103.

Anastasi, R. "Boezio e Massimiano." 2 *Miscellanea di studi di letteratura cristiana antica* (1948), 1–20.

———. "La III Elegia di Massimiano." 3 *Miscellanea di studi di letteratura cristiana antica* (1951), 43–92.

Arcaz Pozo, J. "Passer mortuus est: Catulo (*carm*. 3), Ovidio (*am*. 3, 7) y Maximiano (*el*. 5, 87–104)." 8 *Cuadernos de filologia clásica: Estudios latinos* (1995), 79–88.

———. "Senilis amor: Postura de los elegíacos latinos frente al amor en la vejez." 32 *Analecta Malacitana Electronica* (2012), 3–28.

Arnold, J. *Theoderic, the Goths, and the Restoration of the Roman Empire*. Ph.D. thesis, University of Michigan, 2008.

Barnish, S. "Maximian, Cassiodorus, Boethius, Theodahad: Literature, Philosophy and Politics in Ostrogothic Italy." 34 *Nottingham Medieval Studies* (1990), 16–32.

Bellanova, A. "La lezione nostaligica di Ovidio negli amori senili di Massimiano." 25 *Annali della Facoltà di Lettere e Filosofia dell'Università di Siena* (2004), 99–124.

Bertini, F. "Boezio e Massimiano." *Atti del Congresso Internazionale di Studi Boeziani* (1981), 273–283.

Bjornlie, S. "What Do Elephants Have to Do with Sixth-Century Politics? A Reappraisal of the 'Official' Governmental Dossier of Cassiodorus." 2 *Journal of Late Antiquity* 1 (2009), 143–171.

Boano, G. "Su Massimiano e le sue elegie." 27 *Rivista di filologia classica* (1949), 198–216.

Brewer, "The Ideal of Feminine Beauty in Medieval Literature." 50, no. 3 *Modern Language Review* (1955), 257–262.

Butrica, J. "Review of W. C. Schneider, *Die elegischen Verse von Maximian: Eine letzte Widerrede gegen die neue christliche Zeit: Mit den Gedichten der Appendix Maximiana und der Imitatio Maximiani*." 55, no. 2 *Classical Review* (2005), 562–564.

Carini, M. *Due città per un poeta. Saggi su Magno Felice Ennodio*. Catania: Tringale Editore, 1989.

Carrai, S. "Echi Massimianei nella 'Sylva in scabiem' di Poliziano." 8 *Interpres* (1988–1989), 276–282.

Cawsey, F. "A Note on Maximianus 5, 66." 7 *Liverpool Classical Monthly* (1982), 154.

Chaplin, C. "Maximianus Lacked Consolation of Lady Philosophy and Boethius." *purple motes*, September 27, 2015, 1–10. (http://www.purplemotes.net/2015/09/27/maximianus/boethius)

Chatillon, F. "Sur quelques citations de Fulgence le mythographe, de Boèce et de Maximien dans le florilège d'Oxford (Bodl. 633)." 12 *Revue du Moyen Âge Latin* (1956), 5–26.

Clark, R. "Varia Latina." 27, no. 8 *Classical Review* (1913), 260–261.

Consolino, F. "Massimiano e le sorti dell'elegia latina." In M. Silvestre and M. Squillante (eds.) *Mutatio rerum: Letteratura, filosofia, scienza tra tardo antico e altomedioevo*, 363–400. Naples: Città del Sole, 1997.

———. "L'elegia secondo Massimiano." In R. Cardini and D. Coppini (eds.) *Il rinnovamento umanistico della poesia: L'epigramma e l'elegia*, 183–224. Firenze: Edizioni Polistampa, 2009.

Cooper, K. *The Fall of the Roman Household*. Cambridge: Cambridge University Press,ß 2007.

Courcelle, P. "Tradition platonicienne du corps-prison." 43 *Revue des études latines* (1965), 403–443.

Cubeddu, P. "Il senso della vecchiaia e della morte in Seneca (nat quaest. Libro VI) e in Massimiano Elegiaco (elegie I e VI)." Sassari: Tipografi Associati Sassari, 1984.

Cupaiuolo, G. "A propositio dell'esametro di Massimiano." In D'Alessandro (ed.) *et al Scritti in onore di Giuseppe Morelli*, 381–392. Bologna: Pàtron Editore, 1997.

D'Angelo, E. "Maximianus." In P. Chiesa and L. Castaldi (eds.) *La trasmissione dei testi latini del Medioevo*, 467–473. Firenze: Edizione del Galluzzo, 2005.

Del Barrio, F. "Innovaciones de Maximiano Etrusco en el género elegiaco." In *Los géneros literarios*, 247–253. Bellaterra: Secció Catalana de la Societat Espanyola d'Estudis Clàssics i Servei de Publicacions de la Universitat Autonòma de Barcelona, 1985.

Ellis, R. "On the Elegies of Maximianus." 5, no. 17 *American Journal of Philology* (1884a), 1–15.

———. "On the Elegies of Maximianus II." 5, no. 18 *American Journal of Philology* (1884b), 145–163.

———. "Review of Bröring, *Quaestiones Maximianeae.*" 15, no. 2 *American Journal of Philology* (1894), 233–235.

———. "Review: The New *Maximianus*." 15, no. 7 *Classical Review* (1901), 368–371.

Fielding, I. "Elegy at the End of Pleasure: The Maximianus Collection" in "Later Latin Elegy: A Study of Ovid's Successors in the Fifth and Sixth Centuries." Ph.D. thesis, University of Warwick, 2011, 113–142.

———. "A Greek Source for Maximianus' Greek Girl: Late Latin Love Elegy and the Greek Anthology." In Scott McGill and Joseph M. Pucci (eds.), *Classics Renewed: Reception and Innovation in the Latin Poetry of Late Antiquity*, 323–339. Heidelberg: Winter, 2016.

———. "The Remedies of Elegy in Ovid, Boethius and Maximianus." (forthcoming: 75 pp.).

Fo, A. "*L'Appendix Maximiani* (=*Carmina* Garrod-Schetter): Edizione critica, problemi, osservazioni." 8 *Romanobarbica* (1984–1985), 151–230.

———. "Il problema della struttura della racolta elegiaca di Massimiano." 16 *Bollettino di studi latini* (1986), 9–21.

———. "Una lettura del 'corpus' Massimianeo." 3, no. 8 *Atti e memorie dell'Arcadia* (1986–1987), 91–128.

———. "Significato, tecniche e valore della raccolta elegiaca di Massimiano." 115, no. 3 *Hermes* (1987), 348–371.

Fontaine, J. [Review of Schetter *Studien.*] *Revue des études latines* 48 (1970), 694.

Franzoi, A. "Note massimianee." 28 *Sandalion* (2005), 205–213.

———. "Repertori elettronici, critica del testo, esegesis una verifica su Massimiano elegiaco." In L. Zurli and P. Mastandrea, *Poesia latina, nuova e-filologia: Opportunità per l'editore e per l'interprete*, 401–408. Rome: Herder, 2009.

———. "L'élégie latine tardive: Analyse de procédés compositionnels et expressifs dans les Élégies de Maximien." In L. Sandoz (ed.) *Au-delà de l'élégie d'amour: Métamorphoses et renouvellements d'un genre latin dans l'Antiquité et à la Renaissance*, 159–170. Paris: Garnier, 2011.

Gagliardi, D. "Sull'elegia I di Massimiano." 12 *Koinonia* (1988), 27–37.

Gärtner, T. "Der letzte klassiche Elegiker? Zur Deutung der erotischen Dichtungen Maximians." 7 *Göttinger Forum für Altertumswissenschaft* (2004), 119–161.

———. "Das Gebet des lebensmüden Greises bei Maximian an 'Mutter Erde' und sein antikes Vorbild." 137, no. 4 *Hermes* (2009a), 505–508.

———. "*Fit magis et damnis tristior urna suis* (Max. 1, 170): Zum Fortwirken einer epikureischen Metapher in der Spatanike und im Mittelalter." 30, no. 1 *Elenchos* (2009b), 131–144.

Gauricus, P. (ed.) *Cornelii Galli fragmenta*. Venice: Bernardinum Venetum de Vitalibus, 1501.

Goldlust, B. "Parcours narrative et parcours poétique dans les Élégies de Maximien." 89 *Revue des études latines* (2011), 154–173.

———. "Citations, remplois et imitations dans le *Carmen* 5 de l'*Appendix Maximiani* (=*carmina* Garrod-Schetter)." 84, no. 2 *Revue de philologie, de littérature et d'histoire anciennes* (2012), 217–242.

Green, R. "Review of C. S. Oberg's Versus Maximiani: Der Elegienzyklus textkritisch herausgegeben, übersetzt und neu interpretiert." 50, no. 2 *Classical Review* (2000), 448–449.

Grensted, L. *A Short History of the Doctrine of Atonement*. London: Longmans, Green, 1920.

Gruber, J. "Maximianus 3." 6 *Lexicon des Mittelalters* (1993), 420.

Hartung, A. "The Non-comic *Merchant's Tale*, Maximianus and the Sources." 29 *Mediaeval Studies* (1967), 1–25.

Hollis, A. *Ars Amatoria, Book I*. Oxford: Oxford University Press, 1977.

Hunt, J. "Adnotatiuncula in Maximianus." 33 *La parola del passato* (1978), 59–60.

Jaitner-Hahner, U. "Maximian und der Fucus Italicus: Ein unbekannter Textzeuge." In M. Borgolte and H. Spilling, *Litterae medii aevi: Festschrift für Johanne Autenrieth zu ihrem 65 Geburtstag*, 277–292. Sigmaringen: J. Thorbecke, 1988..

Kennedy, A. "Christine de Pizan and Maximianus." 54 *Medium Aevum* (1985), 282–283.

Kittredge, G. "Chaucer and Maximianus." 9 *American Journal of Philology* (1888), 84–85.

Knox, P. "A Modest Emendation of an Immodest Imitation of Ovid (Maxim. 5, 30)." 154 *Rheinisches Museum* (2011), 411–412.

Kossaifi, C. "Jadis et maintenant: À propos de L'Élégie III de Maximianus." 59 *Bulletin de L'Association Guillaume Budé* (2000), 230–234.

Lemaire, N. (ed.) *Poetae latini minores, vol. septum*. Paris, 1826.

Leotta, R. "Un anonimo imitatore di Massimiano." 16 *Giornale italiano di filologia* (1985), 91–106.

———. "Uno stilema massimianeo." 41 *Giornale italiano di filologia* (1989), 81–84.

———. "Massimiano in Leopardi?" 17 *Orpheus* (1996), 401–404.

Levy, F. "Maximianus." 14, no. 2 *Real-Encyclopädie*, 2529–2533. Stuttgart: Classischen Altertumswissenschoft, 1930.

Lucan. *De bello civili, liber VIII*, trans. J. Postgate. Cambridge: Cambridge University Press, 1917.

Manitius, M. "Über den Dichter Maximian." 44 *Rheinisches Museum* (1889), 540–543.

———. "Zu Maximianus." 50 *Rheinisches Museum* (1895), 642–643.

Mastandrea, P. "Aratore, Partenio, Vigilio coetani (e amici?) di Massimiano elegiaco." 3 *Incontri triestini di filologia classica* (2003–2004), 327–342.

———. "Per la cronologia di Massimiano elegiaco: Elementi interni ed esterni al testo." In M. C. Díaz y Díaz y J. M. Díaz de Bustamante (eds.), *Poesia latina medieval (siglos V–XV): Actas del IV Congreso del "International Mittellateinerkomittee" (Santiago de Compostela, 12–15 de septiembre de 2002)*, 151–179. Firenze: Edizioni del Galluzzo, 2005.

Mather, C. *Magnalia Christi Americana: Books I and II*, ed. K. Murdock and E. Miller. Cambridge, Mass.: Belknap Press, 1977.

Mauger-Plichon, B. "Maximianus un mystérieux poète." 4 *Bulletin de l'Association Guillaume Budé* (1999), 369–387.

Merone, E. "Per la biografia di Massimiano." 1 *Giornale italiano di filologia* (1948), 337–352.

———. "Maximianea." 3 *Giornale italiano di filologia* (1950), 322–336.

Meyers, J. "La figure du vieillard dans les Élégies de Maximien: Autobiographie ou fiction?" In B. Bakhouche (ed.) *L'ancienneté chez les Anciens*, vol. 2, 697–715. Montpellier: Publications de l'Université Paul Valéry, 2003.

Morgan, M. "The Preface of Vitruvius." 44 *Proceedings of the American Journal of Arts and Sciences* (1909), 149–175.

Morrica, U. "Di un nuovo codice delle Elegie di Massimiano." 6 *Athenaeum* (1918), 135–142.

Munro, H. "October 17, 1884 letter to Robinson Ellis." 6 *American Journal of Philology* (1885), 122–123.

Navarro López, J. "El prólogo de Aldo Manucio el Joven a su edición de unos presuntos poemas de Cornelio Galo." 3 *Calamus Renascens* (2002), 147–156.

Neuberger, M. "The Latin Poet Maximianus on the Miseries of Old Age." 21 *Bulletin of the History of Medicine* (1947), 113–119.

Ovid. *Ars amatoria, Book 1*, ed. A. S. Hollis. Oxford: Oxford University Press, 1977.

Petschenig, M. "Zu Maximian und Ammian." 59 *Philologus* (1900), 153–154.

Pinotti, P. "Massimiano elegiaco." In G. Cantanzaro and F. Santucci (eds.) *Tredici secoli di elegia latina*, 183–203. Assisi: Accademia Properziana del Subasio, 1989.

———. "Da Massimiano a Shakespeare: Rappresentazoni del tempo." 3, no. 3 *Vichiana* (1991), 186–216.

Polara, G. "Due note Massimianee (V 99–100; 119–120)." 15 *Sileno* (1989), 197–205.

Pontiggio, G. "Massimiano." 38 *Il Verri* (1972), 137–139.

Prada, G. *Quae inter metri dactylici disciplinam et sermonem latinum in Maximiano poeta existent quaestiones*. Pavia: 1914.

Ramírez de Verger, A. "Parodia de un lamento ritual en Maximiano (el. V 87–104)." 15 *Habis* (1984), 149–156.

———. "Las *Elegias* de Maximiano: Tradición y originalidad en un poeta de última hora." 17 *Habis* (1986), 185–193.

Ratkowitsch, C. "Die Wirkung der Elegien Maximins auf de 'comoediae elegiacae' des Vitalis und Wilhelm von Blois." 100 *Wiener Studien* (1987), 227–246.

——. "Weitere Argumente zur Datierung und Interpretation Maximians (Zu vorliegenden Rezensionem)." 103 *Wiener Studien* (1990), 207–239.

Roberts, M. "Late Roman Elegy." In K. Weisman (ed.) *The Oxford Handbook of the Elegy*, 85–100. Oxford: Oxford University Press, 2010.

Romano, D. "Il Primo Massimiano." 29, no. 4 *Atti dell'Accademia di Scienze e Arti di Palermo* (1968–1969), 307–335; republished in D. Romano, *Letteratura e storia nell'età tardoromana*, 309–329. Palermo: Vittorietti, 1979.

Salanitro, M. "Un titulo e due controversi emendamenti dell' 'Appendix Maximiani.'" 8 *Orpheus* (1987), 138–143.

Salemme, C. [Review of Schetter *Studien.*] 4 *Bollettino di studi latini* (1974), 314–320.

——. "Le nere ciglia di 'Appendix Maximiani.'" 9 *Orpheus* (1988), 98–101.

Sánchez M. and Macanas, O. "Tibulo y Maximiano." In *Simposio Tibuliano: Conmemoración del bimilenario de la muerte de Tibulo*, 391–397. Universidad de Murcia, Departmentos de Latin y Griego, 1985.

Schetter, W. "Neues zur *Appendix der Elegien* des Maximian." 104 *Philologus* (1960), 116–126.

Schneider, W. "Das Ende der antiken Leiblichkeit: Begehren und Enthaltsamkeit bei Ambrosius, Augustin und Maximian." In T. Späth and B. Wagner-Hasel (eds.) *Frauenwelten in der Antike: Geschlechterordnung und weibliche Lebenspraxis*, 412–426. Stuttgart-Weimar: J. B. Metzler, 2000.

——. "Definition of Genre by Falsification: The False Attribution of the Maximianus Verses to Cornelius Gallus by Pomponius Gauricus and the 'Definition' of Their Genre and Structure." 129 *Rivista di filologia e di istruzione classica* (2001), 445–464.

——. "Greis und Geiz, der Mensch ein Grab: Zu zwei schwierigen Stellen und einem entlegenen Bild bei dem Eligiker Maximian und dem Humanistem Joachim Camerarius." 43, no. 1 *Mittelateinisches Jahrbuch* (2008), 1–24.

Sequi, C. "Rassegna di studi su Massimiano elegiaco (1970–1993)." 24 *Bollettino di studi latini* (1994), 617–645.

Shanzer, D. "Ennodius, Boethius and the Date and Interpretation of Maximian's *Elegia III*." 111 *Rivista di filologia e di istruzione classica* (1983), 183–195.

——. "Review of *Maximianus amat: Zu Datierung und Interpretation des Elegikers Maximian* by Christine Ratkowitsch." 60, no. 3 *Gnomon* (1988), 259–261.

Smolak, K. "Maximianus." In O. Schütze (ed.) *Metzler Lexicon Antiken Autoren*, 452–453. Verlag Metzler: Stuttgart-Weimar, 1997.

Spaltenstein, F. "Structure et intentions du recueil poétique de Maximien." 10, no. 3 Études de Lettres, *Bulletin de la Faculté des Lettres de l'Université de Lausanne et de la Société des Études de Lettres* (1977), 81–101.

Stiene, H. "Zu den beiden erotischen Gedichten der Maximian-Appendix." 129, no. 2 *Rheinisches Museum* (1986), 184–192.

Szövérffy, J. "Maximianus a Satirist?" 72 *Harvard Studies in Philology* (1968), 351–367.

Tandoi, V. "Review of Schetter, *Studien zur Überlieferung und Kritik des Elegiker Maximian.*" 25 *Maia* (1973), 140–151.

Tandy, S. "The 'Ode to Mentula' and the Interpretation of Maximianus' Opus." Presentation at the 111th Meeting of Classical Association of the Middle West and South (CAMWS), Boulder, Colorado, March 25–28, 2015.

———. "Boethius as Anti-Boethius: A Re-evaluation of the Role of Boethius in Maximianus' 'Third Elegy.'" Presentation at the 51st International Congress on Medieval Studies (ICMS), Kalamazoo, Michigan, May 12–15, 2016.

Traina, A. "Le busse di Aquilina *(Massimiano 3, 37).*" 115 *Rivista di filologia e di istruzione classica* (1987), 54–57; 116 (1988), 122.

Traube, L. "Zur Überlieferung der Elegien des Maximianus." 48 *Rheinisches Museum* (1893), 284–289.

Uden, J. "The Elegiac *Puella* as Virgin Martyr." 139 *Transactions of the American Philological Association* (2009), 207–222.

———. "Love Elegies of Late Antiquity." In B. Gold (ed.) *A Companion to Roman Love Elegy*, 459–475. Oxford: Wiley Blackwell, 2012.

Uden, J. and Fielding, I. "Latin Elegy in the Old Age of the World: The Elegiac Corpus of Maximianus." 43, no. 3 *Arethusa* (2010), 439–460.

Varela, J. "Identifying the *clarus orator* in Quintilian Inst. 8, 2." 50 *Classical Quarterly* (2000), 314–316.

Vidén, G. *The Roman Chancery Tradition: Studies in the Language of Codex Theodosianus and Cassiodorus' Variae.* Göteborg: Acta Universitatis Gothoburgensis, 1984.

Vogel, F. "Maximianus der Lyriker." 41 *Rheinisches Museum* (1886), 158–159.

Warner, V. "Epithets of the Tiber in the Roman Poets." *Classical Weekly* (November 19, 1917), 52–55.

Wasyl, A. "Maximianus and the Late Antique Reading of Classical Literary Genres." 11 *Classica Cracoviensia* (2007), 353–381.

Watt, W. "Notes on Maximianus." 6 *Eikasmos* (1995), 243–248.

Wedeck, H. "An Analysis of the Techniques of Maximianus Etruscus." 11 *Latomus* (1952), 487–495.

Welsh, J. "Notes on the Text of Maximianus." 15 *Exemplaria classica* (2011), 213–224.

Wilhelm, F. "Maximianus und Boethius." 62 *Rheinisches Museum* (1907), 601–614.

Zurli, L. "L'Aegritudo perdiccae e Maxim. 3." 1 *Bollettino di studi latini* (1991), 313–318.

www.ingramcontent.com/pod-product-compliance
Lightning Source LLC
Chambersburg PA
CBHW030825310726
48980CB00006B/636/J
9780812249798